W9-BTQ-090

SECOND EDITION

Golf

STEPS TO SUCCESS

Paul G. Schempp
Peter Mattsson

HUMAN KINETICS

Library of Congress Cataloging-in-Publication Data

Schempp, Paul G.
  Golf : steps to success / Paul G. Schempp, Peter Mattsson. -- Second edition.
    pages cm
1. Golf. I. Mattsson, Peter, 1970- II. Title.
  GV965.S273 2014
  796.352--dc23
                                            2014007387

ISBN: 978-1-4504-5002-7 (print)

Copyright © 2014, 2005 by Human Kinetics, Inc.

All rights reserved. Except for use in a review, the reproduction or utilization of this work in any form or by any electronic, mechanical, or other means, now known or hereafter invented, including xerography, photocopying, and recording, and in any information storage and retrieval system, is forbidden without the written permission of the publisher.

The web addresses cited in this text were current as of March 2014, unless otherwise noted.

Acquisitions Editor: Tom Heine; **Developmental Editor:** Anne Hall; **Assistant Editor:** Tyler M. Wolpert; **Copyeditor:** Joanna Hatzopoulos Portman; **Permissions Manager:** Martha Gullo; **Graphic Designer:** Keri Evans; **Cover Designer:** Keith Blomberg; **Photograph (cover):** © Frank Röder/imagebrok/age fotostock; **Photographs (interior):** Neil Bernstein; **Visual Production Assistant:** Joyce Brumfield; **Photo Production Manager:** Jason Allen; **Art Manager:** Kelly Hendren; **Associate Art Manager:** Alan L. Wilborn; **Illustrations:** © Human Kinetics; **Printer:** United Graphics

We thank the Boyd Golf Center at the University of Georgia for assistance in providing the location for the photo shoot for this book.

Printed in the United States of America   10 9 8 7 6 5 4 3 2 1

The paper in this book is certified under a sustainable forestry program.

Human Kinetics
Website: www.HumanKinetics.com

United States: Human Kinetics
P.O. Box 5076
Champaign, IL 61825-5076
800-747-4457
e-mail: humank@hkusa.com

Canada: Human Kinetics
475 Devonshire Road Unit 100
Windsor, ON N8Y 2L5
800-465-7301 (in Canada only)
e-mail: info@hkcanada.com

Europe: Human Kinetics
107 Bradford Road
Stanningley
Leeds LS28 6AT, United Kingdom
+44 (0) 113 255 5665
e-mail: hk@hkeurope.com

Australia: Human Kinetics
57A Price Avenue
Lower Mitcham, South Australia 5062
08 8372 0999
e-mail: info@hkaustralia.com

New Zealand: Human Kinetics
P.O. Box 80
Torrens Park, South Australia 5062
0800 222 062
e-mail: info@hknewzealand.com

E5920

We dedicate this book to our children. They make the bogies in life feel like birdies: Adam and Peter Schempp, and Fillip, Elina, and Max Rocksén.

Contents

Foreword

They say it takes a lifetime to master the game of golf. I think it may take even longer than that. In my career as a professional caddy, I have never stopped trying to learn the game and discover ways to help my players become more accomplished golfers. No matter how much success I've enjoyed in this game, I yearn for more.

Part of my journey in golf has included time with the coauthors of this book, Paul Schempp and Peter Mattsson. We have met often at coaching seminars and professional golf events and have discussed coaching strategies and shared ideas on player development. I have found their knowledge, experience, and skill as golf coaches to be a valuable source of information. I'm certain you will find the contents of this book useful.

Enjoying golf requires that you both understand the game and play it to a standard that you find satisfying. *Golf: Steps to Success* will help you on both counts. The progressive steps of this book will familiarize you with the essential skills for playing well—putting, short-game, and full swing. You will also be introduced to fundamental rules, strategies to improve your thinking around the course, and concrete suggestions for continually improving your game and consequently increasing your enjoyment of the sport.

But don't think you can go through this book once and have mastered the game. You will need to revisit each step many times to continually improve and increase your enjoyment. Nobody gets it all the first time around, which is one of the things that makes golf a game for a lifetime. In your development as a golfer, you will realize that you do some things well and other things not so well. Take extra time with the steps in this book that address the things you don't do so well. Often in golf a little knowledge and a lot of practice will help you overcome any challenge you face. You will also come to enjoy practicing and seeing your skills improve—especially by using the drills and activities in this book because they are both fun and challenging.

I have had many wonderful moments on golf courses and look forward to many more. I hope you find the same thing. Golf is a great game, and this book will help you discover that. *Ha så kul!*

Fanny Sunesson

Acknowledgments

No book ever comes to life by the efforts of the authors alone. Many hands have contributed directly or indirectly to what is before your eyes. First, we would like to acknowledge Tom Heine's contribution to this book. When Tom first called to propose this second edition, we said no. We thought the first edition was fine as is. Tom convinced us otherwise—and he was right. This is a much-improved and updated edition. Tom, thank you for your belief in this project and in us as authors, and thank you for your patience with us.

Two other HK staff members went above and beyond in this project: Anne Hall and Neil Bernstein. Anne served ably and admirably as the developmental editor for this project. Her guidance, direction, and enormous patience were instrumental in forming this manuscript into a high-quality book. The photographs are a product of Neil's skill, knowledge, and talent. He was painstakingly thorough in shooting the photos and was also fun to work with. Thank you, Anne and Neil.

The models deserve credit for their time and willingness to contribute. Special thanks, therefore, go to University of Georgia golf team members: Samantha Lee, Mookie DeMoss, Sepp Straka, Dave Cousart, and Josh Shelton. We'd also like to thank coaches Chris Haack and Josh Brewer for their assistance and willingness to allow us to use their players for models.

This book would not be possible if it were not for the players we have had the privilege to work with and call friends. In seeking ways to help them find success on the golf course, we learned much about becoming better teachers and coaches. It would be impossible to include every player's name here, but we would like to extend special thanks to Luke Donald, Niclas Fasth, Mathias Gronberg, David Howell, Anders Hultman, Richard S. Johnson, Per-Ulrik Johansson, Fredrik Jacobson, Catrin Nilsmark, Per Nielsson, Jesper Parnevik, Carl Pettersson, Annika Sorenstam, and Henrik Stenson. Although she is not a player, we would also like to thank Fanny Sunesson, one of the greatest caddies and coaches in the history of golf. Not only has Fanny been supportive of our efforts, but her keen understanding of the game and training athletes has benefitted us both.

The final acknowledgment goes to Pia Nilsson. Years ago, Pia us asked us each independently, "Would you mind if I got you two together?" She did, and the rest, as they say, is history. Takk takk, Pia.

Climbing the Steps to Golf Success

For beginning and intermediate players as well as teachers and coaches, *Golf: Steps to Success* will help ensure a solid foundation of fundamentals and add skills and knowledge to what a player has already achieved. The steps to success are arranged in order, beginning with putting the ball into the hole and progressing back to a smooth and accurate tee shot.

At each step, beginners will benefit from clear, concise information on the basics for every part of the game—skills, strategies, and rules. The explanations and accompanying illustrations not only provide comprehensive instruction for executing each skill, but they also reveal how these skills can be used strategically to speed success on the course.

Golf: Steps to Success offers thorough explanations of fundamental and specialty shots, so intermediate players will have the opportunity to refine their skills with game-specific drills as they move toward advanced performance. They will gain insight into when, why, and how to hit the right shot. They will learn to analyze a golf course and assemble their skills into a game plan that will minimize errors and maximize playing potential.

For teachers, *Golf: Steps to Success* provides an all-inclusive instructional package. The information, drills, activities, and grading methods can be easily adapted to existing instructional programs. Teachers will also find useful information on the history of golf, the latest equipment, rules, course management strategies, sport psychology, and Web-based golf resources. Add to that information key cues in executing a full range of golf shots, as well as strategy, self-paced drills, and methods of evaluating each student, and you have an invaluable teaching resource.

As coaches to amateur and professional golfers, we know that a coach is in constant search of new solutions to familiar problems and tested methods for improving player performance. *Golf: Steps to Success* represents a compilation of the knowledge, skills, strategies, and drills we have used in working with successful golfers at all levels of the game, from complete beginners to accomplished professionals. In each step, coaches will find at least one nugget of knowledge, fresh idea, or unique drill that will help them help their players improve.

Whether you are a recreational golfer or play at a competitive level, you will improve your performance and enjoy the game more as you develop greater competency in the skills and strategies required for successful play. *Golf: Steps to Success* provides a progressive plan for developing golf skills and gaining more confidence on the course. For each step, follow this sequence:

1. Read the explanation of the skill covered in the step, why the step is important, and how to execute the step.

2. Study the illustrations, which show how to execute each skill.

3. Read the instructions for each drill. Practice the drills and record your scores.

4. Have a qualified observer—a teacher, coach, or trained partner—evaluate your skill technique once you've completed each set of drills. The observer can use the success checks included with each drill to evaluate your execution of the skill.

5. At the end of the step, review your performance and total your scores from the drills. Once you've achieved the indicated level of success, move on to the next step.

Legendary golfer Ben Hogan once said, "There are no born golfers. Some have more natural ability than others, but they've all been made." As Mr. Hogan won 62 professional tournaments, including all four major championships, his words carry considerable weight. Use *Golf: Steps to Success* to make you a better golfer. The steps can help you learn the game, expand your skills, teach the game with key cues and effective evaluations, or coach with proven player development strategies. Even advanced players will find drills to hone their shot-making skills and tactics to give them a competitive edge.

People play golf for many reasons. For some, golf is an enjoyable, healthy physical activity in a beautiful outdoor setting. For others, golf provides a venue for social interaction with companions. Others find golf a platform for conducting business in a relaxed atmosphere. And for those who are keen for competition, there is no shortage of tournaments. Wherever your golfing aspirations lead you, *Golf: Steps to Success* will bring you closer to becoming the player you desire to be.

The Game of Golf

Stepping up to the first tee to begin a round of golf usually brings on a bit of nervous anticipation. You wonder, *Will my good golf game show up today, or is disaster waiting for me out there?* The excitement from the hope of playing well blends with the jitters of not knowing exactly what will actually happen out on the course. These feelings follow you as you walk onto the first tee box, push a tee into the ground, place the ball on it, step back for a final stretch, wish your playing partners a good round, take a long look down the fairway to sight your target, and step to the ball.

Golf has been a popular pastime for centuries. So popular was golf in 1457 that King James II of Scotland banned it because it was interfering with archery practice and other military training. It is easy to imagine that people preferred to play golf rather than prepare for war. Fortunately, golf won out over archery at St. Andrews, home of the first golf course in the world. In that sleepy little university town along the east coast of Scotland, you can usually find a game on one of the five public golf courses. The locals still stroll with dogs or baby carriages across the fairways of the famed Old Course on their way to the beach just past the first tee. Regardless of where you play—and today you can find golf courses just about anywhere in the world—you will find certain elements common to most courses.

GOLF COURSE

Carrying on a tradition begun at St. Andrews, today's regulation golf course has 18 holes. Each hole has a teeing ground from where that hole begins and a closely mowed area called the green, into which a hole is cut and a flag is placed.

Comprising the 18 holes is a mixture of par 3, par 4, and par 5 holes (figure 1). Par is the number of strokes that the golf course designer estimates a very good golfer will take to complete a particular hole. Course designers estimate that a very good golfer will take two strokes to get the ball in the hole once he or she gets the ball onto the green. If a designer believes a very good player should take one stroke to get the ball on the green, the hole is a par 3. Put another way, on a par-3 hole a golfer should take one stroke to get the ball on the green and two strokes to get the ball in the hole. Designers also include holes that require two or three strokes to reach the green (par 4 and par 5). In these cases, a fairway is cut between the teeing ground and the green so that a player can land the ball off the tee and then hit an approach from the fairway to the green.

The total length of a golf course varies from 5,000 yards to over 7,000 yards (4,572 to 6,400 meters). Short holes range from 80 to 240 yards (73 to 220 meters), medium holes stretch from 240 to 460 yards (220 to 420 meters), and long holes can run over 600 yards (550 meters). To provide various levels of challenge, multiple tee boxes are placed on each hole. For example, in Pinehurst, North Carolina, from the forward

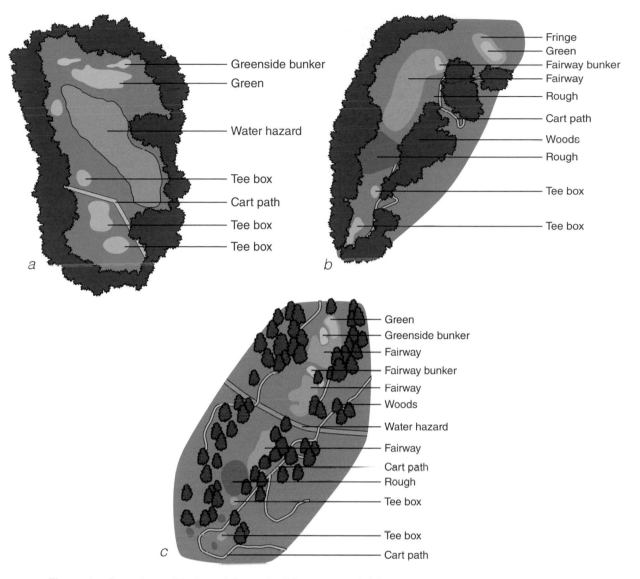

Figure 1   Sample golf holes: *(a)* par 3, *(b)* par 4, and *(c)* par 5.

tees, Course No. 2 covers 5,035 yards (4,604 meters), but played from the back tees the same course is 7,495 yards (6,853 meters), a difference of almost 3,000 yards (2,743 meters)! Golf courses are designed in this manner so that players of all abilities can enjoy the same golf course, one factor that makes golf so popular. At Pinehurst Course No. 2, which is the site of the U.S. Open, a beginning golfer can play the same course played by the greatest golfers in the world. A word of caution for beginners considering playing a course like Pinehurst No. 2: Play the forward tees!

Before venturing out to play a round of golf, you will need to acquire certain equipment, understand how a game is scored, and learn basic rules and etiquette. These elements are covered in this introduction and referred to throughout the book. You will also need to develop critical skills and strategies, which you will learn in the subsequent steps.

EQUIPMENT

To the new player and even to veteran players, equipment can be confusing and overwhelming due to the amount and variety available. However, a player needs only two things: clubs and a ball. A bag to carry your clubs, shoes to ensure good footing, and a few accessories can also increase your enjoyment and skill.

Clubs

The rules of golf state that you are allowed to carry no more than 14 clubs during a round of golf. Selecting the right clubs for you is a matter of knowing the types of clubs available, your level of skill, and the golf course you are playing. There are four types of clubs: metals, irons, wedges, and putters (figure 2). Regardless of the type, all clubs have three parts: the grip, the shaft, and the head (figure 3).

Metal clubs have the largest heads and longest shafts of all the clubs. These clubs were once called woods because the club head was made of persimmon wood. Today they are made with a variety of metals, although titanium is preferred for its strength and elasticity.

Metal clubs are numbered 1, 3, 4, 5, 7, and 9; the higher-numbered clubs have the higher loft. Loft is the angle between the club face and a line at a 90-degree angle from the surface or ground. The more the club face is angled to the sky when it is resting on the ground, the more loft it has. A club with more loft will send the ball higher but a shorter distance than a club with less loft. Club 1 is the driver and seldom has the number on the sole (bottom) of the club head. Clubs 3, 4, 5, 7, and 9 are referred to as fairway metals and are used most often on the fairway.

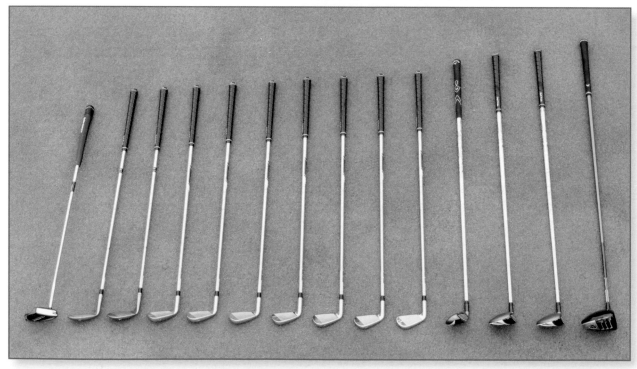

Figure 2   Metals, irons, wedges, and putters make up a set of golf clubs. A golfer can carry no more than 14 clubs on the course.

The most common configuration of metal clubs in the average golfer's bag is driver, 3-metal, and 5-metal. Because they send the ball higher and are easier to hit, many players prefer to add the 7- or 9-metal to their bag and take out some of the long irons.

Iron clubs are numbered 1 through 9. The 1-iron has the least loft and the longest shaft while the 9-iron has the shortest shaft and the most loft; the 9-iron thus sends the ball the highest but also the shortest distance of all the irons. Due to their long shaft and low loft, the 1- and 2-irons are seldom recommended for the average player, and most irons are sold in sets numbered 3 through 9. Iron clubs get their name from the original metal—iron—used in making the head. However, today's iron club heads are a composite of metals.

Because of the difficulty of hitting irons 1, 2, and 3 (and for some golfers 4 and 5 irons as well), club manufacturers have begun making a hybrid club. The hybrid club creates the loft of a fairway metal so that it is easier to get in the air, but it has the shaft length of an iron club so that the club is easier to control and the ball will not fly as far as

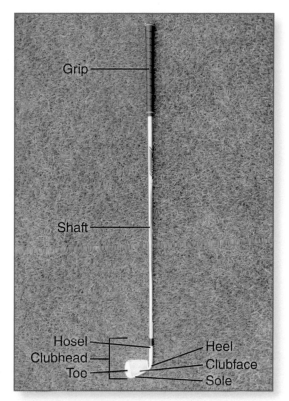

Figure 3 All clubs have a grip, shaft, and head.

with a fairway metal. Hybrids have become standard clubs found in the golf bags of many players of any level, from beginning golfer to touring professional.

Two types of club heads are used in irons: forged and perimeter-weighted. Forged irons place more weight in the center of the club head while perimeter-weighted irons distribute the weight on the outside of the club head. For advanced players who consistently strike the ball in the middle of the club face, forged irons give a better feel and performance. For the average player who does not always hit the center of the club face, the perimeter-weighted club head is more forgiving and gives a better result with shots that are struck slightly off-center. In recent years, perimeter-weighted clubs have become the iron of choice for most players, including touring professionals.

Wedges are irons that have slightly modified soles to help move the club head through sand or green-side rough. Typical wedges include the approach wedge, pitching wedge, sand wedge, and lob wedge. LPGA (Ladies Professional Golf Association) Tour player Annika Sörenstam carries four wedges in her golf bag, but most players carry only a pitching wedge and a sand wedge.

Because wedges have the greatest loft, they produce the most spin on the golf ball, allowing the ball to bite or stop on a hard green. Wedges also have the shortest shafts, making them easier to control. With the greatest loft and shortest shafts, they are designed for short or scoring shots. Practicing with wedges is a sure way to lower your scores.

Putters come in many shapes and lengths. Players can choose from a long putter, belly putter, or standard putter. With a long putter, the end of the shaft is held near to, but not on, the chest. The top hand grips the top of the club, and the lower hand grips the middle of the shaft. With a belly putter, the end of the shaft is pressed against the inside of the arm closest to the hole. With a standard putter, the end of the shaft is gripped with both hands. The most common length by far is the standard putter. As for putter heads, many varieties are on the market, and new ones appear each year. When selecting a putter, it is best to simply try several until you find one that feels comfortable and puts the ball in the hole. Performance is more important than looks, so go for the putter that does the job for you. Step 1 will discuss putters and putting strokes in greater detail.

A final thought on clubs: Get fitted. Just as you wouldn't walk the golf course in shoes that weren't a proper fit, you shouldn't play golf with clubs that aren't a proper fit. Most club shops can fit you for a set based on your swing. If you are buying new clubs, this service is usually free. If the shop does not offer this service, see a professional who is certified by the PGA (Professional Golf Association) of America or LPGA to fit clubs to players. You will be fitted for the proper length and flex of the shaft, optimal lie and loft for each club head, and grip size. The time and money you put into this process will pay off in years of good service from your clubs; the investment is well worth it. However, it is bet to first commit to your golf game before you decide to invest in fitted clubs.

Golf Balls

Golf ball technology has seen many advancements over the years. All advances have benefited the player. Today's golf balls fly farther and with less sidespin. (Sidespin is the force that redirects an otherwise perfectly good shot with a big, sweeping curve called a slice.) Like clubs, golf balls come in many varieties. The differences in golf balls are both internal and external. The design characteristics of a golf ball are on the packaging, not the ball itself, so read labels carefully.

Internally, golf balls have a one-, two-, or three-piece core. Multicore centers produce more backspin, which gives better players more control over their shots. Some multicore balls gain greater distance from the accelerated club-head speed of a good golfer. Balls with a solid or single-piece core spin less but tend to fly a bit farther, characteristics appreciated by beginning and intermediate golfers and golfers with lower swing speeds.

Externally, golf ball covers come in soft and hard varieties. Soft covers provide a better feel, particularly on short shots and putting, but only good players can detect this characteristic. Soft covers tend to be more expensive and less durable. Hard covers are more durable, spin less, and are less expensive. These qualities appeal to the beginning to intermediate player.

Which ball should you use? With so many choices available, this question can be difficult to answer. If you are just beginning, look for a solid-center golf ball with a durable cover. These balls are less expensive, last longer, go farther, and spin less, giving you straighter shots. At this level, your golf shots will be affected more by your swing technique than the ball, so focus more on your skills and don't fret too much about the ball. You will also likely lose balls to water hazards, in tall grass or woods, or out of bounds. Losing an inexpensive ball is not nearly as painful as losing a ball that cost several dollars. As your skill level increases, try a variety of mid- to upper-priced balls until you find one that fits your game. If you get serious about your game, you can seek advice directly from ball manufacturers. This information is easily accessible on the Web. The Callaway Golf website (www.callaway.com) is a good source of information on golf balls.

Accessories

A set of clubs and a golf ball are all the tools you really need to play golf. A few accessories can make your game more efficient, comfortable, and enjoyable. Unless you want to walk a golf course with 14 different clubs hanging loose under your arm, you will need a golf bag. Two common types of golf bags are stand bags and cart bags. Stand bags are used by players who prefer to walk the course as they play a round of golf. These bags are smaller and lighter than cart bags and come equipped with a stand mechanism that opens automatically when the bottom of the bag is placed on the ground. The stand keeps the bag upright and angles the clubs toward the golfer for easy club selection. A cart bag is larger and heavier and is designed to be strapped to the back of a golf cart for those who prefer to ride the course. All golf bags come with pockets for storing golf balls, tees, a sweater or rain suit, and other items of necessity. Loops for holding an umbrella and golf towel come on most golf bags, as does a hood cover.

Balance is a critical factor in a golf swing, and golf shoes are specifically designed to hold your feet firmly to the ground during the swing. Golf shoes have the added benefit of being waterproof; rain or heavy dew can soak your feet in a hurry. Considering that an average round of golf takes four to five hours, the support offered by comfortable, well-fitted golf shoes makes them a recommended accessory. Like any other sport shoes, it is best to try them on before making a purchase. A knowledgeable golf store employee should be able to give you advice on quality, durability, and price.

You should also consider carrying an umbrella on the course. Depending on your geographical location, it may often rain when you are playing. To keep dry and comfortable, an umbrella is necessary, preferably a windproof golf umbrella. These umbrellas have large canopies so you can keep yourself and your golf bag dry during a downpour. Windproof umbrellas have a vent near the top so that wind can escape the canopy and not bend or break the umbrella.

If your hands sweat easily, are soft, or are easily irritated, you may want to consider wearing a golf glove. The glove is worn on the target-side hand on all full-swing shots to provide a better grip. Wearing a glove is a matter of personal preference.

Additional accessories to put in your golf bag include a mark repair tool to fix ball marks on the green, tees for teeing your ball, and sunscreen.

SCORING

Success in golf is measured by the number of strokes it takes you to move the ball from the teeing ground into the hole; the fewer strokes, the better the player. In a round of golf, the count begins on the first tee and ends when the ball drops in the 18th hole. One stroke is counted each time you attempt to strike the ball whether you make contact or not.

Every golf course has a par rating. Par represents the strokes a highly competent player would need to complete all 18 holes. As previously mentioned, each hole on the golf course has a par rating, and the sum or total of the par ratings of all 18 holes is the par rating for the course. Par-3 holes are short because the highly competent golfer should reach the green from the tee box in one stroke and then take two putts to complete the hole. Par-4 holes require two shots to reach the green, one from the tee box to the fairway and one from the fairway to the green. Par-5 holes allow for three strokes from the tee box to the green. The typical 18-hole golf course is comprised of 4 par-3 holes, 10 par-4 holes, and 4 par-5 holes, for a course par of 72.

Golf has terminology to describe how you played each hole relative to par. If you took one stroke from the tee box to hole out the ball (this normally occurs only on par 3s), this is called an *ace* or a *hole in one*. If your score on a hole is two under par, this is called an *eagle*. Both the ace and the eagle are rare occurrences. One under par on a hole is a *birdie* and a prized score. It is common for beginning and intermediate players to shoot scores that are over par. One over par is a *bogey*, two over par is a *double bogey*, three over is a *triple bogey*, and so on.

How you play a hole and where your ball lands affects your score. If your ball stops in the fairway on your tee shot, this is called a *fairway hit*. If you put the ball on the green in the allocated number of strokes (on a par 3, that would be one stroke), you are said to have reached the *green in regulation*. If you miss the green but are able to chip or pitch the ball on the green and then hole the ball out with one putt, this is called an *up and down*. An up and down from a greenside bunker is called a *sand save*. The number of putts you take to complete a round represents your putting proficiency. Par is 36 putts. If you hit fewer putts than that, you are considered a *good putter*. These terms are important indicators of your success as a golfer; the greater your proficiency in any of these areas, the better golfer you are.

KEEPING A SCORECARD

When you check in for your tee time, you will be provided with a scorecard for the course. At some courses, they place the scorecard in the golf cart or in a box on the first tee. The scorecard will list the holes, the par for each hole, the distance from each set of tee boxes to the hole, and the handicap for each hole (figure 4). The handicap indicates the difficulty of the hole in comparison to the other holes on the course. The hole with the lowest number (1) is the most difficult, and the hole with the highest number (18) is the least difficult. Also listed on the scorecard are the course rating and slope. These numbers indicate the course difficulty in comparison to other courses. A course with a higher rating is more difficult than a course with a lower rating. For example, a course with a rating of 70.6/132 is more difficult than a course with a rating of 67.6/121.

Although the scorecard provides information regarding the course and the holes, its primary purpose is for you to record your score in stroke play. As you play a round, write down the number of strokes you took for each hole, including penalty strokes. Most players simply write down the number of strokes, but some players prefer to add a bit more information. For example, if you score a birdie on the hole (one under par for the hole), you circle the number that you record. If you eagle the hole (two under par), you circle the number twice. A bogie (one over par) is indicated by drawing a box around the number. A double bogie number receives two boxes, a triple bogie receives three boxes, and so on.

It is customary in tournament play for players to swap scorecards and keep the score of their opponent. In recreational play, players can keep their own score, or one member of the group can keep the scores for everyone on a single card. A word of caution: When playing a tournament, carefully check the hole-by-hole score and the final score. If you sign the scorecard and turn it in to tournament officials and it is later discovered that you signed an incorrect scorecard, you will be automatically disqualified from the tournament. In 1968, Roberto De Vicenzo had apparently won one

Hole	1	2	3	4	5	6	7	8	9	Out	Initial	10	11	12	13	14	15	16	17	18	In	TOT	Rating
Gold	402	495	428	197	450	182	445	406	522	3527		400	451	210	510	229	331	405	548	456	3590	7117	M74.5/136
Blue	368	487	398	169	427	176	410	382	507	3324		388	401	186	500	189	367	368	535	400	3334	6658	M72.1/130
White	337	471	370	145	405	160	380	353	477	3098		363	370	164	487	160	345	331	506	390	3116	6214	M70.4/125
Green	315	439	348	117	391	132	353	322	432	2849		354	347	149	462	124	315	305	426	346	2828	5677	M67.8/115
Par	4	5	4	3	4	3	4	4	5	36		4	4	3	5	3	4	4	5	4	36	72	Net — HCP / Net
Handicap	5	11	13	15	3	17	1	7	9			14	12	16	2	18	10	6	8	4			
Green	315	439	348	117	391	132	353	322	432	2849		354	347	149	462	124	315	305	426	346	2828	5677	W72.8/131
Red	294	405	316	98	354	107	348	289	417	2628		329	313	126	415	112	273	275	421	325	2589	5217	W70.6/123
Par	4	5	4	3	4	3	4	4	5	36		4	4	3	5	3	4	4	6	4	36	72	
Handicap	3	9	1	15	5	17	11	13	7			8	12	16	2	18	10	14	6	4			

Date: _____   Scorer: _____   Attest: _____

Figure 4 Sample scorecard.

of the most prestigious tournaments in golf, the Masters, until it was discovered that he had inadvertently signed an incorrect scorecard and was consequently disqualified. If your score is supposed to count, be sure to count it carefully!

BASIC RULES

The fundamental goal of golf is to get the ball in each hole on the course in the fewest number of strokes. The rules of the game provide a framework that regulates what a player can and cannot do in this quest. The rules permit fair and impartial competition between players and with the course (you play against par). The better you understand the rules, the better you understand golf and the more enjoyment you can derive from the game.

The rules of golf are often defined in terms of the penalties a player incurs for certain actions and events on the course. Violation of a rule results in a one- or two-stroke penalty or a disqualification. The rules also provide options for certain course conditions. The rules specify a player's actions when preparing to strike the ball, conditions surrounding the ball at rest, and course conditions not under a player's control.

The rules of golf are intended to maintain the integrity of the game. As a golfer, you are expected to know the rules and adhere to them. If you are uncertain of a rule, you may ask your playing partners or opponents to state the rules. At all times, you must abide by the rules; otherwise you are not playing golf.

As you will see in the following rules, in many situations you must replay a ball from its original position. If you believe your ball may be lost, in a hazard, or out of bounds, you may declare your belief that your ball is unplayable and hit a provisional ball, which you hit from the original spot in case your first ball must be returned under the rules. This courtesy is intended to keep the pace of play by not making a player walk back on the course. If, after hitting the provisional ball, you discover that your first ball is playable, you can pick up the provisional ball and play your original ball. If the first ball is unplayable, declare it so and play your provisional ball as the ball in play, assessing the required penalty.

This section reviews the key rules of stroke play, the most common scoring system, and typical situations that occur in a round of golf. However, as you get more serious about the game, particularly if you are going to be competitive, you need to familiarize yourself with the rules of golf as established and published by the USGA (United States Golf Association; www.usga.org).

Relief and Free Drops

On the golf course, the ball may come to rest in certain situations that are beyond your control and therefore result in no penalty. In such cases, you may elect to play the ball as it lies (always an option in golf), or seek relief from the obstruction with a free drop. The latter option allows you to relocate the ball fairly (figure 5).

To exercise the free-drop option, you must stand outside the trouble area at the closest point where an unencumbered strike at the ball is possible. At this point, you raise the ball to shoulder height, extend your arm, and drop the ball within one club length of your spot. The ball must come to rest no closer to the hole than the original spot from which you are seeking relief.

Figure 5 Free drop.

Conditions from which you are entitled to seek relief include but are not limited to the following:

- Ground under repair (usually marked with a sign or white paint)
- Man-made objects (such as paved cart paths, sprinkler heads, and metal grates) embedded in the course
- Holes made by burrowing animals
- Casual water (water not normally on the course) left by rain or sprinklers
- Staked trees or shrubs (no relief from trees and shrubs not staked; they are considered a natural part of the course)

One-Stroke Penalties

Some situations result in a one-stroke penalty. For a one-stroke penalty, one stroke is added to your score even though you did not strike at the ball. Further procedures govern how you continue play once you have been assessed the penalty.

- **Lost ball.** If you cannot find your ball after a 5-minute search, the ball is declared lost. As a result, you must strike another ball from the spot at which you struck the original ball, plus you receive a one-stroke penalty. In the score, you count both the original stroke (lost ball) and the penalty stroke. It is known as loss of stroke and distance.
- **Out of bounds.** If your shot passes the white stakes on the perimeter of a golf course, it has gone out of bounds (OB). If any portion of the ball lies inbounds, the ball is considered inbounds. Like a lost ball, the penalty for OB is loss of stroke and distance. You play the next shot from the place of the previous shot, with a one-stroke penalty.
- **Direct water hazard.** A water hazard marked by yellow stakes is a direct water hazard. If your ball comes to rest inside the yellow stakes, you have three options. First, you may play the ball as it lies with no penalty stroke assessed, although your club cannot touch any object within the hazard until you initiate your swing to strike the ball or you will be assessed a one-stroke penalty. Second, you may replay the ball from the previous spot from which

it was struck, with a one-stroke penalty. Third, keeping in line with the point at which the ball entered the hazard and the hole, you may back away from the hole as far as desired and drop the ball, with a one-stroke penalty.

- **Lateral water hazard.** A water hazard marked with red stakes is a lateral water hazard. Lateral water hazards normally run parallel to the course. You have four options if your ball comes to rest within a lateral water hazard. First, you may play the ball as it lies with no penalty as long as your club does not contact any object within the hazard until you make a fair strike at the ball. Second, you may return to the original location of the shot and replay the stroke with a one-stroke penalty. Third, you may determine where the ball entered the hazard and, with a one-stroke penalty, drop a ball within two club lengths of this spot, no closer to the hole. Fourth, you may go to the far side of the hazard directly across from where the ball entered. Keeping the hole and the point of hazard entry on line, drop a ball as far as desired and in line with the hole and point of entry, again with a one-stroke penalty.

- **Unplayable lie.** If you determine that a ball is unplayable (for example, if it is against a tree or under a thick bush), you may declare it unplayable and assess yourself a one-stroke penalty. Now you have three options. First, you may replay the ball from the original spot. Second, you may drop the ball within two club lengths of the spot in which it came to rest. Third, you may go back as far as desired to drop the ball on a line from the hole through the unplayable point.

- **Accidentally moving the ball.** When a ball has been struck from the tee but not yet holed out, if you move the ball from its original position while it is in play, you must return it to the original position and take a one-stroke penalty. If you fail to return the ball to the original point of play, you are assessed a two-stroke penalty.

Two-Stroke Penalties

Some situations result in a two-stroke penalty, in which two strokes are added to your score even though you do not strike at the ball. Additional procedures govern how you continue play once you have been assessed the penalty.

- **Grounding the club in a hazard.** If your club touches the ground or any object affixed to the ground (for example, a tree or a post) while in a hazard (for example, a water hazard or sand bunker) before you initiate a swing, you are assessed a two-stroke penalty.

- **Playing the wrong ball.** If you strike a ball that is not the ball in play, you are assessed a two-stroke penalty and must find your own ball and continue play. It is appropriate for players to mark their golf balls for the purpose of identification. You may not alter the playability of the ball as you mark it. A waterproof marker works best. It is customary to use a line, symbol, dots, or initials as markers. Professional golfer and Irishman Darren Clarke draws a distinctive green shamrock on his golf ball, making it easy to spot on the golf course.

- **Striking the flag or another ball when putting from on the green.** If you play a ball from the putting green and your ball strikes either the flag stick or another player's ball, you are assessed a two-stroke penalty. You should play the next stroke where your ball came to rest but return your opponent's ball to its original location. It is your responsibility to have the flag tended or removed before playing a ball from the putting green. No penalty is assessed for hitting the flag stick when shooting the ball from off the green. If you believe your opponent's ball lies within your putting line, ask your opponent to mark the placement of the ball with a small object and remove the ball from the green.

- **Asking advice.** If you are playing a competitive round, you may not ask for any advice that will aid your play, such as which club to play or how to swing. You may, however, ask for general course information such as the location of yardage markers or the hole. This rule would not apply if you were receiving on-course instruction and were not planning to use your score for a competition or for handicap purposes.

Disqualification

You can be disqualified, or not have your score count in a competition, if you play the wrong ball and do not correct the error before teeing off on the next hole. As mentioned, scoring errors also may result in disqualification. Scoring errors usually result from recording an incorrect score on a particular hole. If you incur a penalty on a hole and do not assess yourself for that penalty, you have recorded an incorrect score and could be disqualified.

ETIQUETTE

The rich history of golf has left a legacy of social protocol that will enhance your enjoyment and improve playing conditions. No penalties are assessed for violating the rules of etiquette, but such offenses are considered rude. By following the rules of etiquette, you allow all golfers to enjoy the game and you send the message that you understand the sport. Most of the golfers you meet on a course won't be concerned about your skill level, but they will be concerned if you do not exhibit the social graces of the sport. Following are 10 keys to courtesy on the golf course.

10 KEYS TO COURTESY

1. Play in a group. If the starter places you with another group, take advantage of the opportunity to get to know other golfers.
2. Keep your tee time. Tee off in the correct order.
3. Follow the correct order of play.
4. On the green, follow the correct order of play, mark your ball, and tend the flag. Do not stand or walk in a putting player's line of sight, target line, or line of return. Remain quiet and still when another player is putting.
5. Maintain an appropriate pace of play. Be ready to play your shot when it is your turn and let faster groups play through.
6. Maintain the golf course.

7. Be safety conscious.
8. Operate the golf cart correctly.
9. Dress appropriately for the course, following the course's dress code.
10. Be courteous to your opponents, other golfers, and those who take care of the course.

Group Play

A round of golf is traditionally played in groups of two, three, or four, known as twosomes, threesomes, or foursomes. You may play alone, but group play is the norm. If you show up at a golf course alone, the starter may place you with another group. Consider it an opportunity to get to know other golfers.

Tee Time

It is traditional to schedule a tee time by calling the golf course within a week of the round you intend to play. You will be scheduled a time to start your round, at which time you are expected to be on the course striking your first shot off the first tee. Come to the course up to an hour before your tee time to make sure you have all the equipment you need, check in with the starter, and warm up by stroking some putts on the practice green and hitting some balls on the practice range.

The first person to tee off is said to have the honors. On the first hole, guests usually have the honors; otherwise, a flip of the coin can determine honors. For every hole after the first, the honor goes to the player who scored the lowest on the previous hole. If two golfers had the same score on the previous hole, the honor carries over from the previous hole.

Order of Play

After all golfers tee off, the distance from each ball to the hole determines the order of play. The player whose ball is farthest from the hole hits first. The other golfers should remain behind the player until the shot is struck. The golfers then continue to the next farthest ball from the hole. After a hole is finished, the order of play at the next hole is determined by score, from lowest to highest.

On the Green

Etiquette on the green is particularly important due to the proximity of other players and the number of activities taking place. Rules and etiquette ensure that players can attend to their business fairly and without undue delay.

The order of putting is similar to the order of play from the fairway. The player farthest from the hole is the next player to putt. This applies whether or not all players are on the green. For example, if one player is 20 feet (6 meters) from the hole and on the green and another is 10 feet (3 meters) from the hole but in the green-side rough, the player farthest away has the honors, in this case the player on the green. However, the group would typically give the player in the rough the option to play first so that all players are on the green before putting begins. The player in the rough can decide whether to play onto the green or wait.

It is common courtesy to mark your ball once you reach the green. This will be explained in greater depth in step 1, but briefly, marking your ball means placing a small object such as a coin behind your ball and removing your ball from the green until it is your turn to putt. When it is your turn to putt you replace the ball in front of your marker, remove the marker from the green, and then putt.

If one of your playing partners has a putt that is so long it is difficult for him or her to see the hole, it is courtesy to tend the flag. Tending the flag requires a player to stand beside the hole with one hand on the flagstick, allowing the putting player to easily see the location of the hole on the green. After the putt is struck, the flag tender removes the flagstick from the hole so that the putting player won't be assessed a two-stroke penalty for hitting the flag. A golfer playing a shot from off the green has the option of removing the flag or letting it remain in the hole, because there is no penalty for striking the flag with a ball played from off the green.

Several rules of etiquette determine where—more precisely, where *not*—to stand or walk on the green. First, you should not stand in a putting player's line of sight during a putt. The line of sight is the area where the putter can immediately view the ball and the hole as well as directly behind the ball and beyond the hole. Standing in another player's line of sight is considered poor sporting behavior because it distracts the player. When another player is putting, or taking any stroke for that matter, you should remain quiet and still.

Second, you should not walk on your opponent's target line or line of return. The target line is the potential path the ball will roll on the green. The line of return is the line the ball will likely follow should it go past the hole and need to be putted back to the hole. Because greens are sensitive, they are susceptible to being scuffed, and footprints leave small depressions. These marks can unfairly deflect a well-struck putt away from the hole.

Pace of Play

Pace of play refers to the amount of time it takes to play a round of golf. On most courses, pace of play can take 3 1/2 to 4 1/2 hours depending on the length of the course and its difficulty. You can do several things to keep the pace of play going without rushing your preparation for or execution of a shot.

First, always be ready to play your shot when it is your turn. Because order of play is determined by the ball farthest from the hole, you should always know when it is your turn. Begin to plan your shot as you approach the ball and while your opponents are hitting their shots. Doing so will allow you to know what shot you want to play and have the club in your hand when it is your turn. Don't rush your swing, but be quick to get to your ball. Do as much preparation as possible before your turn. If socializing is an important part of the game for you, do so while walking to your shot, but be prepared to play when it is your turn. Most golfers do not mind playing with a beginner, but they do mind playing with someone who is unprepared when it is time to play and thus slows play down.

Once you complete a hole, leave the green quickly so that it is open for the group behind you. Record your score while walking to the next tee. Once you reach the next tee, determine who has honors and hit your tee shots.

There will be times when a group behind you is playing more quickly than your group. If you notice the group behind you has to wait for you to finish before they can play their shots and no one is in front of you, it is courtesy to let them play through. For example, if someone in your group has lost a ball and you're going to take time to look for it, consider waving the group behind you through. Once you wave them through, stand aside the fairway or far from the green so that they can play their shots without interference. This courtesy keeps the pace of play up for everyone.

Golf Course Maintenance

Imagine walking to your ball in a bunker and seeing it deep in someone else's footprint. Or, imagine seeing a large ball mark between your ball and the hole. In either case, you would naturally feel you were being disadvantaged by someone else's lack of courtesy. If the player before you had raked the bunker or repaired the ball mark, you would have a considerably better shot. Because we all play the golf course, we must all take part in maintaining it so that those who come after us find the course in the best condition possible. You should expect and give no less.

On the green, be particularly careful to leave the putting surface as smooth as possible. When removing the flag from the hole, be careful to place it on the green; do not drop it. Take care as you walk so as not to harm the grass. Place your golf bag and other equipment off the green. Always repair any ball marks you make when hitting the green. To repair a ball mark, insert a tee or ball-mark repair tool into the ground around the mark, and lift the ground back to its original level. Then tap down uneven areas with your putter.

On the fairway, replace any divots you make when striking your ball, or fill them with sand if it is provided on a golf cart (figure 6). To replace a divot, pick up the piece of grass and soil unit that you cut from the ground with your club, return it to the bare spot, and step down on it.

Because you must play the ball as it lies, bunkers also need particular care. Be sure you leave the bunker looking as well as you found it, if not better. Rake any ball marks and footprints you may have made. Rake a bunker by walking backward out of it, gently covering your marks as you leave (figure 7). Return the rake to a safe area with the spikes turned down.

Safety Consciousness

Fortunately, few injuries occur in golf, in part because golfers take care of the two sources of danger they carry with them—clubs and balls. Be certain the area is clear before you swing a golf club, especially when you take warm-up swings, because others may not be aware that you are about to swing the club. Also, know where your golf ball and the golf balls of your partners are located. Don't play a shot if there is a danger of hitting someone. If you hit a shot that looks as if it might strike someone, loudly yell "Fore!" (as in, "Be forewarned!"). Don't be embarrassed to yell this warning; everyone hits an errant shot from time to time. People on a golf course expect an errant shot every now and again, but they also expect and deserve an appropriate warning.

Figure 6 Repairing a divot on the fairway.

Figure 7 Raking the bunker.

Cart Operation

Golf carts are common on courses today. While walking a beautiful course is the best option, sometimes that option simply isn't available. When operating a golf cart, drive the cart only where allowed, and never drive on or near a green. Park the cart where it will not interfere with another player's shot or line of sight. If you are required to leave the cart on the cart path, take as many clubs as you think you may need for the shot and perhaps a few more, because walking back to the cart to retrieve more clubs will slow the pace of play. If you are sharing a cart, drive it to a place that is mutually convenient for both players to play their shots.

Looking Like a Player

Most golf courses have a dress code, and playing the course requires you to adhere to the code. In general, the dress code is slacks or dress shorts, golf skirts, golf shirts, and soft-spiked shoes or athletic shoes. The last point is particularly important, because street shoes or heavy-soled shoes can damage the greens. When in doubt, dress conservatively and neatly. Dress for success!

Golfing With Courtesy

Good sporting behavior is a fundamental principle of golf. Golf is the only sport in which even at the highest levels players call penalties on themselves; there are no referees. Courtesy should be present in every part of your game. Make no mistake, you can retain decorum and courtesy and still be highly competitive.

Golf courtesy begins with the way you treat your playing partners. Be quiet and still when they play their shots. Don't get in another player's line of sight, and don't allow your shadow to fall on another player's ball or on the line on which another player is putting. If a player leaves equipment near you, return it to the right person. Tend the flag when necessary, or hand a player a rake for the bunker if you are close. The same courtesies will be returned to you.

You should also be courteous to players not in your group. Keep loud noise to a minimum; someone in a group near you may be playing a shot. Maintain the course and the pace of play. When necessary, let others play through.

Finally, show courtesy to the people operating the golf course. A simple "Please" and "Thank you" will show your respect and appreciation. Masters champion Phil Mickelson is renowned for his kindness and expressions of appreciation for the people who organize and conduct the tournaments and golf courses he plays. He simply treats others as he himself would like to be treated.

Golf has a rich and rewarding heritage. Few sports are played in settings so natural or lovely. All people, young and old, can enjoy golf; it is a game for a lifetime. Golf is one of the few sports in which people from all walks of life can play together regardless of age or ability.

Now that you have been introduced to the basics of the golf course, scoring, equipment, rules, and etiquette, turn your attention to developing your skills and deepening your knowledge. In the following chapters, you will take several steps to golf success. Whether you have never touched a club before or have been playing for several years, these steps will help you gain a level of skill and confidence to make golf an enjoyable and rewarding game.

Putting the Ball Into the Hole

The object of golf is simple: Get the ball into the hole in the least number of strokes. If you keep that purpose in mind, you will dramatically decrease your score and increase your enjoyment of the game. Crafting a beautiful swing, striking long drives, or sporting expensive equipment means little if next to your name on the scorecard is a high number. If success in golf is what you seek, then begin developing and improving your game with the skill that most often gets the ball into the hole—putting.

Becoming a successful golfer requires you to become a good putter. Harvey Penick, one of the greatest golf teachers of all time, once wrote, "Golf should be learned starting at the cup and progressing back toward the tee . . . If a beginner tries to learn the game at the tee and move on toward the green, postponing the short game until last, this is one beginner who will be lucky ever to beat anybody" (Penick, *Harvey Penick's Little Red Book: Lessons and Teachings From a Lifetime in Golf*, 41). In other words, learning to putt is the first step to success in golf.

According to the rules, you can make a putt with any club in your bag. However, this skill is so important and so unique that putters are designed specifically for this stroke. Putters come in many shapes and sizes, so it is best to experiment with various putters to determine which one leads to the best results. For most players, a traditional putter works well, and it is a good place for beginners to start.

One unique characteristic of a putt is that the ball is intended to roll along the ground and never become airborne. To accomplish this task, the putter has a near-vertical face with little or no angle. Consequently, the ball rolls with topspin. All other shots in golf are struck to impart backspin, which helps the ball move up into the air. The topspin of a ball not only keeps the ball on the ground, it allows the ball to track (roll) more accurately on the intended target line. Another unique quality of the putt is that of all the shots in golf, it requires the least amount of force.

PUTTING RULES AND ETIQUETTE

Putting rules and points of etiquette include the unwritten rules of the putting green. In other words, while you will not incur a penalty stroke for violating them, your playing partners will not appreciate your violations, and they will mark you either as a naive novice or as someone who is simply discourteous.

The first rule allows you to lift your ball once it has come to rest on the green (*USGA 2012 Rules of Golf*, rule 16.1B). Once you lift the ball, you may clean it if you so desire. A ball with a collection of dirt or grass clung to it will not roll smoothly, so cleaning it ensures a smoother roll. Once you have cleaned it, return the ball to the spot from which it was lifted. Failure to return the ball to its original location results in a two-stroke penalty. To mark the location of this spot, place a small coin or similar object behind the ball before lifting it (figure 1.1). You should also mark your ball if it interferes with another player's putting line. When you return the ball to its original spot on the green, remember to remove the marker before stroking your putt.

The second rule states that when playing a ball from the putting green, your ball must not hit the flag or flagstick (*USGA 2012 Rules of Golf*, rule 17.3) or another player's ball at rest on the putting green (*USGA 2012 Rules of Golf*, rule 19.5A). Should

Figure 1.1   Marking the ball on the green.

you strike the flag, flagstick, or another player's ball at rest on the green while putting, you incur a penalty of two strokes. It is your responsibility to have the flag or an opponent's ball removed if there is any chance your putt may strike it. This rule applies only if your ball has come to rest on the putting green. Hitting the flag, flagstick, or another player's ball with a stroke taken from off the putting green incurs no penalty. Play your ball from wherever it came to rest off the green; if you hit another player's ball on the green, that player simply replaces the ball where it was before it was struck.

It is proper etiquette for the player who is farthest from the hole to putt first. Continue putting the ball farthest from the hole until all players have holed out. It is also proper etiquette for the player closest to the flag to remove the flag from the hole before anyone putts. Because the grass on a putting green is particularly sensitive and cut very low to the ground, be careful to not scuff the green with your shoes or leave deep depressions with your steps or equipment. Damage to the greens caused by carelessness will affect the quality of play for the golfers who follow you, and due to the delicate nature of the grass, it can take a long time for the greens to heal properly.

Etiquette on the green requires you to avoid walking or standing on another player's line of play. The line of play is an imaginary line that extends from the ball to the hole as well as beyond both the ball and the hole. Walking where other players must roll their ball to the hole creates depressions on the target line at best and leaves spike marks at worst, which can deflect a well-struck putt away from the hole. According to the rules, a player cannot fix spike marks before putting, so it is unfair and discourteous to create such a situation. Standing on the line of play, either behind the ball or behind the hole, while another player is putting can be distracting to the player attempting to line up and make a putt. As your partners line up and stroke their putts, stay well to the side of their line of play.

After all players have holed out, the first player to have holed a ball replaces the flag. Good etiquette recommends you repair any marks made by your ball when it hit the green and at least one other that might have been left by another player (figure 1.2).

Figure 1.2 Repairing a mark on the green.

Ball marks are repaired using a tee or a ball-mark repair tool (an inexpensive tool for repairing indentations in the green). Push the tee or tool into the ground alongside the indentation and push the ground toward the center of the indentation, continuing until you have gone completely around the ball mark. With your putter head, tamp down the spot until it is smooth. This will leave the green smooth for the players who follow you and help the green heal more quickly from being struck by your ball.

PUTTING TECHNIQUES

Given the variety in both equipment and player preferences, there are multiple ways of stroking a putt. With recent and impending rule changes relative to putting technique, the number of techniques will continue to change. We therefore recommend that a player master the conventional method of putting using a standard length putter. Once that technique has been mastered, he or she may experiment with different putters and techniques. In this step, we will describe a conventional method of putting and offer an alternative technique known as the *arm lock.*

The governing bodies of golf, the USGA (United States Golf Association) and the R&A (Royal and Ancient Golf Club), have recently created a rule change regarding putting technique. The proposed rule change falls under Rule 14-1b (*USGA 2012 Rules of Golf*), and it states that during the execution of a putting stroke a player may not anchor the club, either "directly" or by use of an "anchor point." To clarify the rule, two notes are provided. Note 1 states that "the club is anchored 'directly' when the player intentionally holds the club or a gripping hand in contact with any part of his body, except that the player may hold the club or a gripping hand against a hand or forearm." Note 2 states that "an 'anchor point' exists when the player intentionally holds a forearm in contact with any part of his body to establish a gripping hand as a stable point around which the other hand may swing the club." In short, with the exception of the forearm, a player's hands or club may not have sustained contact with any part of the body during the stroke. Both the conventional putting stroke and the arm-lock technique presented in this step conform to these new rules. The two techniques presented also accommodate a player's choice of putters. Currently putters are available in these three lengths:

1. Conventional putters (shaft length of 28-35 inches; 71-89 centimeters)
2. Belly putters (shaft length of 40-45 inches; 101-114 centimeters)
3. Long putters (shaft length of 46-55 inches; 116-140 centimeters)

The distinguishing characteristic in each of these putters is the length of the shaft. Putters also come with a variety of heads. The most common putter heads are blade and mallet putters. While the length of the putter shaft influences the putting technique, the type of putter head does not.

Conventional Putting

As the name implies, this stroke is used with putters of conventional length. It is also the most common stroke used by current and past players—both professionals and amateurs. This technique has stood the test of time for producing consistent results. It also contains all the fundamentals for a technically efficient and effective stroke, so particularly for beginners, it is a good technique to learn as the first step in becoming a good putter.

The first step of the putting stroke is lightly gripping the putter in the palms of your hands. To create an efficient and controlled stroke in a conventional putting stroke, the hands should be directly opposite each other, as if you were clapping (figure 1.3a). Next, set the putter face behind the ball so that it is square to the target line (the line you intend your ball to track along to the target). Assume a comfortable posture in which you feel relaxed. Your arms and hands should be under your shoulders, your eyes directly over the ball, your knees slightly bent, and your weight evenly distributed over both feet, which are about shoulder-width apart. To allow for a straight putt, your shoulders, hips, knees, and feet should all be parallel with the target line. The ball should be slightly closer to the target side of the center of your stance.

The putting stroke is a pendulum action, much like the swing of the pendulum at the bottom of a large grandfather clock. Using a rocking action with the shoulders, bring the putter back and then forward through the ball with an even tempo (figure 1.3b). The arms and wrists have very little or no independent movement in a good putting stroke. Bring the putter back approximately the same distance as you bring it forward, just like the pendulum on a clock. The length of the stroke controls the distance of the putt, not how fast you swing the putter. Using the length of the stroke to control the distance the ball travels permits the greatest control over the putter head. The length of the stroke is, therefore, directly related to the length of the putt: The longer the stroke, the longer the putt. An unrushed, rhythmic, straight-back and straight-through stroke helps bring the putter head to the ball with the face of the putter directly facing the target line of the putt, allowing you to contact the ball squarely in the center of the putter, also known as the *sweet spot*.

Several key factors promote solid contact between the ball and putter head. The first is a steady body. A player needs to be relaxed during the stroke, but there is very little movement in the lower body (no weight shift, little or no movement of the hips or legs), no lateral movement of the upper body, and little movement from the arms or wrists. The shoulders turning around a fixed spine provide almost all the necessary movement. The angle of the spine should remain constant throughout the putting stroke. Keeping the body steady makes it much easier to bring the putter head squarely in contact with the ball. A moving body makes the putting stroke seem as though you are trying to hit a small, but moving target.

A second key to a solid putt is light grip pressure. A light grip allows the shoulders, arms, and hands to respond naturally in the stroke without conscious thought. A light grip also keeps the putter on the target line longer, because it gives you the feeling of stroking the ball into the hole rather than slapping the ball and hoping it ends up somewhere near the hole. Finally, maintaining a light grip on the putter makes it easier to relax the entire body and thus allows your natural muscle responses to help you putt successfully.

A final key to consistent, confident contact is a preshot routine. The preshot routine is discussed in more detail in step 11. A few brief notes here, however, will prove helpful as you develop your putting stroke as the preshot routine should be seen as an integral part of executing a putting stroke. Simply put, a preshot routine is a series of activities you routinely perform before each stroke. A preshot routine includes picking your target (where you want the ball to go), identifying your target line (the path the ball will take to get to the target), setting up to the ball, and stroking the ball along the target line to the target. These actions are linked in a continuous, relaxed flow. Most players select the target and target line while standing or squatting behind the ball. It provides a better view of the green than you get while standing alongside the ball. After picking the target and line, step up to the ball, place your putter head behind the ball along the target line, assume your putting address position, look at the hole, look at the ball, and stroke your putt. The time from initiating your routine to completing the stroke should be as minimal as possible, without feeling rushed. No single routine is applicable to every golfer, so you will need to experiment a bit to find the routine that fits you best. To ingrain a preshot putting routine, you need to practice it on the practice green. The Preshot Routine drill will help you develop this vital part of your putting stroke.

After the putter strokes the ball, several factors in a follow-through help ensure a successful putt. First, the wrists should be locked or firm as the putter head comes through the ball all the way to the finish (figure 1.3c). This position promotes square contact with the ball during impact. Flipping or moving the wrists changes the angle of the putter head, making solid contact with the ball almost impossible. The putter head should accelerate through the ball; it is a stroke, not a strike. Finally, if the putt is made with a rhythmic stroke, the follow-through will be the same length as the backstroke.

To help keep the body stable and to maintain the angle of the spine throughout the stroke, many good players keep their heads still and don't even look up to watch the ball after they stroke it. Rather, they listen for the ball to fall into the hole. In addition to ensuring that the angle of the spine remains steady, listening rather than watching keeps the shoulders (and consequently the arms) from moving away from the target line, making it easier to stroke the ball along the intended target line. Not only does listening to the ball fall promote good putting technique, it is a sweet sound every golfer enjoys hearing.

Figure 1.3 EXECUTING THE PUTT

Preparation

1. Take your grip by turning the palms toward each other.
2. Putter head is square to the target line.
3. Shoulders, hips, and thighs are square to the target line.
4. Feet are set shoulder-width apart, and the weight is evenly distributed on both feet.
5. Eyes are directly over the ball.
6. Grip pressure is light and relaxed.

Execution

1. Shoulders, arms, and hands move as one unit.
2. Shoulders, arms, and hands move in a pendulum motion.
3. Putter head moves back along the target line.
4. Lower body remains still throughout the stroke.
5. Backswing and forward swing are the same in terms of distance and tempo.

Follow-Through

1. Putter head comes through and follows along the target line.
2. Wrists remain firm throughout the swing (no breaking).
3. Putter head comes through the ball at the same tempo as the backswing.
4. Listen (rather than watch) for the ball to fall into the cup.

MISSTEP

The ball consistently misses left or right on straight putts.

CORRECTION

This misstep is usually caused by body misalignment. Ensure that the feet, thighs, hips, and shoulders are all parallel with the target line. Try the Two Clubs drill. Another cause may be that the putter's face is not square at impact with the ball. The putter head must track along the target line at the point of impact. Try the Target Line drill.

Conventional Putting Stroke Drill 1   **Grip**

Rest the putter head on the ground with the grip leaning against your target-side thigh. Place your hands on either side of the putter's grip with the palms facing each other. Put your target-side hand on the club by wrapping your fingers lightly around the grip with the thumb pointing straight down the middle of the club. Place your other hand on the club with the thumb pointing straight down the middle of the club. Wrap the fingers of this hand lightly around the club. Lift the putter head off the ground, and swing it gently back and forth three times. Repeat this drill five times on each side.

Success Check

- The palms are turned toward each other.
- The thumbs point straight down the middle of the club.
- You grip the putter lightly so that it swings easily in your hands.

Score Your Success

Have a partner evaluate your performance. Give yourself 1 point for every grip that includes the following:

Palms facing each other

Thumbs pointing down the middle of the club

Light grip pressure, allowing the putter to swing easily backward and forward along the target line

Your score _____ (out of 15 possible points)

Arm Lock Putting

For some people, the conventional putting stroke can be challenging to master. If you have given the conventional technique a good attempt without success, or if you are just looking to try another type of putting stroke, one that has proven useful for players is the arm lock putting stroke with a longer shafted putter. PGA Tour champion Matt Kuchar has had consistent success with this technique, as have other players. Arm lock putting is most common with belly length putters—putters with a shaft length between 40 and 45 inches (101-115 centimeters). This technique is particularly helpful for people who have difficulty maintaining firm wrists during the putting stroke. Breaking the wrist while stroking a putt makes it difficult to consistently return the putter head squarely into the ball. The arm lock putting stroke eliminates this problem.

In the setup, the stance is very similar to conventional putting. The only significant difference is in the grip. Arm lock putters should be used with the grip resting a few inches below the elbow and against the lead arm. For a right-handed golfer, the lead arm is the left arm. With the upper portion of the putter grip pressed against the forearm, the wrists are unable to break during the stroke. It also minimizes forearm rotation. Players often encounter these two problems with the conventional putting stroke.

With the lead (left) arm fully extended, place the left hand comfortably on the grip with the palm squarely facing the putter grip. Next, bring the right hand up, as you would in the conventional putting grip, and wrap the fingers around the putter grip with the palm squarely facing the putter grip and the palm of the left hand.

The stroke is made identically to the conventional length. Because the end of the putter grip is stabilized against a golfer's lead forearm, the stroke will be dominated by the rocking of the shoulders, not the movement of the hands and forearms. In this stroke technique, the left arm does the work and the right arm simply helps guide the left arm along.

Arm Lock Putting Drill 1   One-Hand Putting

The purpose of this drill is to get you accustomed to stroking the putt with the dominant target side arm. First, rest the putter head on the ground behind a golf ball on a flat green 3 feet (.9 meter) from a hole. Extend the left arm down the shaft of the club (for a right-handed golfer; a left-handed golfer extends the right hand down the shaft of the club). The top of the grip should rest on the inside of the arm just below the elbow. Second, grip the club by placing the palm of your left hand against the putter grip, and gently wrap your fingers around the grip. Your right hand remains on the right side of your body. Lift the putter head off the ground, and swing it gently back 2 feet (60 centimeters) and forward 2 feet (60 centimeters) three times. Repeat five times.

When the one-hand stroke feels comfortable and you are able to maintain a relatively straight path with the putter head, repeat the drill. This time, attempt to putt a ball into the hole with each stroke. When putting a ball, rather than make three swings as you did in the first part of the drill, bring the putter head back and through the ball only once to contact the ball. Repeat the drill 10 times.

Success Check

- Palm is facing the putter grip squarely; the back of the hand is facing the hole.
- The thumb is pointed straight down the middle of the club.
- The top of the grip rests on the inside of the forearm just below the elbow.
- The putter is gripped lightly so that it swings easily.
- The putter head follows a relatively straight path back and a straight path forward.

Score Your Success

For every stroke, give yourself 1 point for each of the following:

Maintain contact with the inside of your forearm with the top of the putter grip, and

the putter head follows a relatively straight path back 2 feet (60 centimeters) and forward 2 feet (60 centimeters).

When putting a ball, give yourself 1 additional point for every putt holed.

Your score _____ (out of 25 possible points)

PUTTING DRILLS

You can perform these drills either with the conventional putting technique or with the arm lock technique. If you are new to golf, you should first attempt to master the conventional putting stroke, because most golfers have found success with this stroke. If, after completing these drills with the conventional technique, you believe your performance may be enhanced with the arm lock technique, then grab a longer putter and repeat the drills using the alternative technique.

Putting Stroke Drill 1   Preshot Routine

A consistent preshot routine will increase your confidence and improve your putting consistency. For this drill, take one ball onto the practice green and practice a preshot routine to different golf holes. In your preshot routine, determine the target, target line, and the pace at which the ball must travel to reach the target. Then step up to the ball, take a few practice strokes if desired, and stroke the putt. Vary the distance for each putt, and attempt to follow the same routine for each putt. Repeat the routine 10 times.

Success Check

- Stand behind the ball to determine the target and target line.
- Visualize the pace of the ball as it rolls along the target line and drops into the hole.
- Step up to the ball and take your putting stance.
- Take a few practice strokes, if desired.
- Stroke the putt.

Score Your Success

Consistent preshot routine = 1 point per hole

Making the putt = 1 point per hole

Your score _____ (out of 20 possible points)

Putting Stroke Drill 2   Pendulum Progression

The putting stroke is a pendulum action; the shoulders provide the power to the arms, hands, and putter, which work as a unit like a pendulum. This drill is designed to ingrain this important action in your stroke.

Without a putter, assume a putting posture with the palms of both hands lightly pressed together directly over a ball. Rock your shoulders, letting the arms and hands swing back and forth over the ball in a straight line about 3 feet (.9 meter) long. If done correctly, the wrists should stay firm and your spine angle should not change.

Repeat the drill with a putter, but this time, remove the ball. Grip pressure should be light, and the arms, hands, and putter should function as one unit. Concentrate on creating pendulum-like strokes with the putter head moving in a straight, 3-foot (.9-meter) line. Maintain your spine angle. The head should not move, and the wrists should stay firm. Once you feel comfortable with both parts of the progression, you are ready to score yourself. Repeat the first part of the progression (ball and no putter), but place two ball markers on a putting green approximately 2 feet (.6 meter) apart. Attempt 10 strokes, giving yourself 1 point every time your hands pass over the ball and both markers when you stroke. Repeat the second part of the progression (putter and no ball). Attempt 10 strokes, giving yourself 1 point every time your putter head passes over the ball and both markers when you stroke.

TO DECREASE DIFFICULTY

- Without a putter, stand with one foot back and move arms and hands in a 2-foot (.6-meter) line over the ball.
- With a putter but without a ball, stand with one foot back and move the putter in a 2-foot line.

TO INCREASE DIFFICULTY

- Place two tees 3 feet (.9 meter) apart on the practice green. Repeat both parts of the progression.
- Passing over or touch the tees on each stroke.
- To develop a feel for the pendulum action, repeat both parts of the progression with your eyes closed.

Success Check

- Back and forward swings stay the same length.
- Arms, hands, and putter act as a single unit.
- Wrists remain firm, and spine angle does not change on the stroke.
- Lower body remains still during the entire stroke.

Score Your Success

Hands pass over the ball and both markers = 1 point each time

Putter passes over both markers = 1 point each time

Your score _____ (out of 20 possible points)

Putting Stroke Drill 3   **Ball Position**

In order for you to apply a solid stroke to the ball, the ball must be in position to be struck in the middle of a square putter face. A mis-hit will likely be short and travel either left or right of the intended target line. To begin, place a ball on a practice green 3 feet (.9 meter) from a hole. Align the small lettering or brand name on the golf ball so that it is pointing at the hole. The lettering should be directly over the target line. Aligning the lettering on the ball with the target line will help you identify the target line when you take your stance over the ball in preparation for putting. Hold the putter in your dominant hand, and take an extra ball in your other hand. Place the putter head behind the ball along the target line, and take your normal putting posture. Place the extra golf ball on the bridge of your nose between your eyes, and drop the golf ball. If your eyes are aligned properly over the ball, the ball you dropped should strike the ball on the green. Repeat 10 times.

Score Your Success

Dropped ball hits the ball on the green = 1 point each time

Your score _____ (out of 10 possible points)

Putting Stroke Drill 4   **Two Clubs**

Figure 1.4   Setup for Two Clubs drill.

A consistent club path leads to better directional control. Place two clubs parallel to each other on the ground with the grip ends alongside a hole on the practice putting green (figure 1.4). The clubs should be a little farther apart than the length of the putter head. Practice a pendulum-like putting action; the putter head should remain square to the hole and move between the clubs without touching them. Repeat 10 times.

After you are able to take 10 strokes without touching the golf clubs with the putterhead, place a ball between the clubs, approximately 3 feet (.9 meter) from the hole. Repeat the drill, attempting to clear the clubs and putt the ball into the hole. Repeat 10 times.

Repeat the drill with your eyes closed, first without a ball for practice. Then repeat the drill with your eyes closed and a ball between in the clubs. Repeat 10 times with the ball.

TO DECREASE DIFFICULTY

- Try to keep every other stroke from touching the clubs on the ground.

TO INCREASE DIFFICULTY

- Move the clubs to a distance between 6 and 9 feet (1.8-2.7 meters) from the hole, and repeat the drill.
- Remove the clubs, and draw a line from 6 feet (1.8 meters) away to the hole using carpenter's chalk. Make the putter head follow this line on the backswing and forward swing. Place a golf ball on this line, and putt the ball along the line into the hole.

Success Check

- Length of backward and forward swings should be the same.
- Make a rocking motion with the shoulders to create pendulum action.
- Keep the wrists firm throughout the entire stroke.

Score Your Success

Stroke between two clubs as if putting, no ball, putter head doesn't touch either club = 1 point each stroke

Stroke between two clubs, putting with a ball 3 feet (.9 meter) from the hole, make the putt, putter head doesn't touch either club = 1 point each made putt

Stroke between two clubs, putting with a ball 3 feet from the hole, eyes closed, make the putt, putter head doesn't touch either club = 1 point each made putt

Your score _____ (out of 30 possible points)

Putting Stroke Drill 5   Distance Control

Controlling the distance your ball rolls is vital to your success. Putts struck too firmly or too lightly not only have no chance to go in the hole, they often can make the second putt far more difficult.

Three factors influence the distance a putted ball will travel: the solidness of the strike, the length of the swing, and the slope of the green. This drill helps you develop distance control. Pay particular attention to the length of the swing and the influence of the green's slope on the ball.

Place three balls on the putting green (figure 1.5). Select three different holes. One hole should be a short distance away (3 feet/.6 meters or fewer), one hole a medium distance (6 to 12 feet/1.9-3.8 meters), and one hole a longer distance (15 feet/4.5 meters or more). Putt the balls in order from closest to farthest holes. Walk to the first ball struck, and continue putting until you hole the ball. Remove the ball, and place it near the hole. Putt it to the medium-distance hole. Continue putting both the first ball and the second ball until both balls are holed, always putting the ball farthest from the hole first. Remove the two balls from the second hole, and place them near the hole. Putt these balls to the farthest hole. Continue putting to this final hole until you hole all three balls. Complete the drill 3 times.

(continued)

Putting Stroke Drill 5 *(continued)*

Figure 1.5   Setup for Distance Control drill.

TO DECREASE DIFFICULTY

- Place three golf clubs at a distance of about 3, 6, and 9 feet (about 1, 2, and 3 meters) from the hole. Putt to the golf clubs instead of holes. Attempt to have the ball come to rest within 6 inches (15 centimeters) of the targeted golf club.
- Place three golf balls in the middle of the practice putting green. Putt to the fringe of the putting green, attempting to get the ball as close to the fringe as possible without the ball going off the green.

TO INCREASE DIFFICULTY

- Incorporate an uphill putt, a downhill putt, and a sidehill putt into the drill.
- Putt to tees placed into the putting green rather than holes. Place tees at short, medium, and long distances. The smaller targets make this variation more difficult.
- Listen for the ball to fall into the hole; do not look up to watch it.
- Putt to holes at distances of 10, 20, and 30 feet (about 3, 6, and 9 meters).

Success Check

- Backswing and forward swing should be the same distance on each stroke.
- Shoulders, arms, hands, and putter work together as a single unit.

Score Your Success

Count the total number of strokes you need to complete the drill.

27 putts or more = 0 points

21 to 26 putts = 5 points

15 to 20 putts = 10 points

11 to 14 putts = 15 points

10 putts or fewer = 20 points

Your score ____ (out of 20 possible points)

Putting Stroke Drill 6   Par-2 Golf Course

Select nine holes on the practice putting green, and order them 1 through 9. This is your par-2 golf course. You will putt to each hole in order from 1 to 9. Each hole has a par of 2 strokes. Once you have selected your course, place a ball approximately 6 feet (about 2 meters) from the first hole, and putt the ball into the hole in as few strokes as possible. Remove the ball from the hole. Place it 3 feet (about 1 meter) from hole 1, and putt to hole 2. Continue putting until you have putted the ball into hole 2. Repeat until you have putted to all 9 holes. Count the total number of strokes you need to complete the round of 9 holes.

Success Check

- Use your best putting technique.

Score Your Success

More than 27 putts = 0 points

21 to 27 putts = 5 points

18 to 20 putts = 10 points

Fewer than 18 putts = 20 points

Your score ____ (out of 20 possible points)

Putting Stroke Drill 7   Nautilus

Use 10 balls. Start putting at 2 feet (1.6 meters) from the hole, or close enough so that you surely would not miss. Then, move back in a nautilus shell shape, increasing the distance about 3 feet (about 1 meter) per ball. Score 1 point per holed putt. Use only one putt per ball.

Your score ____ (out of 10 possible points)

Putting Stroke Drill 8   **Geometry**

There are three geometry drills: line, circle, and triangle. For the line drill, place nine balls in a line, each ball 1 foot (30 centimeters) from the next with the first ball 1 foot from the hole. Begin with the ball closest to the hole, and putt each ball in turn. Hole each ball before moving on to the next ball.

For the circle drill, place six balls in a circle 3 feet (.9 meter) from the hole, six balls in a circle 6 feet (1.8 meters) from the hole, and six balls in a circle 9 feet (2.7 meters) from the hole (figure 1.6). Begin in the innermost circle. Putt the balls from the inner circle into the hole, working your way to the outermost circle. Hole each ball before moving to the next one.

For the triangle drill, create a triangle with three balls, each ball 2 feet (.6 meters) from the hole (figure 1.7). Use three more balls to create a second triangle, each ball 4 feet (1.2 meters) from the hole. Finally, create a third triangle with three balls, each ball 6 feet (1.8 meters) from the hole. Begin with the balls closest to the hole. Putt each ball in turn, working around the triangle. Hole each ball before moving on to the next ball.

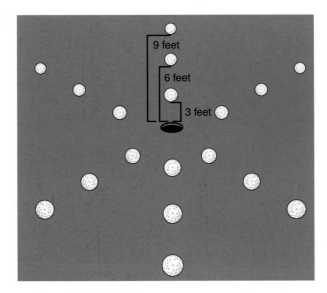

Figure 1.6   Circle drill.

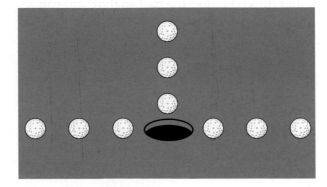

Figure 1.7   Triangle drill.

TO DECREASE DIFFICULTY

- Shorten the distance of the balls to the hole by 1 foot (30 centimeters).

TO INCREASE DIFFICULTY

- Use a hole that has uphill, downhill, or sidehill undulation.
- Attempt to make all putts in all three drills consecutively. If you miss a putt, reset the line, circles, or triangles and begin again.

Success Check

- Keep the wrists firm on every stroke.

Score Your Success

Line drill: 1 point for each putt holed with a single stroke

Circle drill: 1 point for each putt holed with a single stroke

Triangle drill: 1 point for each putt holed with a single stroke; 1 additional point for every consecutive putt

Your score _____ (out of 42 possible points)

Putting Stroke Drill 9   **Long Holer**

Choose the longest putt you can find on the green, and putt three balls. Hole out each one. Score 1 point for two putts and 3 points for holing it in one stroke. Then choose the next longest putt, and repeat the drill. Complete the drill 3 times.

Your score _____ (out of 12 possible points)

READING THE GREEN

It cannot be said too often that the purpose of golf is to get the ball in the hole in the least number of strokes. Putting is normally the final stroke that gets the ball in the hole. In addition to sound technique, a vital part of putting is being able to *read the green*. In other words, a player must be able to estimate how the slope and conditions of the green will affect the ball as it rolls to the hole.

Here is a common procedure for reading the green. First, as the ball sits on the putting green, bend or squat down behind the ball so that you can see the ball, the green, and the hole. Next, imagine how the ball will roll along the putting surface and drop into the hole. In other words, determine how the ball will move from where it sits to the bottom of the cup. When reading the green, try to answer three questions:

1. How fast does the ball need to go to just reach the hole?
2. In what direction does the ball need to start so that the slope of the green will take the ball to the hole?
3. How far does the ball need to travel to fall into the hole?

The first factor is pace, the second is line, and the third is putt length.

Pace

Pace is the speed the ball travels as it makes its way to the hole. If the ball lacks pace or has too much pace, it will stop short of or past the hole, resulting in a difficult second putt. With the right pace, the ball will finish close to, if not in, the hole. The length (not the speed, which should remain constant to maintain good rhythm) of the putting stroke determines the pace. For more pace, increase the length of the backswing and forward swing. For less pace, decrease the length of the backswing and forward swing. Remember, in a good putting stroke the backswing and forward swing have the same length and pace.

In addition to the length of the putting stroke, factors affecting pace include the slope of the green, the distance of the ball to the hole, and the type and length of grass. Uphill putts must be struck with more force than when the surface is flat. Downhill putts must be struck with less force, because gravity will increase the speed of the ball as it rolls. Obviously a longer putt requires more pace than a shorter putt. A green that has been tightly mowed allows the ball to travel faster than a green with taller grass.

On most golf courses, practice greens near the first tee resemble the greens found on the golf course. Allow yourself a few minutes of putting practice before teeing off so that you can get a feel for the pace the greens require for that particular day. It is important to concentrate on the influence of the green on pace when warming up, so avoid the temptation to concentrate on technique or even holing putts at this time. Get a feel for the greens just before you tee off.

MISSTEP

You lack distance control; the ball rolls too far or not far enough.

CORRECTION

You may not be keeping your wrists firm. If your wrists waver during the stroke, the putter head will not consistently contact the ball solidly, causing a lack of distance control. Practice using Putting Stroke Drill 2: Pendulum Progression. Another cause might be uneven lengths of the backward and forward swings. Uneven tempo in the golf swing makes it difficult to consistently pace the ball. Try the Two Clubs, Distance Control, and Ladder drills.

Line

The slopes and undulations of the green affect the path the ball takes to the hole. Putting surfaces are not perfectly flat. The more undulation in the green, the more effect it has on the ball as the ball rolls to the hole. Therefore, you must select a path, or line, that the ball can successfully travel to the hole after it is struck.

Study the green to determine whether the undulations will cause your ball to move left or right as it rolls toward the hole. If the slope of the green will move the ball from right to left, you need to start the ball to the right of the hole and let the natural slope feed the ball into the hole. The amount of left or right movement caused by the green is called *break,* because the ball breaks from the direction in which it originally started. On greens that severely slope from left to right or right to left, play for more break.

To play for break, simply align the ball along the line you want to start the putt rather than align the putt to the hole. Once you have aligned the ball, align your body along the same line. If necessary, take a practice stroke or two to get a feel for the pace needed to get the ball into the hole, then concentrate on stroking the ball along the target line. If you read the green correctly, the ball will follow the target line and the slope of the green will carry the ball to the hole.

The pace of the ball will influence the target line, because a slower ball is more affected by the break than a faster ball. Good players know this and are keenly aware of the slope of the green near the hole; the ball will slow down as it approaches the hole. Learning to read greens properly and develop a good feel for line and pace takes considerable practice and experience.

MISSTEP

The ball breaks too little or too much as it approaches the hole.

CORRECTION

If your ball is breaking in ways you had not predicted, you may be misreading the green. You need to understand how the slope of the green and the speed of the putt affect the roll of the ball. Try the Hand-Putting drill.

Putt Length

The length of the putt partly determines both the pace and the line you choose to play. Because the ball must travel a greater distance on a long putt, it will be more affected by the undulations of the green, making selection of a line more difficult. Concentrate on the pace of long putts to ensure that your ball travels the proper distance to the hole. In other words, although the green undulation may cause the ball to go a little more to the left or right of the hole, proper pace will ensure that the ball does not finish too far from the hole.

Lag putts are when players attempt to get the ball close to the hole on a long putt. Lag putts are intended to simply snug the ball close to the hole but take the risk out of putting the ball too far or too short. When lag putting, your primary focus is on the length of the putt, which is a pace issue. The precise line the ball takes, while not completely forgotten, is not your main focus.

Putts that are just a few feet from the hole are less affected by undulation, because they do not have as far to travel. However, it is still possible for the green undulation to take the ball away from the hole if the putt is struck with insufficient pace. Aim short putts into the hole and putt with a bit more pace so that any existing undulation will not deflect the ball from its target. This is known as putting the ball firm. A good place to aim would be the center of the back of the cup.

Strategic Putting Drill 1   *Hand-Putting*

If you were to follow a professional player's caddie on any pretournament practice round, you would see the caddie rolling golf balls by hand to different places on the green for every hole on the golf course. The caddie is learning the necessary line and pace for the most probable hole locations during the tournament. The tournament committee cuts the holes in different places on the green every day of the tournament, and this exercise allows the caddie to help the player determine the line and pace of the putts to be faced in the tournament.

Hand-putting is an effective method for learning to read greens. To hand-putt, bend down at various places on the practice green, then roll the ball with your hand to various holes (figure 1.8). Notice how the ball tracks differently to the hole when you change speed and direction (pace and line). Next, from one position and using one hole, hand-putt the ball, changing the pace and line to determine which target line and pace offer the best chance for getting the ball into the hole. Select a hole that provides a moderate amount of break between you and the hole. You should be at least 10 feet (3 meters) from the hole. Hand-putt 10 balls.

Repeat the drill for a score, hand-putting so that the ball just drops into the hole. When you successfully hand-putt the ball into the hole, select a new hole.

Figure 1.8   Hand-Putting drill.

TO DECREASE DIFFICULTY

- Hand-putt from a distance of 5 feet (1.5 meters) or less.
- Hand-putt on a flat surface, concentrating only on the pace of the putt.

TO INCREASE DIFFICULTY

- Use a hole with a large amount of break between you and the ball.
- Select a hole that has both a right-to-left break and left-to-right break as the ball approaches the hole.
- Use a putter instead of your hand, watching the ball track to the hole after it has been struck.

Success Check

- Putt with sufficient pace so that the ball either drops into the hole or stops within 3 feet (.9 meter) of the hole.
- You should be able to see which direction the ball breaks as it approaches the hole.

Score Your Success

Based on the second part of the drill, give yourself 1 point if the ball stops within 2 feet (.6 meter) of the hole and 3 points if the ball is holed.

Your score _____ (out of 30 possible points)

Strategic Putting Drill 2   Target Line

Successfully stroking a putt into the hole requires that you be able to identify and putt along a target line. A target line is the path the ball follows as it rolls across the green and into the hole. This drill will help you take a stance that allows you to clearly see your target line as you putt.

Place a ball on a practice green 3 feet (.9 meter) from a hole. Align the small lettering or brand name on the golf ball so that it is pointing at the hole. The lettering should be directly over the target line. Aligning the lettering on the ball with the target line helps you identify the target line when you take your stance over the ball in preparation for putting. Set the center of your putter head directly behind the ball lettering in order to line up the putter head and ball with the target line. Finally, stroke the putt by driving the center of the putter head through the lettering on the ball. Repeat 10 times.

TO DECREASE DIFFICULTY

- Repeat the first part of the drill with the ball 1.5 to 2 feet (45 to 60 centimeters) from the hole.

TO INCREASE DIFFICULTY

- Repeat the first part of the drill with the ball 10 to 15 feet (3 to 4.5 meters) from the hole.

(continued)

Strategic Putting Drill 2 *(continued)*

Success Check

- Maintain your spine angle throughout each stroke.
- Keep the body in balance.

Score Your Success

Make the putt with the ball 3 feet (.9 meter) from the hole = 1 point each time

Your score ____ (out of 10 possible points)

Strategic Putting Drill 3   Strategic Putting Minicourse

Set up a minicourse of nine holes on the practice green. Each hole should be at least 6 feet (1.8 meters) from the previous hole. Hand-putt to each hole in order from hole 1 to hole 9. Play the course a second time and attempt to lower your score.

Success Check

- Putt with sufficient pace so that the ball either drops into the hole or stops within 3 feet (.9 meter) of the hole.
- You should be able to see which direction the ball breaks as it approaches the hole.

Score Your Success

Three-putt hole = 1 point

Two-putt hole = 3 points

One-putt hole = 5 points

Your score ____ (out of 90 possible points)

Strategic Putting Drill 4   Croquet Putting

Set up croquet hoops on the putting green, and play croquet using a golf ball and a putter. Complete this drill as a game against an opponent rather than a drill for points. The purpose of this drill/game is to improve your ability to determine the line, pace, and distance of a putt without the concern for holing a putt.

PUTTING SUCCESS SUMMARY

Your skill in putting plays a large role in determining your success in golf. A long drive or an accurate iron shot can help you play well, but it is only when you master the ability to put the ball in the hole that you will get low scores. Being able to putt well can often compensate for a lack of skill in other areas of the game, but no skill can compensate for poor putting. Simply put, good putters need fewer strokes to get the ball in the hole, and consequently they have better scores on their scorecards.

The good news is that putting is the easiest stroke to learn, practice, and master. Virtually anyone can become a good putter if they understand a few fundamental principles and spend time practicing. Because it is not influenced by physical size or strength, putting is the great equalizer in golf. Developing a technically sound stroke, practicing distance control, and studying how greens affect the roll of the ball are the three keys to successful putting. Learn the information and practice the drills in this step, and you will be well on your way to becoming a successful putter and golfer.

In the following list, record your point totals from each of the drills in this step, then add them together. If you scored at least 180 points, you're ready for the next step. If you scored fewer than 180 points, review the drills that gave you the most trouble before moving on to the next step.

SCORING YOUR SUCCESS

Conventional Putting Stroke Drill
1. Grip   ___ out of 15

Arm Lock Putting Drill
1. One-Hand Putting   ___ out of 25

Putting Stroke Drills
1. Preshot Routine   ___ out of 20
2. Pendulum Progression   ___ out of 20
3. Ball Position   ___ out of 10
4. Two Clubs   ___ out of 30
5. Distance Control   ___ out of 20
6. Par-2 Golf Course   ___ out of 20
7. Nautilus   ___ out of 10
8. Geometry   ___ out of 42
9. Long Holer   ___ out of 12

Strategic Putting Drills
1. Hand-Putting   ___ out of 30
2. Target Line   ___ out of 10
3. Strategic Putting Minicourse   ___ out of 90

Total   ___ **out of 354**

Now that you have developed your skill as a putter, the next step is to get the ball onto the green where your putting skills can help you score low. While the putting stroke has many elements in common with shots hit with the other clubs, they have some basic differences. In the next step, you will look to master the fundamentals of a sound setup for a reliable, consistent golf swing. These setup fundamentals apply to short shots near the green as well as long drives that get the ball off the tee and into play.

Setting Up for the Shot

Great golf shots are often attributed to powerful, rhythmic swings. But great golf shots are as much a result of the setup as they are the swing. In fact, a successful swing is usually impossible without a sound setup. A successful golfer approaches each shot with a deliberate, methodical process that insures a proper setup before moving the club to strike the ball.

The setup is the foundation upon which a successful golf swing is built. Too often golfers dismiss the setup and practice only swinging golf clubs at golf balls. These are the frustrated players you see spraying the ball around a course or practice range. If you want to experience success as a golfer, give your setup the attention it needs. The good news is that mastering a sound setup for a golf shot is relatively easy.

In this step, you will be taken through the fundamentals of a successful setup for shots with wedges, irons, and metal clubs. Specifically, you will be progressively guided through the principles of a proper grip, alignment, and setup. These universal principles apply to almost all full and partial golf swings. Many problems people experience in their golf swings are traceable to the grip, alignment, or some other element of the setup. Master these skills, and you will be on your way to success.

GRIP KEYS

There are three common golf grips, and they all share four common elements. This section focuses on the four key elements of a good grip.

The first element in a good golf grip is having the palms turned toward each other with the hands square to the target line. When the palms face each other, the hands work in unison; when the hands are square to the target line, they bring the club head back to the ball aimed directly at the target. Here are two checks to see if your hands are properly positioned on the golf club: First, place your hands on the grip end of the club, palms turned toward each other, hands square to the target line. Looking down at your hands, two knuckles from your target-side hand should be visible to you. If you can't see two knuckles or you see more than two, realign your hands so that only two knuckles are visible.

Second, keep your hands on the club as you did in the first check. Look to see the location of the Vs formed by your thumbs and forefingers. They should be pointing between your nontarget-side ear and shoulder. If two knuckles are visible and the Vs formed by your thumbs and forefingers are pointing toward your nontarget shoulder, your hands are properly placed on the club (figure 2.1*a*).

The second key element in a good golf grip is holding the club in the fingers (figure 2.1*b*). Begin by placing the target-side hand at the top of the club's grip. For a right-handed golfer, it will be the left hand. The grip of the club should rest in your fingers and press diagonally into your palm. The butt end of the club should rest under the fleshy part of the palm. The left thumb points down the right center of the club shaft (for a right-handed golfer).

The third key element is to grip the club with the nontarget-side hand using the middle two fingers with the palm turned toward the target line (figure 2.1*c*). The two middle fingers should lightly contact the forefinger of the target-side hand. The thumb of the nontarget-side hand rests on the target side of the club, not on top.

MISSTEP

It is difficult to release the club head at contact.

CORRECTION

You are holding the club in the palms of the hands rather than in the fingers. Hold the club in the fingers between the first and second knuckles.

The final element of a good grip is to bring your hands together by closing the fleshy part of the lower hand over the thumb of the upper hand. The Vs formed by the thumb and forefinger of each hand should be angled somewhere between the right shoulder and the right ear. Two knuckles from the target-side hand, and one knuckle from the nontarget-side hand should be visible (figure 2.1*d*). If you lifted the club head off the ground and held it parallel to the ground, the grip would be resting completely in the fingers with the right hand facing directly away from the target and the left hand facing directly at the target (for a right-handed golfer). Gripping the club in this manner allows the club to return to this position on the downswing with the clubface square to the target. Grip pressure should be as light as possible; you should be able to hold on to the club, but your wrists should hinge naturally and easily. On a scale of 1 to 10, 10 being as tightly as you could grip the club, a grip pressure of 4 to 6 would be ideal.

Figure 2.1   **GRIP KEYS**

First Key: Hands-On Grip

1. The palms should face each other.
2. The hands should be square to the target line.

Second Key: Target-Side Hand

1. Two knuckles of the target-side hand should be visible.
2. Thumb and index finger of the target-side hand should be touching.
3. V should be to the side of the rear ear.
4. Club should rest in the fingers and be lightly pressed diagonally across the palm.
5. Butt of club should rest under the fleshy part of the palm.

Third Key: Nontarget-Side Hand

1. One knuckle of the nontarget-side hand should be visible.
2. Thumb and index finger of the nontarget-side hand should be touching.
3. Turn the palm toward the target.
4. Hold the club primarily with the middle two fingers of the nontarget-side hand.
5. Thumb should rest to the target side (not on top) of the club.

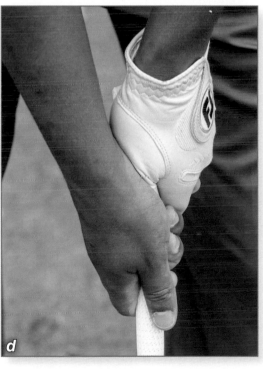

Fourth Key: Both Hands

1. Vs formed by the index finger and thumb should point at or slightly past the nontarget-side ear.
2. Two knuckles of the target-side hand should be visible.
3. One knuckle of the nontarget-side hand should be visible.
4. Fleshy part of the nontarget-side hand should completely cover the thumb of the target-side hand.
5. Use light grip pressure.

MISSTEP

The grip is turned so that the Vs formed by the index fingers and thumbs point outside the rear shoulder or directly at the chest.

CORRECTION

Position the hands so that the Vs point just to the right side of the ear on the nontarget side of the body.

The Vs of your hands are a visible checkpoint. If the Vs point to your nontarget-side ear or shoulder, the hands are positioned to return the club head squarely to the golf ball. If the Vs point toward your nose or past your nontarget-side shoulder, the club face will not return squarely to the ball. Use the Vs to ensure that your hands are properly positioned on the club.

GRIP STYLES

Now you know the key elements of the grip, it's time for you to discover a grip style that will best fit your hands. Currently three styles are popular for gripping a golf club: the overlap grip, interlock grip, and 10-finger (baseball) grip. No one universal style is best for all golfers.

Currently, the overlap grip is most popular among golfers. The overlap grip gets its name by having the smallest finger of the right hand resting on top of and overlapping between the forefinger and middle finger of the left hand (figure 2.2*a*). Arnold Palmer, Zach Johnson, Jesper Parnevik, Jim Furyk and the majority of golfers today use this grip. This grip is most comfortable for players with average or large hands.

A slight variation to the overlap grip is the interlock grip. To grip the club using an interlock style, the smallest finger of the right hand links or hooks with the forefinger of the right hand (figure 2.2*b*). Jack Nicklaus made this grip popular, but it is also used by Tiger Woods, Michelle Wie and Rory McIlory. Players with smaller hands and shorter fingers generally find this grip more comfortable.

The 10-finger (baseball) grip requires each finger of both hands to directly and completely contact the golf club. The fingers of both hands are placed on the golf club (figure 2.2*c*). This grip works well for children, women, and senior players who may lack strength in their hands, but it is also used by professional golfers such as Bob Rosburg and Beth Daniel.

To discover the most comfortable and most effective grip for you, give each of the three styles a try. The drills that follow will help you do that, but it is also beneficial to simply spend some time on the driving range experimenting with each grip. Afterward, reflect on which grip felt most comfortable and—more important—which grip produced the greatest results. You may also experiment with the various grips on the golf course to see which one holds up best under playing pressure. For example, you may play three holes with the overlap grip, followed by three holes using the interlock grip, and finally three holes with the 10-finger grip.

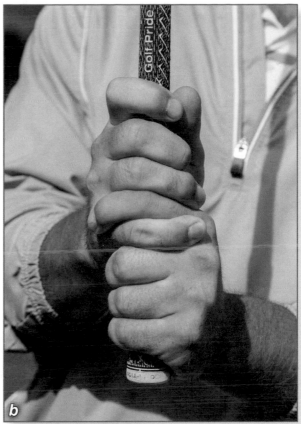

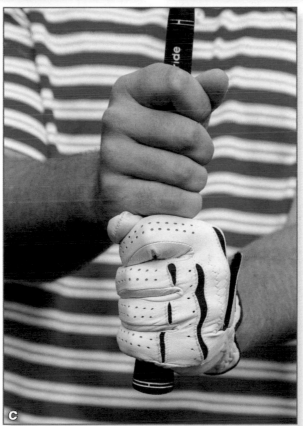

Figure 2.2 Grips: *(a)* overlap, *(b)* interlock, and *(c)* 10-finger (baseball).

MISSTEP

You grip the club too tightly.

CORRECTION

A good method of determining the appropriate grip pressure during a golf swing is to imagine the club grip as a tube of toothpaste. With the cap off and the top turned toward you, hold the club firmly enough to swing it but not so tightly that you squeeze toothpaste out and onto yourself as you swing.

Grip Drill 1   Get a Grip

With the head of the golf club resting on the ground, let the grip lean against your thigh. Begin placing your target-side hand on the top of the grip using the keys mentioned earlier in this chapter. Next, grip the club with your nontarget-side hand below your top hand, again using the keys described earlier in this chapter. Then, raise the club so that your arms are straight out in front of you and the club points up (figure 2.3). Return the club to the ground, and take a swing without using a ball. Repeat this drill using first the overlapping grip, then the interlocking grip, and then the 10-finger grip. Repeat this drill until you have practiced all three grips five times each.

Figure 2.3   Get a Grip drill.

TO DECREASE DIFFICULTY

- Focus on just one grip at a time. The baseball grip is the easiest to learn, so begin there.

TO INCREASE DIFFICULTY

- Repeat the drill with your eyes closed as you take the grip. Concentrate on feeling the proper finger positions and pressure.
- After you have raised the club and checked your grip, finish the drill by bringing the club back to the ground and taking a full swing at a ball.

Success Check

- Palms are turned toward each other.
- The club is gripped primarily with the fingers and not the palms.
- The Vs formed by the thumbs and index fingers of both hands are pointing over your right shoulder (for a right-handed golfer).

Score Your Success

Have a partner evaluate your performance. Give yourself 1 point for every grip that includes the following:

Two knuckles of the target-side hand are visible.

One knuckle of the nontarget-side hand is visible.

Vs formed by the index finger and thumb are pointing over the nontarget-side shoulder.

Fleshy part of the nontarget-side hand completely covers the thumb of the target-side hand.

Grip pressure is light.

Your score _____ (out of 15 possible points)

Grip Drill 2 Coin

After you have taken a grip with your top (target-side) hand, place a dime or penny between the thumb and index finger. Hit 10 balls while keeping the coin in place. If the coin slips, it is an indicator that you did not maintain the proper grip through the swing. Score 1 point for every full swing made without the coin moving or falling.

Your score _____ (out of 10 possible points)

Grip Drill 3   **Random Grip**

Have a partner call out a grip style (overlap, interlocking, or baseball). Grip the club using that style. Repeat the drill until your partner has called out each style five times.

Success Check

- Palms are turned toward each other.
- The club is gripped primarily with the fingers and not the palms.
- The Vs formed by the thumbs and index fingers of both hands are pointing over your right shoulder (for a right-handed golfer).

Score Your Success

Correct grip = 1 point

Your score _____ (out of 15 possible points)

Grip Drill 4   **Pressure Test**

On a scale of 1 to 10 (1 is the lightest and 10 is the hardest), grip a club with a pressure of 3. Hit 10 golf balls with a pressure of 3. For each ball hit without putting any more pressure on the grip than a 3 at anytime, score 1 point. Next, hit 10 balls with a pressure of 5, and score 1 point for each swing made without increasing or decreasing the pressure on the club. Next, hit 10 balls with each grip pressure up to 7, scoring 1 point for every swing made without changing grip pressure. Finally, select a grip pressure that allows you to swing the club head freely and in control; hit 10 balls, scoring 1 point for every swing where the pressure never changes. *Note:* If you are swinging with an appropriate grip pressure, you should feel the weight of the club head throughout the swing.

Success Check

- Turn your palms toward each other
- Grip the club with the fingers, not the palms.
- Vs formed by thumbs and index fingers of both hands point just past the right ear for a right hand player.

Score Your Success

Pressure 3_____

Pressure 5_____

Pressure 7_____

Choose Pressure_____

Total _____ (out of 40 possible points)

PROPER SETUP

The setup, also called address, is the position a golfer takes in preparation for striking a golf ball. The setup has a significant effect on the ultimate shape, direction, and distance of the golf shot. The importance of the setup cannot be overstated, and an improper address is often the cause of many poor golf shots. A proper setup allows you to generate a powerful, efficient, and accurate stroke. Investing the time to understand and practice a good setup will pay large dividends in your development as a successful golfer.

A good setup begins several yards behind the golf ball, facing your target (figure 2.4a). The first step is to identify your target (i.e., where you want the ball to land and roll to a stop). Next, imagine a line coming from the target back to the ball. This is your target line. It is common for the very best golfers to visualize the ball flight to the target in this stage of the setup. Once you identify the target line, pick out an intermediate target on the line, such as an oddly-shaped blade of grass, an old divot, or a twig, that is a step or two in front of the ball but directly between you and the target. Next, walk up to the ball and take your stance alongside the ball, perpendicular to the target line you have just visualized.

Once you have positioned yourself alongside the ball and perpendicular to the target line, place your club head on the ground behind the ball. Align your club head with the intermediate target. Using an intermediate target helps you gain proper aim and alignment much more easily and effectively than trying to align to a target that may be several hundred yards away.

MISSTEP

The ball consistently goes left or right of the target line.

CORRECTION

This error is common for many golfers. Taking a position that is perpendicular to the target line makes it challenging to get properly aligned in the setup. To help with alignment and get your ball flying down the proper target line, position a club on the ground directly in front of your feet and parallel with your target line. The club will make it easier for you to align your thighs, hips, and shoulders to the target line.

Place your club behind the ball and in line with the intermediate target. Align your shoulders, hips, and thighs so that they are parallel with this target line (figure 2.4b). When your body is not properly aligned, it is almost impossible to hit your shots straight. Therefore, it is imperative to practice taking a stance in which your body is parallel with the target line. The Alignment drill will help you develop proper alignment in your setup.

To complete the setup, bend forward from your hips as if you were about to sit on a high stool (figure 2.4c). Your knees should be slightly bent with your arms hanging directly under your shoulders. To allow the club to swing freely under your shoulders, the back must remain straight throughout the swing and your chin should be up so that your shoulders can turn completely and easily on the backswing. Your weight should be evenly distributed between your feet.

When setting up with a driver or fairway club, the ball should be in line with the left heel. When setting up for an iron shot, the ball should be just to the target side of the middle of your stance. The difference in location is due to the length of the club shafts: The shorter the shaft length, the closer to the middle of your stance the ball should be.

MISSTEP

The ball is positioned too far forward, causing you to pull the ball to the left.

CORRECTION

Practice setting up with an iron by placing a club on the ground between your feet; the grip end points at your ball. This setup makes it easy to identify the ball position during the setup.

Figure 2.4 PROPER SETUP

Identify the Target Line

1. From behind the ball, select a target.
2. Imagine a line running from the target directly to the ball. This is the target line.
3. Identify an intermediate target on that line a few inches in front of the ball.
4. Visualize your ball flying over the target line on a proper trajectory to your target.

Set Body to Ball Position

1. Step up to the ball.
2. Place the club head behind the ball and in line with the intermediate target.
3. When using a metal club, be sure the ball is in front of the left heel.
4. When using an iron, the ball is slightly to the target side of the center of the stance.

Set Up for the Shot

1. Position the feet shoulder-width apart.
2. Evenly distribute your weight over both feet.
3. Align the thighs, hips, and shoulders parallel with the target line.
4. Bend forward from the hips, keeping your back straight and your chin up.
5. Position the target-side shoulder slightly higher than the nontarget-side shoulder.
6. Let your arms hang comfortably and directly under the shoulders.

MISSTEP

You bend from the waist rather than the hips, making it difficult to maintain a straight back.

CORRECTION

Check yourself in a mirror or have a partner observe your setup to ensure that your back is straight and not curved when in setup position.

As will be explained in the next steps, in some situations you will want to modify the setup. When your feet, thighs, hips, and shoulders are aligned directly parallel with the target line, you are in a normal stance (see figure 2.5a). If you pull your target-side foot back from the target line and align the rest of your body with your feet, you are in an open stance (figure 2.5b), because your body is open to the target. An open stance is used for pitch shots, bunker shots, and fade shots. As will be explained in Step 4, a pitch shot is a short, high shot struck with a wedge. A fade shot is a shot hit with an iron, fairway wood, or driver whereby the ball turns gently to the right as it comes down for a right-handed golfer. Because the pitch, bunker, and fade shots all fly a bit higher than regular shots, an open stance helps promote a higher moving shot, or shots that move from left to right as in fade. Moving your target-side foot closer to the target line and realigning your body along this line closes your stance, because your body is turned away from (closed to) the target. When hitting a draw shot, it is common for golfers to close the stance. A draw shot is the opposite of a fade in that the ball does not flight as high and moves from right to left for a right-handed golfer. A closed stand helps promote a lower shot and one that moves right to left.

Figure 2.5 Stance variations: *(a)* open stance and *(b)* closed stance.

Setup Drill 1 Intermediate Target

Step a few yards behind a ball, pick out a target about 100 yards (91.4 meters) away from your ball. Next, identify a target line to your ball and an intermediate target just in front of your ball. Approach the golf ball, and take your address position. Have a partner hold a golf club over your intermediate target and the club face of your golf club. The club should point directly at your target. Repeat this drill five times.

TO DECREASE DIFFICULTY

- Place one tee in the ground 2 feet (.6 meters) in front of your golf ball and one tee 2 feet behind your golf ball. When you take your address position, use the tees to help you align your golf club with the target line.

TO INCREASE DIFFICULTY

- Use a different target, target line, and intermediate target each time.

Success Check

- Shoulders, hips, and knees should be parallel with the intended target line.

Score Your Success

Clubface and intermediate target point directly at the target = 1 point

Your score _____ (out of 5 possible points)

Setup Drill 2   Alignment

With a club and a ball, pick out a target and target line, and take your address position. Have a partner check your alignment by placing the shaft of a club against your shoulders, hips, and knees to make sure they are parallel with your intended target line (figure 2.6). Repeat this drill five times. Score 1 point each time your shoulders, hips, and knees are all parallel to your target line.

TO DECREASE DIFFICULTY

- Place a club behind the golf ball with the handle of the club pointing toward the target. When you take your address position, use the golf club to help you identify your target line.

TO INCREASE DIFFICULTY

- From behind the ball, pick out a target and an intermediate target, then move to the ball and take your setup. Repeat this drill five times using five different targets.

Success Check

- Shoulders, hips, and knees should all be parallel with the intended target line.

Score Your Success

Shoulders, hips, and knees parallel with the target line = 1 point

Your score ____ (out of 5 possible points)

Figure 2.6 Alignment drill.

Setup Drill 3   **Parallel Clubs**

Place two clubs parallel on the ground along the target line, approximately 1 foot (30 cm) apart. The clubs should have enough space between them to place and stroke a golf ball (figure 2.7). Address the ball with your feet, hips, and shoulders aligned with the nearest golf club (and your target line). Then stroke the ball with a 7-iron. Repeat 10 times.

TO DECREASE DIFFICULTY

- Chip the ball rather than take a full swing.
- Execute the shot using a pitching wedge or 9-iron.

TO INCREASE DIFFICULTY

- Use five different clubs to execute the shot. Use each club twice before changing clubs. Start with a higher-lofted club, progressing to a lower-lofted club.

Success Check

- Visualize each shot from behind the ball.
- As you step to the ball, place the club head square to the intermediate target.

Score Your Success

Execute the shot with the shoulders, hips, and feet parallel to the golf clubs = 1 point

Your score _____ (out of 10 possible points)

Figure 2.7   Parallel Clubs drill.

Setup Drill 4   Baseball

The principles of proper techniques in one sport often translate to techniques in other sports. This drill is appropriate for golfers who have played baseball or softball. As you begin, imagine that you are facing a baseball or softball pitcher, and assume a batting position as if you were going to hit the next pitch thrown to you. From this position, relax your arms, letting the club head fall to the ground. The position you are now in should be a proper setup position. Repeat this drill 10 times. If you can move from the baseball batting stance into a proper setup without moving any body parts other than your arms, then score 1 point.

Your score _____ (out of 10 possible points)

Setup Drill 5   Partner Evaluation

Approach a golf ball from behind, and take the proper setup, concentrating on the points covered earlier in this chapter. Have a partner check that you are set to the target line, your body is properly positioned to the ball, and your body posture is set up for the shot. Repeat five times.

TO DECREASE DIFFICULTY

- Assume your setup without a ball or golf club.

TO INCREASE DIFFICULTY

- Change clubs with each setup.
- Pick a different target line each time you take your setup.

Success Check

- Your setup should meet all the points covered in figure 2.4.

Score Your Success

Place the club head behind the ball and in line with the intermediate target = 1 point

For a metal club, the ball is directly in line with the left heel; for an iron, the ball is slightly to the target side of the middle of your stance = 1 point

Feet are shoulder-width apart = 1 point

Weight is evenly distributed over both feet = 1 point

Thighs, hips, and shoulders are parallel with the target line = 1 point

Forward bend is forward from the hips, your back is straight, and your chin is up = 1 point

Target-side shoulder is slightly higher than the nontarget-side shoulder = 1 point

Arms hang comfortably and directly under shoulders = 1 point

Your score _____ (8 points possible for each setup; 40 points possible for the drill)

SETUP STRATEGY

The setup requires three strategic decisions. The first decision will be target selection. For example, on a par-5 hole, where do you want your second shot to land? Can you reach the green with your second shot, or are you better off to lay up to hit your third shot closer to the hole? What are the risks and rewards for both of these options? As a general rule in golf, it is better to play more conservatively, because penalty strokes from lost balls, out of bounds, water hazards, and poor lies add many more strokes than an extra stroke from playing to a closer target.

The second strategic decision in the setup is determining the appropriate shot shape. Given the conditions, is it best that the shot to go left to right (a fade for a right-handed golfer and a draw for a left-handed golfer; explained later in this section), right to left (a draw for a right-handed golfer and a fade for a left-handed golfer; explained later in this section), or straight toward the target? Because a beginner often struggles simply to get the ball airborne, the idea of stroking a ball so that it moves in a predictable path may seem daunting, but getting the ball to fade or draw is not all that difficult, because this path is determined primarily in the setup. Shaping the shot is most often determined by minor adjustments to the grip and foot position, along with a great deal of practice. To be clear, shaping a golf shot is an advanced skill that comes with a great deal of practice. In the next several paragraphs, the adjustments in the setup that produce various shot shapes are explained.

Most golfers attempt to hit the ball straight to the target. The traditional setup has this goal in mind. So, to make the ball flight, the Vs formed by the index fingers and thumbs should point toward the nontarget-side ear. The shoulders, hips, and knees all should be parallel to the target line. You are now set up for a straight shot.

A ball that moves left to right in flight for a right-handed golfer is known as a fade, and for a left-handed golfer this same shot shape is called a draw. This shot is useful for directing a ball over or around a hazard. For example, if a water hazard lines a fairway on the right, you might want to start the tee shot on the left side of the fairway with a small amount of left-to-right turn so that it moves back to the middle of the fairway in flight. If you slightly mis-hit the shot and it goes straight, you will still be in the fairway and far from the hazard.

To execute this shot for a right-handed golfer, move the Vs until they point closer to your nose. The club face should point to where you want the ball to land. Open your stance by moving your left foot back and away from the target line about an inch or two (a few centimeters). The knees, hips, and shoulders should align to the target line where you want the ball to begin its flight path. A fade won't travel as far as a straight shot, so consider using a club with a little less loft than usual for the distance you need the shot to travel.

A ball that moves from left to right during flight is a draw for a left-handed golfer. To execute a draw, a left-handed golfer moves the Vs of the thumb and forefinger so that they point just past the nontarget-side shoulder. The hands, rather than the club, should be moved to achieve the desired results. The club face should be facing directly at the intended target. Next, close your stance by moving your right foot back an inch or two (a few centimeters) and aligning your knees, hips, and shoulders to the line you want the ball flight to initially follow. A draw will travel farther than a straight shot, so consider using a club with slightly more loft than usual.

A ball that moves from right to left during flight is a draw for a right-handed golfer and a fade for a left-handed golfer. Like the fade, a draw is useful for maneuvering a ball around hazards and natural objects on the course. To execute a draw, a right-handed golfer moves the Vs of the thumb and forefinger so that they point just past the nontarget-side shoulder. Make sure you move the hands, not the club, to achieve the desired results. The club face should be facing directly at the intended target. Next, close your stance by moving your right foot back an inch or two (a few centimeters) and aligning your knees, hips, and shoulders to the line you want the ball flight to initially follow.

To execute this shot for a left-handed golfer, move the Vs until they point to your chin. The club face should be pointed to where you want the ball to land. Open your stance by moving your right foot back and your knees, hips, and shoulders so that they align to the target line where you want the ball to begin its flight path.

Once the decision has been made regarding the target and shot shape, your final decision is *Which club do I select?* This decision will be based primarily on the distance to the target, the shape of the shot (straight, fade, or draw), and conditions that affect ball flight (e.g., wind, elevation). If you are hitting a straight shot, choose a club that, on average, goes the distance you are standing from the target. For example, if you are 120 yards (109 meters) from a target, select the club that you normally hit that distance. If you are hitting a fade, the ball will not go the full distance, so choose a club that will hit the ball, for example, 130 yards (118 meters). If you are hitting a draw, the ball will travel further, so select a club that normally sends the ball 110 yards (100 meters). Regardless of the club, club selection only influences ball position in the setup. With shorter-shafted irons, the ball is played closer to the center of the stance. Longer metal clubs require you to move the ball more in line with your left heel. Step 6 explores club selection in greater depth.

Setup Strategy Drill 1   Target, Club, Shape

On the practice range, pick out a target that you believe you can reach that is between 25 and 200 yards (22 and 182 meters) away from you. Next, after considering wind and elevation, determine which shot shape would be most appropriate for reaching this target. Finally, determine the club that will take the ball to the target on the path (shot shape) you have selected. Execute this drill five times, using a new target each time. Each time you complete the drill, record the distance, club, and short shape in the Success Check (table 2.1) that follows. Award yourself 1 point each for determining target, shot shape, and club. Shaping shots will be a skill further explained and developed in Step 6.

Success Check

* Each time you repeat the drill, the first decision (target) helps determine the second decision (shot shape), which in turn influences the third decision (club).

Table 2.1   Success Check

Target	Shot	Club	Score

Your score _____ (out of 15 possible points)

Setup Strategy Drill 2   **Ball Position**

You will need four clubs for this drill: a pitching wedge, 6-iron, 3-iron, and driver. The shorter the shaft, the more the ball is played in the middle of the stance. Place a golf ball on the practice range, and lay the 3-iron so that the grip points toward the golf ball and the club head points toward your body when you are addressing the golf ball. The shaft of the 3-iron should be perpendicular to the target line.

Begin the drill behind the ball. Pick out a target, and go through your normal setup routine. The only change is the position of the ball in your stance, which is determined by the club you are using. First, set up using a pitching wedge, positioning the golf ball so that it is aligned in the middle of the stance between both feet. Second, set up using the 6-iron. The ball should be approximately 2 inches (5 centimeters) closer to the target than the middle of the stance. Third, set up with the driver and the ball on a tee. The ball should be in line with the heel of your target-side foot. Each time you set up, use the 3-iron on the ground to check for proper ball position. Repeat the drill five times with each club.

Success Check

- With the pitching wedge, the ball should be in the middle of stance.
- With the 6-iron, the ball should be approximately 2 inches (5 centimeters) closer to the target than the middle of the stance.
- With the driver, the ball should be in line with the target-side heel.

Score Your Success

Correct setup with pitching wedge = 1 point each time

Correct setup with 6-iron = 1 point each time

Correct setup with driver = 1 point each time

Your score ____ (out of 15 possible points)

Setup Strategy Drill 3   **Straights, Fades, and Draws**

Use a driver, 3-metal or 5-metal. To gain maximum benefits from this drill, place the ball on the tee. Hit a straight shot, then a fade, then a draw, each time making the appropriate adjustment in grip and stance. Remember, a straight shot requires a standard setup, a draw requires an closed stance and a stronger grip, and a fade needs an open stance and a weaker grip. Repeat the cycle of three shots 10 times. Be patient; this skill takes time to develop.

TO DECREASE DIFFICULTY

- Take half swings, bringing the club only halfway back and swinging it halfway through. This provides more control, making the shots easier to hit. The ball will not fly as far in the air, but the shape of the shot— straight, fade, or draw—will let you know if your setup was correct. Once you are comfortable shaping the shot, return to the full swing.

TO INCREASE DIFFICULTY

- Alternate between a 3-metal and a 7-iron after each three-shot cycle.
- Hit all shots to the same target.

Success Check

- For a straight shot, Vs should point between the nontarget ear and shoulder, and knees, hips, and shoulders should be parallel with the target line.
- For a fade, Vs should point toward the nose, and the stance should be open to the target (a right-handed golfer would appear to be aimed left of the target).
- For a draw, Vs should point past the nontarget shoulder, and the stance should be closed to the target (a right-handed golfer would appear to be aimed right of the target).

Score Your Success

Correct stance and grip on straight shot = 1 point each shot

Straight shot goes straight = 1 point each shot

Correct stance and grip on fade shot = 1 point each shot

Fade shot moves left to right (right-handed golfer) = 1 point each shot

Correct stance and grip on draw shot = 1 point each shot

Draw shot moves right to left (right-handed golfer) = 1 point each shot

Your score _____ (out of 60 possible points)

Setup Strategy Drill 4   Called Shots

The European Tour Pro, Niclas Fasth, likes to finish a long day of practice by hitting a variety of golf shots simply for the joy of hitting the ball. At the 2003 World Golf Championship World Cup, the sun was setting but Niclas was still on the practice range. To provide a bit of a challenge, others called out shots for him to hit—straight, fade, or draw. To increase the challenge, they called out the shot just as he reached the top of his backswing.

Find a partner. One of you takes 10 swings as the other calls out the shot (straight, fade, or draw). Call out the shot when your partner is addressing the ball so that he or she can make the grip and stance adjustment before starting the swing.

TO DECREASE DIFFICULTY

- Have your partner call the shot before you take your stance.
- Execute the shot using a pitching wedge or 9-iron.

TO INCREASE DIFFICULTY

- Have your partner call the shot just as you begin to take the club away.
- Increase the amount the ball turns as it fades or draws by altering your grip and stance.

(continued)

Setup Strategy Drill 4 *(continued)*

Success Check

- For a right-handed player hitting a draw shot, the Vs of the thumb and forefinger should point past the left shoulder, and the stance should be closed (facing to the left of the intended target).
- For a right-handed player hitting a fade shot, the Vs of the thumb and forefinger should point toward the nose, and the stance should be open (facing to the right of the intended target).

Score Your Success

Called shot is successfully executed = 2 points

Your score _____ (out of 20 possible points)

SETUP SUCCESS SUMMARY

A good setup is a prerequisite to a good golf shot. Put another way, without a good setup it will be challenging to hit consistently good golf shots. Many of the problems players have with their golf swings can be traced to deficiencies in the setup. Consequently, investing time in understanding the keys to a good setup and undertaking the practice activities in this step will pay large benefits in your golf game. Golfers who overlook or skip this information because they believe it is unimportant are destined to remain novices for a long and frustrating time.

Maintaining a good setup requires constant vigilance. Fortunately, you can practice your setup anywhere. To reinforce the good habits you are building in this step, keep a golf club handy at home or at the office and periodically practice taking a grip, checking the key elements of your setup. You can also check and practice the setup with or without a ball or even with or without a club. A full-length mirror is helpful when checking the setup, particularly checking your posture. Revisit these areas of your game often. When a problem occurs in your swing, check grip and setup first; many problems in a golf swing can be traced to these two factors. Fortunately, these areas often are the easiest to practice and correct.

Record your point totals from each of the drills in this step, and add them together. If you scored at least 150 out of 260 points, you're ready for the next step. If you scored fewer than 150 points, review the drills that gave you the most trouble before you move on to the next step.

SCORING YOUR SUCCESS

Grip Drills

1.	Get a Grip	___ out of 15
2.	Coin	___ out of 10
3.	Random Grip	___ out of 15
4.	Pressure Test	___ out of 40

Setup Drills

1.	Intermediate Target	___ out of 5
2.	Alignment	___ out of 5
3.	Parallel Clubs	___ out of 10
4.	Baseball	___ out of 10
5.	Partner Evaluation	___ out of 40

Setup Strategy Drills

1.	Target, Club, Shape	___ out of 15
2.	Ball Position	___ out of 15
3.	Straights, Fades, and Draws	___ out of 60
4.	Called Shots	___ out of 20
Total		___ **out of 260**

In this step, you have learned that to have a good golf stroke, you need to have a good grip and setup. These techniques are the foundation upon which a golf game is built. In his book *Tom Watson's Getting Back to Basics*, Tom Watson, a five-time British Open champion, wrote, "I can almost always predict when my 15-handicap friends are going to hit a good shot, because they will be set up well" (28).

Now that you understand and have practiced these fundamentals, you are ready to apply them to a golf shot. In keeping with the philosophy that golf is best learned from the hole back to the tee, the next step introduces you to the chip. The chip shot gets a ball that is just off the green onto the green and close to, if not in, the hole. If you can chip and putt, you can play with anyone—because you can score. You already know about putting, so take what you learned in this step and move to the next: Chipping to the Green.

3

Chipping to the Green

Getting the ball on the putting green with an approach shot is not easy. Golf course architects design a course so a good golfer can get the ball on the green in one, two or three shots, and then allow 2 putts to get the ball in the hole. Hence, we have Par 3 holes (1 stroke to get to the green, plus 2 putts make a par 3 hole), Par 4 holes (2 strokes to get to the green, plus 2 putts make a par 3 hole), and Par 5 holes (3 strokes to get to the green, plus 2 putts make a par 3 hole). Getting your golf ball onto the putting green in the number of strokes the course designer intended is known as a 'green in regulation' and it is not easy to do for most golfers. Even professional golfers find it challenging to hit the green in regulation more than half the time. You will often find yourself just a few yards from the green with high grass or some other obstacle between the ball and the putting green. In these situations, you will need to use a chip shot.

A chip shot is a low-trajectory shot intended to land on the green and roll close to or into the hole. A good chip shot will either go into the hole or close enough for a single putt to put the ball into the hole. Because it demands a superb touch to control the distance of a chip shot, it takes hours of practice to become a good chipper. However, the shot itself is relatively easy to execute.

Producing a low-trajectory shot with sufficient roll requires the use of an iron club. The clubs commonly used in chipping are 6-, 7-, 8-, and 9-irons. The lower the iron, the lower the trajectory. The lower the trajectory, the quicker the ball lands on the green and the more roll is produced toward the hole. For example, if you hit a chip shot with a 6-iron, the ball will land on the green sooner and produce more roll than if you hit the same stroke with a 9-iron. Practicing chipping with different irons will help you learn the ball flight and roll characteristics that you can achieve with each club.

To assist you in learning and mastering this key skill, this step is divided into four sections. First, it explains and illustrates the setup or address for the chip shot. Second, it explains the proper technique for executing the shot. Third, drills that have proven effective are provided to give you the opportunity for practicing the chip shot. Fourth, chipping strategies are discussed. In Step 4, additional information will describe the decision-making process used to determine when the chip shot should be used.

CHIP SHOTS

Like any golf shot, preparation helps ensure solid ball contact and the desired flight pattern. The chip uses the standard golf setup presented in step 2 but with three modifications:

1. The majority of weight (approximately 80 percent) is on the target-side foot.
2. The ball is in front of the back (nontarget-side) foot.
3. The hands are forward of the ball, in front of target-side thigh.

These three adjustments work together to give the club head a slightly descending angle into the ball, resulting in the crisp contact necessary for a controllable chip shot. Because the chip shot requires a short swing with little force, the feet are closer together than on a full swing and the target-side foot is turned out a bit more.

Accuracy is a critical element of a successful chip shot. To improve the accuracy of a chip shot, begin by standing behind the ball looking at the hole. Next, pick out a target (landing area). Visualize the ball landing on your target and then rolling along a line to and into the hole. Finally, pick out an intermediate target (something in front of and near the ball that will help you set up directly parallel to the target line). Move up to the ball, place your club behind the ball, and square it to your intermediate target. Then make the three adjustments to the setup: First, place about 80 percent of your weight on your target-side foot, and keep it there throughout the swing. Second, position the ball back in the stance, directly in front of the big toe of your nontarget-side foot. Third, grip down on the handle so that you almost touch the shaft and position the grip of the club in front of your target-side thigh. These three adjustments will help you make clean, solid contact with the golf ball and produce a predictable flight and roll.

Because the ball does not travel a great distance in a chip, the shoulders provide all the power necessary for this shot. Setting the lower body by bending the knees and maintaining that position throughout the swing makes the chip shot easier to execute. In the chip shot, the lower body is used only for balance; too much lower-body action makes it difficult to contact the ball squarely. Once you set your feet, legs, and hips, they should be relaxed but move little throughout the swing.

With the body set in the proper address (figure 3.1a), the next phase is the stroke. Think of the stroke as a rocking motion of the shoulders, much like a putt. Initiate the backswing by turning your shoulders away from the target (figure 3.1b). Initiate the downswing by returning the shoulders back to and through their original position. The arms and shoulders form a triangle; the hands and club represent the apex. Because the shoulders provide most of the movement, the triangle is maintained throughout the swing. To promote a steeper angle back to the ball and achieve a crisper shot, the wrists hinge slightly up on the takeaway. The length of the shot determines the length of the backswing. The farther the ball must travel, the longer the backswing must be.

The chip shot is a single, smooth motion. The club travels back from the ball and then returns to and through the ball with the golfer in a balanced position (figure 3.1*c*). Because the weight is loaded to the target side during the address, there is little lower-body movement. The primary chipping motion is made with the shoulders; the hands and arms naturally follow the shoulders.

Allow the club to follow through to finish about the same distance as the club traveled on the backswing (figure 3.1*d*). In the follow-through, body weight is primarily on the target-side foot, the left wrist (for a right-handed player) remains straight, the hips and shoulders angle toward the target, the club face points directly on the line the ball just traveled, and the body is balanced.

MISSTEP

You hit on top of the ball, resulting in no loft.

CORRECTION

Flipping the wrists when contacting the ball normally causes this error. If the wrists bend, the sole of the club, rather than the club face, strikes the ball. Keep your wrists firm and practice the Address drill.

MISSTEP

You hit behind the ball, striking the ground first and losing distance on the shot.

CORRECTION

If too much weight is on the back foot at the point of contact, you will hit behind the ball. At address, shift approximately 80 percent of your weight to the target side of your body, and keep it there throughout the stroke.

Figure 3.1 **EXECUTING THE CHIP SHOT**

Preparation

1. Grip down on the club so that the hands are close to the shaft.
2. Position the hands ahead of the ball, in front of the target-side thigh.
3. Bend the knees.
4. Position the ball in front of the back (nontarget-side) foot.
5. The body weight favors the target side of the body.
6. Use the lowest lofted club that will carry the ball 3 to 6 feet (.9 10 1.8 maters) onto the green and allow it to roll to the hole.

Backswing and Downswing

1. Follow your preshot routine (same as for putting).
2. The hands remain ahead of the club head all the way through the stroke.
3. Use the shoulders to turn away from and then back to and through the ball.
4. The club face is square to the target line on contact.
5. The backswing and downswing are approximately the same length.
6. Keep the head and lower body still for better club and ball control.

Follow-Through

1. Finish with your weight on the target side of the body.
2. The shoulders and hips face the target.
3. The forward swing is the same length as the backswing.
4. Keep the target-side wrist straight.

MISSTEP

The ball goes too far or stops short of the hole.

CORRECTION

Try checking the loft of the club. A lower loft results in a lower trajectory and more run to the ball (i.e., the longer the ball will roll on the green toward the hole), while a higher loft results in a higher trajectory, softer landing, and less run (i.e. the less the ball will roll toward the hole). Practice the Club Selection drill. Also make sure the length of the backswing and forward swing are the same. Practice the ladder drill.

MISSTEP

The ball consistently goes offline to the left or right.

CORRECTION

Be sure your knees, hips, and shoulders are parallel with the intended target line. Practice the Parallel Clubs drill and the Alignment drill with a partner.

Chip Shot Drill 1 Address

Set a ball 3 to 5 feet (.9 to 1.5 meters) from a putting green. Approach the ball, and get in the address position for a chip shot. Check the three key factors for a proper setup (ball back in stance, weight primarily on target side, and hands ahead of the ball, in front of thigh). Repeat the drill five times each with a 5-iron, 7-iron, and 9-iron. Give yourself 1 point each time you assume the correct setup.

With a proper setup, practice the chipping motion, emphasizing keeping the target-side wrist straight. For a right-handed player, the left hand leads and pulls the club through the contact zone. You should feel as if you are pulling the starting cord of a lawn mower with your left hand. After each shot, your left wrist should be straight, not bent. Repeat the motion 10 times. Receive 1 point for every stroke made with a straight wrist.

Hit 10 chip shots to three different holes with an 8-iron. Check for proper address with each chip. Have a partner observe that the ball position is correct, your hands are ahead of the ball, and your weight is on the target side of the body. Give yourself 2 points for every chip you finish with your hands ahead of the club head.

TO DECREASE DIFFICULTY

- Set up without a ball. Execute chip shots, emphasizing the shoulder turn with minimal arm and hand movement. The club face should just brush the grass.

TO INCREASE DIFFICULTY

- Repeat the drill with the ball on an upward slope to the green.
- Repeat the drill with the ball on a downward slope to the green.

Success Check

- Your weight should be primarily on the target-side foot.
- Keep your hands ahead of the club head at all times.
- Grip down on the club.

Score Your Success

0 to 10 points = 2 points

11 to 20 points = 4 points

21 to 30 points = 6 points

31 to 40 points = 8 points

41 to 45 points = 10 points

Your score _____ (out of 30 possible points)

Chip Shot Drill 2   Pyramid

This drill develops distance control. Use a 7-iron to chip a ball approximately 10 feet onto a practice green. Chip the next ball so that it stops 3 to 5 feet (.9 to 1.5 meters) past the first ball and 1 to 3 feet (.3 to .9 meter) to the left. Repeat until you have chipped five balls. The last ball should stop approximately 30 feet (9 meters) directly in front of you. Then reverse the drill so that each ball comes to rest 3 to 5 feet short of the previous chip shot and 1 to 3 feet to the left. When you have completed the drill, the 10 chip shots should form a pyramid (figure 3.2).

TO DECREASE DIFFICULTY

- Chip five balls so that each ball passes the previous chip.
- Chip five balls so that each ball stops closer to you than the previous chip.

TO INCREASE DIFFICULTY

- Attempt to make the pyramid apex no farther than 20 feet (6 meters) away.
- Use a different club for each distance.
- Perform the drill on an undulating portion of the practice green.

(continued)

Chip Shot Drill 2 *(continued)*

Figure 3.2 Pyramid drill.

Success Check

- Perform the stroke with a pendulum-like action, using the shoulders.
- At the finish the hands and wrists should be firm and ahead of the club head.
- Maintain the spine angle throughout the stroke.

Score Your Success

More than two shots off = 0 points

Two shots off = 5 points

Perfect pyramid = 10 points

Your score _____ (out of 15 possible points)

Chip Shot Drill 3   Club Chips

Place three clubs on a practice green at distances of 10, 20, and 30 feet. Place the clubs so that the shafts are square to you and completely visible; in other words, do not place two clubs in a direct line running from you. Chip a ball to the club closest to you, chip a second ball to the club 20 feet (6 meters) away, and chip a third ball to the club 30 feet (9 meters) away. Repeat 10 times for a total of 30 chip shots.

Success Check

- Perform the stroke with a pendulum-like action, using the shoulders.
- At the finish the hands and wrists should be firm and ahead of the club head.
- Maintain the spine angle throughout the stroke.

Score Your Success

The ball stops within 3 feet (.9 meter) of the target club = 1 point each shot

Ball comes to rest against the target club = 2 points each shot

Your score _____ (out of 60 possible points)

Chip Shot Drill 4   **Hole in One**

Spread 20 balls approximately 3 feet (.9 meter) apart, 3 to 5 feet (.9 to 1.5 meters) from the green. Go through the proper setup, picking a hole that you believe you can chip the ball into in a single stroke. Repeat the process for the remaining 19 balls. Award yourself 10 points for every chip shot holed, and 3 points for every chip shot that stops within one club length of your intended target hole.

TO INCREASE DIFFICULTY

- Chip to holes at least 20 feet (6 meters) away.
- Select holes that have uphill, downhill, or sidehill slopes.
- Repeat the drill using three different irons (5, 7, and 9 or 6, 8, and pitching wedge).
- Have a chipping contest with a partner. Whoever holes out first wins the contest.

Success Check

- Keep the hands ahead of the club head throughout the stroke.
- Keep the lower body set so that it moves little throughout the stroke.

Score Your Success

Chip shot stops within one club length of the hole = 3 points

Holed chip shot = 10 points

Your score ____ (out of 200 possible points)

Chip Shot Drill 5   **Three Clubs and Three Holes**

This drill will help you understand which clubs are best suited for which length chip shots. For this drill, select a chipping spot 4 to 6 feet (1.2 to 2.8 meters) from the green. Then choose three different holes: One that is approximately 10 feet (3 meters) from this spot, one approximately 20 feet (6 meters) away, and the third hole should be approximately 30 feet (9 meters) away. You will need a sand wedge, a 9-iron, and a 7-iron for this drill.

Begin with the sand wedge, and chip 3 balls to each of the 3 holes (9 balls total). Score 3 points for each ball within a club length of the hole, and 10 points for each ball holed. Collect the balls, and repeat the drill with the 9-iron then again with the 7-iron. When you have finished the drill, you should have chipped a total of 27 balls.

TO DECREASE DIFFICULTY

- Chip five balls to hole 1, then five balls to hole 2, and then five balls to hole 3. This modification will help you gain a better feel for distance.

TO INCREASE DIFFICULTY

- Select three holes that are 20 feet (6 meters), 40 feet (12 meters), and 60 feet (18 meters) away from your chipping spot.

(continued)

Chip Shot Drill 5 *(continued)*

Score Your Success

Chip shot stops within one club length of the target hole = 3 points

Holed chip shot = 10 points

Your score _____ (out of 270 possible points)

Chip Shot Drill 6   Up and Down

Many golf instructors and touring pros consider this drill to be the most effective method for lowering scores. Chip a ball to a hole, take a putter, and continue putting until you hole the ball. Attempt to get the ball in the hole with one chip shot and one putt. Repeat the shot 10 times with 10 different holes.

TO DECREASE DIFFICULTY

- Complete the drill using only one hole that is within 6 feet (1.8 meters) of you.

TO INCREASE DIFFICULTY

- Vary the distance of the holes. The closest hole should be no farther than 10 feet, and the farthest hole should be at least 60 feet (18 meters).
- Select a different iron for each chip according to the distance you wish the ball to travel in the air and roll on the green.
- Select holes with different undulations—left-to-right break, right-to-left break, uphill, and downhill.

Success Check

- Maintain the triangle of shoulders, arms, and club throughout the shot.
- Slightly hinge the wrists on the takeaway for longer shots.
- Maintain balance.

Score Your Success

Three strokes to hole the ball (a chip and two putts) = 1 point

Two strokes to hole the ball (a chip and a putt) = 3 points

Holed chip shot = 5 points

Your score _____ (out of 50 possible points)

Chip Shot Drill 7   **Chipping Course**

Select nine different holes on a practice green, and number them 1 through 9. Chip and putt a ball into each hole in order. You may change clubs or use the same club for all nine holes. Each hole represents a par 3 (one shot to get on the green and two strokes to putt out). Count the total number of strokes needed to complete the nine holes.

Success Check

- Maintain the triangle of shoulders, arms, and club through the shot.
- Hinge the wrists slightly on the takeaway for longer shots.
- Maintain balance.

Score Your Success

29 strokes or more needed to complete the course = 5 points

24 to 28 strokes needed to complete the course = 10 points

18 to 23 strokes needed to complete the course = 15 points

17 strokes or fewer needed to complete the course = 20 points

Your score _____ (out of 20 possible points)

CHIPPING STRATEGY

As is the case for any golf shot, the first decision to be made in executing a chip shot is to determine where you want the ball to go (target). The second decision is to figure out how you want it to get there (ball flight, landing, and roll). Most good golfers do this by visualizing the chip shot and imagining the trajectory of the ball, where the ball will land on the green, and the path it will take as it rolls to the hole.

To execute a chip shot with a low trajectory, that lands on the green quickly, and rolls to the hole, club selection is critical. This decision will determine both the trajectory and the amount of roll achieved in a properly executed chip shot. If you are 2 or 3 feet (.6 to .9 meter) from the green, a low-lofted club such as a 4-, 5-, or 6-iron may be the best choice. If you are 10 to 15 feet (3 to 4.5 meters) from the green, an 8- or 9-iron or even a pitching wedge may be the best choice. Stroking chip shots to different targets using different clubs will help you learn which clubs provide the ball flight and roll characteristics you need for the best chance of holing the shot (see Club Selection Drill 1).

Determining the path the ball will take as it rolls on the green is the next strategic decision you need to make. This process is referred to as *reading the green* and was described in step 1. A chip shot and a putt have a great deal in common as the intent of both shots is for the ball to roll into the hole. After visualizing the shot and choosing the club and ball path, the next step is to properly execute the shot.

Chipping Strategy Drill 1 Club Selection

Select a hole on the practice green within 30 feet (9 meters) of your golf ball. Experiment with various clubs to discover which club gets the ball consistently closer to the hole. Note changes in where the ball lands on the green and the path it takes as it rolls to the hole. Using a 6-, 7-, 8-, and 9-iron, hit at least three chip shots with each club.

To score the drill, hit a chip shot with 5-, 7-, and 9-irons to a single hole that is 10 to 15 feet (3 to 4.5 meters) away. Hit three shots with each club.

TO DECREASE DIFFICULTY

- Chip the ball to a towel placed on the practice green rather than to a golf hole.
- Select one club (6-, 7-, 8-, or 9-iron), and determine which hole on the practice green you can consistently chip closest to with that club.

TO INCREASE DIFFICULTY

- Chip to a hole that is uphill. Does this change your club selection?
- Chip to a hole that is downhill. Does this change your club selection?

Success Check

- Visualize the landing area, and roll to the hole for each chip.
- Read the green to determine whether you need more or less club loft to compensate for an uphill or downhill chip shot.

Score Your Success

Chip lands on the green = 1 point

Ball stops within 6 feet (1.8 meters) of the hole = 2 points

Holed chip shot = 3 points

Your score _____ (out of 27 possible points)

Chipping Strategy Drill 2 Modified Hazard

A chip shot is often used to clear a hazard between the ball and the putting green, and this drill simulates such a situation. Place a golf bag approximately 10 yards (9 meters) in front of your ball. Chip over the bag to golf clubs placed on the green at 20, 30, and 40 feet (6, 9, and 12 meters; figure 3.3). Experiment with clubs with different lofts, and note their effect on the trajectory of your shot.

Now you are ready to score the drill. Place four golf clubs at 3, 6, 9, and 12 feet (about 1, 2, 3, and 4 meters) onto the green. Chip the first ball so that it lands between the first and second clubs, chip the second ball so that it lands between the second and third clubs, and chip the third ball so that it lands between the third and fourth clubs. Repeat five times for a total of 15 chip shots.

TO DECREASE DIFFICULTY

- Repeat the drill with a pitching or sand wedge.

TO INCREASE DIFFICULTY

- Repeat the drill, setting clubs at 5, 10, and 15 feet (1.5, 3, and 4.5 meters) from the edge of the green.
- Practice chipping over a bunker to a practice green.
- Repeat the drill, setting clubs at 50, 60, and 70 feet (15, 18, and 21 meters).

Figure 3.3 Modified Hazard drill.

Success Check

- Visualize the trajectory and roll of the ball before stroking each chip shot.
- Focus on where you want the ball to land, not on the obstacle.

Score Your Success

Chip shot lands in the intended target area = 2 points

Your score _____ (out of 30 possible points)

CHIPPING SUCCESS SUMMARY

During almost any round of golf, you will find yourself close to, but not quite on the green on several occasions, and sometimes more. The purpose of golf is to get the ball in the hole in the least number of strokes; a well-practiced and executed chip shot will help you do just that. If you become a very good chipper, you will occasionally chip your balls into the hole. The more proficient you become at chipping, the greater your success on the scorecard will be. Like putting, chipping is not one of the most glamorous skills in golf. It is, however, critical to your success and therefore requires continued practice. Because this shot is a short-distance shot favoring accuracy over power, it is easier to gain proficiency with practice. Use the drills in this step to increase your skill and the Score Your Success scores to assess your progress. When you play, monitor your ups and downs because you will find that many strokes can be saved with a good chip shot.

Record your point totals from each of the drills in this chapter, and add them together. If you scored at least 400 out of 702 points, you're ready for the next step. If you scored fewer than 400 points, review the drills that gave you the most trouble before moving on to the next step.

SCORING YOUR SUCCESS

Chip Shot Drills

1.	Address	___ out of 30
2.	Pyramid	___ out of 15
3.	Club Chips	___ out of 60
4.	Hole in One	___ out of 200
5.	Three Clubs and Three Holes	___ out of 270
6.	Up and Down	___ out of 50
7.	Chipping Course	___ out of 20

Chipping Strategy Drills

1.	Club Selection	___ out of 27
2.	Modified Hazard	___ out of 30
Total		**___ out of 702**

A chip shot is the best shot for getting a ball that is just off the green onto the green and rolling toward or into the hole. Practice this shot often, and you will shoot lower scores.

Sometimes you will find yourself too far from the green for an effective chip shot but not far enough for a shot requiring a full swing. Other times, you may need the ball to land softly on the green and roll very little. Both of these situations call for a pitch shot, which is covered in the next step.

Pitching From Farther Away

A pitch shot is similar to a chip shot in that the ball flies through the air to reach the green and then rolls to the hole. However, a pitch shot is used when the ball must fly farther or higher to reach the green and then stop rather quickly. Generally speaking, a chip has a low trajectory and uses conditions of the ground (rolls over a mound, down a slope, etc.), while a pitch aims to fly over any obstacles or inconveniences in the ground and land on a flat surface close to the hole. Typically a pitch shot is used when the ball is 10 to 90 yards (9 to 82 meters) from the green. With its high trajectory and modest roll, the pitch shot gets the ball over bumps in the fairway, past the rough, over a green-side bunker, or even beyond a small pond and still allows the ball to sit when it lands and not roll off the green. Because the majority of shots in a round of golf are played from fewer than 100 yards (90 meters) from the hole, a player who becomes proficient at putting, chipping, and pitching—the skills of the short game—will make significant progress in shooting lower scores.

PITCH SHOTS

A successful pitch shot requires accuracy and distance control, and proper setup is key to both. As with a chip shot, the pitch shot does not require a full, powerful swing, so begin the setup by identifying precisely where you would like the ball to land on the green. When selecting the landing target, remember that the ball will roll gently when it lands.

With the target firmly in mind, set up in a relatively narrow, balanced stance with the feet less than shoulder-width apart (figure 4.1a). To promote a smooth swing, open the stance a bit by pulling the target-side foot back a few inches and pointing the toes toward the target. Because pitching wedges have shorter shafts, play the ball in the middle of the stance to promote clean, crisp contact. Move the hands slightly ahead of the ball.

Once you are locked onto your target and have set up properly, you are ready to begin the swing (figure 4.1b). Turn the shoulders away from the target, letting the shoulders draw the club back. The arms and hands will naturally follow the turn of the shoulders, as will the hips and legs. The backswing is the key to distance control: The shorter the backswing, the shorter the shot. With practice, you will learn how far the backswing needs to go for the ball to land on target.

Distance control and accuracy are possible only when you execute the pitch shot in a relaxed, rhythmic manner. A pitch shot uses the same smooth, easy motion as tossing a ball underhanded into a bucket. Begin the downswing (figure 4.1c) by shifting the weight from the back foot to the target side and letting the rest of the body follow. The club should feel as if it is simply dropping back to the ball as the shoulders and chest unwind toward the target. The speed of the shot slowly accelerates through contact and a high finish. At impact, your left wrist is straight, your focus is on stroking the ball firmly toward the target, and your hands are ahead of the club head. Don't rush the downswing.

In the follow-through, the club follows the ball toward the target (figure 4.1d). You should finish on balance with your body weight on the target-side foot, hips and chest facing the target, and hands about as high as they were in the backswing. This finish will help to create a rhythmic movement where the back and forward motion follow a similar pattern. Before you lift your eyes to see your shot, focus on the location where the ball was before contact. In other words, resist the temptation to look up too soon, because it may cause the shoulders to pull the club offline. Make sure the ball is well gone before you look for it.

If you have trouble hitting the ball with loft, check your wrist position. If you flip your wrists in an effort to lift the ball into the air, you may hit the top of the ball and not get any loft. Many players attempt to scoop the ball up using their wrists. When the left wrist bends, the sole of the club rather than the club face strikes the ball, causing the dreaded skulled shot. Execute the shot by turning the shoulders and chest, letting the arms, hands, and club simply follow.

Decision Making

A number of factors dictate what shot to hit. When considering the pitch shot, here are some guidelines that might help you make the best decision:

1. If every possible trajectory were available, how would you want the ball to travel from where it is to where you want it to finish? Try to imagine the ball in the air, how it behaves on the green, and if it rolls or if it is possible to stop.

Figure 4.1 **EXECUTING THE PITCH SHOT WITH CORRECT WRIST POSITION AND BODY WEIGHT DISTRIBUTION**

Preparation

1. Set up in a narrow, balanced stance.
2. Position the feet less than shoulder-width apart.
3. Pull the target-side foot back a few inches, and point the toes toward the target.
4. Play the ball in the middle of the stance.
5. Position the hands slightly ahead of the ball.

Backswing

1. Turn the shoulders away from the target to begin the swing.
2. Allow the arms, hands, and club to naturally follow the turn of the shoulders.
3. Allow the hips and legs to turn naturally in response to shoulder turn.
4. Use the length of the backswing to determine flight distance.

Downswing

1. Begin the downswing by shifting weight from the back to the front foot.
2. Drop the club back to the ball as the shoulders and chest unwind to the target.
3. Build shot speed slowly to accelerate through the ball.
4. At impact, keep the left wrist firm and square to the target.
5. Execute the shot in a relaxed, rhythmic manner.

(continued)

Figure 4.1 *(continued)*

Follow-Through

1. Let the club follow the ball toward the target.
2. Finish with the body weight on the target-side foot, elbows high.
3. Focus on the spot where the ball was before contact, then lift your eyes to follow the ball.

2. If you were to create that ball flight using a club and a swing, what would it be like? Can you imagine yourself doing it?

3. Is this practically possible? In other words, does the lie of the ball allow for such a shot? If not, return to item 1 on this list and select another way for the ball to travel. Once you have found the way you want the shot to be, then ask the questions *What club will you need?* and *What swing do you want to use?*

When the questions presented result in a clear answer—a high trajectory shot that flies to the green and stops quickly—you have arrived at the pitch shot!

To achieve the higher trajectory and less roll that characterize the pitch shot, a higher-lofted iron is required. Wedges, a special category of irons, are used for pitch shots. Common wedges include the pitching wedge (45 to 52 degrees of loft), sand wedge (52 to 58 degrees of loft), and lob wedge (58 to 64 degrees of loft). The higher the loft of the club, the higher the trajectory of the ball, the shorter distance the ball will fly, and the less distance the ball will roll when it lands. A proficient player will also be able to put backspin on the ball, at least on shots that are slightly longer, which will cause the ball to stop more or less immediately or even move backward after landing on the green.

Controlling the Ball

As mentioned previously, a good player is likely to be able to put backspin on the ball, influencing the ball's flight in the air and its behavior upon landing on the green. A number of factors influence the way the ball reacts. The more proficient the player, the more control he or she will have over these factors and hence over the ball. Of course, factors such as the speed of the club head and the loft of the club face influence the ball. A good player will be able to vary these factors by adjusting the length of the swing as well as the speed of the swing. The loft will vary depending on the position of the hands and body at impact. Given the same club head speed and loft, there are still some factors that will determine the players' ability to control the ball. Some can be influenced by the player, while others are dependent on external conditions such as these:

- **The golf ball.** Generally speaking, the softer the golf ball, the better the chance of controlling the ball. Tour players use the so-called multilayer ball, which is more or less a requirement when wishing to create backspin.

- **The lie.** Good ball control requires the club face to make clean contact with the ball. In other words, a ball sitting on a closely mown fairway, ideally on rather firm ground, will be easier for the club to get to than a ball in a lie in the rough where grass is likely to prevent clean contact. Of course, a fairway on a course where tour players play their tournaments will be prepared in a different way than a normal course, so it may be that this greatly limits your chances to create backspin and have good ball control!

- **The club.** There has been great debate over the last few years about the importance of the grooves of the club. So-called square grooves that increased the amount of spin possible to put on the ball, especially from the rough, have now been banned in an effort to increase the importance of hitting the fairways. What players can do is to make sure that the face of the club is clean and the grooves are free from dirt, which can improve the contact with the ball.

- **The wind.** Playing with the wind will make putting backspin on the ball a lot more difficult. Playing against the wind means the angle at which the ball will come into the green and the spin on the ball will cause the ball to stop in shorter distance once it has hit the green.

- **The green.** Whether the green is firm or soft will greatly influence what the ball does when it hits the ground. A soft green will increase the possibility of the ball spinning back, while a firm green will cause the ball to bounce high and forward.

MISSTEP

You hit the top of the ball, resulting in no loft.

CORRECTION

The most common problem occurs when less experienced golfers hit the top of the ball while trying to pitch. The natural tendency is to try to help the ball get airborne by breaking the wrists at impact. This happens when the player tries to lift the ball rather than rely on the loft of the club face doing its job. Ideally when hitting a pitch shot, the hands are above or slightly in front of the ball at impact. If not, there is great risk that the club has already reached its lowest point in the swing, which means the head is on its way up when hitting the ball. A posture problem may also be the cause of this error. Wedges are the shortest clubs in the bag and require greater bend in the knee to properly hit down on the ball. Check your posture, particularly during the swing. You may have the tendency to raise up as the club approaches the ball. Maintain proper posture from address to follow-through.

MISSTEP

You hit behind the ball, striking the ground first and losing distance on the shot.

CORRECTION

Ironically this problem can stem from the same issue as the previous misstep, especially in combination with resting the weight on the non-target-side foot. It can easily happen because the pitch shot uses an abbreviated swing. Be sure to move your weight to the target-side foot before contacting the ball.

MISSTEP

You fail to hit the ball clean, resulting in poor distance control.

CORRECTION

If you are having problems hitting the ball in a consistent way, you may be decelerating on the downswing. The pitch shot demands distance control. A common error is to overswing on the backswing and then compensate by decelerating on the downswing. This error results in poor contact with the ball. Shorten the backswing, and be mildly aggressive on the downswing. You'll find it easier to make solid contact, which makes it easier to control the distance the ball travels.

MISSTEP

The ball consistently goes off the target line.

CORRECTION

Check your alignment. Be sure your knees, hips, and shoulders are all parallel with the intended target line. Try the String drill.

MISSTEP

The ball goes too far or falls short.

CORRECTION

Check your swing length. Evaluate the length of the backswing and forward swing on the pitch shot; they should be the same. Practice the Ladder drill.

Pitch Shot Drill 1   String

To hit crisp pitch shots, your weight must be forward and you must bring the club to the ball so that you contact first the ball and then the turf. This drill improves your contact and thus your control. Lay a piece of string, a small branch, or another object approximately 1 foot (30 centimeters) long on the ground perpendicular to you. Take your stance so that the string runs directly out from your nontarget-side foot. Place a golf ball in the middle of your stance. From this position, execute the pitch shot, concentrating on getting the club head past the string before it contacts the ball (figure 4.2). Repeat the drill 10 times.

Figure 4.2 String drill.

TO DECREASE DIFFICULTY

- Use a high-lofted wedge (56 to 60 degrees), and open the club face.

TO INCREASE DIFFICULTY

- Pitch to targets at 15, 20, and 25 yards (14, 18, and 23 meters).
- Use different wedges (pitching, sand, and lob).
- Move the string so that it is only a couple of inches from the ball.

Success Check

- The weight should be on the target-side foot at contact.
- Execute the shot in a relaxed, rhythmic manner.

Score Your Success

Club strikes the ground on the target side of string = 1 point

Club strikes the ball first, then the ground = 2 points

Your score _____ (out of 20 possible points)

Pitch Shot Drill 2   See the Spot

This drill is designed to help you contact the ball before the ground. Pitch the ball to the practice green (no specific target is needed). Before looking up to see the ball in flight, locate the spot where the ball was before you struck it. Once you see the spot, look up to see where your shot landed. Repeat this drill 10 times.

TO DECREASE DIFFICULTY

- Take a shorter backswing
- Narrow your stance

TO INCREASE DIFFICULTY

- Pick a landing target before executing the shot. Hit the shot, locate the spot the ball occupied before being struck, and then look up to see how close the ball comes to your target.

Success Check

- Weight should be on the target-side foot at contact.
- Execute the shot in a relaxed, rhythmic manner.

Score Your Success

Locate the spot where ball was before looking up = 1 point each shot

Your score _____ (out of 10 possible points)

Pitch Shot Drill 3   Pitch Shot Appreciation Check

This drill works best when done with a partner, because you can discuss and judge each other's thinking and performance. On your own it requires honesty and a bit of creativity; there may be other ways to hit the shot than what you first thought.

The purpose of the drill is to check your thinking, your decision making, and your ability to perform what you set out to do. Choose a situation that you think will require a pitch shot, such as where the pin sits tightly on the green and there is no room for the ball to roll after landing, a lie where you need to hit the shot over a bunker, or something similar. Imagine how the ball travels through the air, lands on the green, and comes to rest where you want it to rest. Once you are happy with your vision of the shot, and if you have a partner you are in agreement, decide on club and the way you want to hit the shot. Now turn to the way you need to swing the club, and try to get a clear sense of what it is like. Perform the shot, and judge the outcome. Repeat the drill 10 times from different positions, and score you success. Give yourself 5 points if you manage to pick the right type of shot (trajectory, roll, etc.), manage to perform it the way you want, and the ball comes to rest where you wanted it to; 3 points if two out of three (type of shot, performance, result) is all right; and 1 point for one out of three.

TO DECREASE DIFFICULTY

- Use the same spot for each of the 10 shots to allow yourself to learn from previous experience.

TO INCREASE DIFFICULTY

- Vary the lies and length of shots so that each shot requires you to make a new assessment.

Success Check

- Make sure that you perform the shot twice—once in your mind and once in reality.
- The two shots, the Imagery shot and the real shot, should match each other.

Score Your Success

10 points or fewer = 5 points

11 to 19 points = 10 points

20 to 29 points = 15 points

30 to 39 points = 20 points

40 to 50 points = 25 points

Your score _____ (out of 25 possible points)

Pitch Shot Drill 4   Target Towel

Distance control is vital to a successful pitch. You must be able to land the ball on a specific target on the green so that it can roll to the hole. This drill is designed to help you develop this vital touch. Remember, to achieve distance control you need to regulate the length of the backswing, not change the speed of the swing.

Place golf towels at 20, 40, and 60 yards (18, 37, and 55 meters) from the hole. From a good lie, pitch 10 balls to each target in turn, beginning with the nearest target towel (figure 4.3). Try to land the ball on the target. Give yourself 5 points if the ball lands on the target, 3 points if the ball lands within 10 yards of the target, and 1 point if the ball comes to rest on or within 10 yards of the target. Hit 10 pitch shots to each target for a total of 30 pitch shots.

Figure 4.3 Target Towel drill.

(continued)

Pitch Shot Drill 4 *(continued)*

TO DECREASE DIFFICULTY

- Place one golf towel at 25 yards. When you are able to consistently land 5 balls out of 10 within 10 yards of this target, return to the original drill.
- Put the ball on a tee before hitting the pitch shot.

TO INCREASE DIFFICULTY

- Pitch the balls from slight or moderate rough. Pitch shots are often hit from these conditions.
- Pitch the balls with your eyes closed.

Success Check

- Play the ball from the middle of your stance.
- Regulate distance by changing the length of the backswing, not by changing the speed of the swing.

Score Your Success

25 points or fewer = 5 points

26 to 50 points = 10 points

51 to 75 points = 15 points

76 to 100 points = 20 points

101 to 125 points = 25 points

126 to 150 points = 30 points

Your score _____ (out of 30 possible points)

Pitch Shot Drill 5 Pitch and Putt Practice

Place a golf ball approximately 15 yards (14 meters) from the edge of a practice green and 30 yards (27 meters) from the hole on the practice green. Pitch the ball to the green, then putt the ball into the hole. The goal is to take the fewest number of strokes to hole the ball. Give yourself 20 points if you hole the pitch shot, 10 points if you use a pitch shot and a putt, 5 points if you use a pitch shot and two putts, and 1 point if you use a pitch shot and three putts. Repeat five times.

TO DECREASE DIFFICULTY

- Place the ball 5 yards (4.5 meters) from the green in a good lie.
- Instead of a hole, pitch and putt to a club or umbrella placed on the green.

TO INCREASE DIFFICULTY

- For each pitch and putt, select a new hole and distance.
- Repeat the drill using a lob wedge, sand wedge, and pitching wedge.

Success Check

- Maintain the spine angle throughout the swing.
- At the finish, your weight should be on the target side of the body and the elbows should be high.

Score Your Success

25 points or fewer = 5 points

26 to 50 points = 10 points

51 to 75 points = 15 points

76 to 100 points = 20 points

Your score _____ (out of 20 possible points)

Pitch Shot Drill 6   Pitch and Putt Stroke Play

Select nine holes on a practice green. Place a golf ball approximately 10 yards (9 meters) from the edge of the practice green but in line with the target hole; no other holes should be between your ball and the target hole. Pitch the ball to the green, then putt the ball into the hole. Repeat until you have played all nine holes, taking each hole in turn.

Success Check

- Maintain the spine angle throughout the swing.
- At the finish, your weight should be on the target side of the body and the elbows should be high.

Score Your Success

Complete all nine holes in 36 strokes or more = 5 points

Complete all nine holes in 31 to 35 strokes = 10 points

Complete all nine holes in 26 to 30 strokes = 15 points

Complete all nine holes in 25 strokes or fewer = 20 points

Your score _____ (out of 20 possible points)

Pitch Shot Drill 7   **Pitch and Putt Match Play**

Once you've completed pitch and putt stroke play, get a partner and play a match of nine holes. Begin 10 to 15 yards (9 to 14 meters) away from the practice green, and select a golf hole on the practice green. Both of you should pitch your ball to the hole and then putt out. The golfer who has the fewest strokes to the hole wins the hole. If you both take the same number of strokes, the hole is halved. Repeat until you have completed all nine holes.

Success Check

- Maintain the spine angle throughout the swing.
- At the finish, your weight should be on the target side of the body and the elbows should be high.

Score Your Success

Give yourself 2 points for every hole you win and 1 point for each hole that is halved.

Your score _____ (out of 18 possible points)

Pitch Shot Drill 8   **Hazard**

A pitch shot is often used to stroke the ball high over a hazard—water, tall rough, a small tree, or a bunker—and make the ball land softly on the green. Golfers often find a pitch shot over a large hazard quite challenging, so the hazard drill allows you to practice your technique under conditions similar to those on a course.

Find a practice green that has a hazard, preferably a sand bunker, nearby (figure 4.4). You should be at least 25 yards (23 meters) from the green. Place 10 golf balls a few feet from the hazard. Pitch the balls to the middle of the green.

Once you are comfortable with the pitch shot, try pitching 10 balls over a green-side hazard to a golf hole or target.

TO DECREASE DIFFICULTY

- Replace the hazard with your golf bag. Place the bag upright between you and the practice green, then pitch 10 balls over the bag and onto the green.

TO INCREASE DIFFICULTY

- Pitch the balls to specific target holes.
- Place the golf balls 50 yards (46 meters) from the green-side hazard.
- Hit each of the 10 pitch shots from a different distance.
- Use a different wedge for each shot.

Figure 4.4 Hazard drill.

Success Check

- Build shot speed slowly so that the club accelerates through the ball.
- The club should follow the ball toward the target.
- At the finish, your weight should be on the target-side foot and the elbows should be high.

Score Your Success

Ball lands and remains on green = 2 points each shot

Your score _____ (out of 20 possible points)

PITCHING STRATEGY

The first key to pitching strategy is knowing when to hit the pitch shot. The second key is deciding where to land the ball. The pitch shot requires accuracy, so choosing a clear, precise target for the ball is an important strategic decision.

Because a chip permits greater accuracy and control, it is preferred over a pitch. There are, however, occasions when it may be wiser to pitch than to chip. Due to the ball flight characteristics of a pitch shot—high trajectory and little roll—a pitch is a good choice when the hole is close to the edge of the green. A pitch may also be the shot of choice if significantly more flight or airtime than roll is desired. For example, if a golfer has 40 yards (37 meters) of fairway and 10 yards (9 meters) of green to get the ball to the hole, a pitch shot is probably the way to go. Finally, when an obstacle, such as a bunker, deep rough, or water, lies between the ball and the green, you should use a pitch shot because it will carry the ball over the obstacle and stop it near the hole. Keep in mind that it takes a great deal of practice to develop the distance control necessary for an effective pitch shot.

In short, consider a chip shot when you have a poor lie or a downhill lie, the green is hard, there is a lot of wind, or you are under stress. Consider a pitch shot when you have a good lie or an uphill lie, the green is soft, or an obstacle is in the way.

The second strategic decision is where to land the ball before it rolls to the hole. If the pitch shot is played to clear an obstacle, then the target should be sufficiently far from the obstacle to ensure that the ball does not land in the trouble area. The purpose of the shot is to simply get the ball on the green. In some cases, this may mean selecting a landing target that is at or even past the hole. The player must ensure that the next shot after a pitch is no worse than a putt. Too often players get greedy when attempting to clear an obstacle and choose a landing target that just clears the hazard, and with a slight mis-hit they find their ball in the hazard they were attempting to clear. It is wiser to choose a landing target that takes the ball comfortably clear of the trouble.

If you choose the pitch because the ball has to carry more of the fairway or rough but doesn't have to roll so much on the green, a good target is the hole itself. In other words, try to land the ball directly in the hole. Due to slight mis-hits, most golfers tend to land shots shorter than they intended, and few amateur players hit the ball past the hole even when they try. Choosing the hole as the target ensures that even though the ball may land a little short or a little long, it is still somewhere near the hole; a properly struck pitch shot does not produce much ball roll once it hits the green. However, do not use the hole as the target if it is too close to a hazard or a danger spot. A successful golfer avoids trouble on the golf course.

Pitching Strategy Drill 1   Chip or Pitch?

Place 10 balls approximately 5 yards (4.5 meters) from the edge of a practice green. Pick out one hole, and chip five balls. Now pitch five balls to the hole. Which stroke consistently gets the ball closer?

Place 10 balls 5 yards (4.5 meters) apart in a line moving away from the practice green. The first ball should be 5 yards from the green and the last ball should be 50 yards (45 meters) from the green. Select a hole near the middle of the practice green. Decide whether the shot calls for a pitch or chip, select the appropriate club, and pitch or chip the 10 balls to this hole.

TO INCREASE DIFFICULTY

- Pitch and chip from 20 yards (18 meters) away from the green.
- Pitch and chip from 20 yards away with a hazard between you and the green.

Success Check

- Consider the lie and landing area before each shot.

Score Your Success

For the second part of the drill, give yourself 3 points for every shot within 5 yards of the target hole.

Your score _____ (out of 30 possible points)

Pitching Strategy Drill 2   Mission Impossible

This drill is one of the most popular drills with the players on the Swedish national team. With a partner or opponent, select a spot within 50 yards (45 meters) of a practice green that offers a challenging ("Impossible") shot to the green. Both of you should play a ball from this spot into the hole. The player to hole the ball in the fewest strokes wins the hole. If you both take the same number of strokes for a hole, the hole is halved. Play six holes.

TO DECREASE DIFFICULTY

- Place the balls within 25 yards (23 meters) of the practice green.

TO INCREASE DIFFICULTY

- Place a hazard (e.g., sand bunker, tree, thick rough) between the spot of your first shot and the green.

Success Check

- Assess the lie, hazards, wind, and other pertinent factors before each shot.

Score Your Success

Halve the hole = 3 points

Win the hole = 5 points

Your score _____ (out of 30 possible points)

PITCHING SUCCESS SUMMARY

If you learn to pitch the ball successfully, you will lower your scores. Pitching is fun. To throw the ball high into the air and have it land softly on the green gives a feeling of success and provides excellent practice for the full swing. However, the pitch is not an easy shot. It requires sound mechanics and dedicated practice to develop the necessary touch to execute it properly. Fortunately it is an easy shot to practice, because it doesn't require much room or even a regular practice area; a backyard or local park will do. Review the fundamentals in this step, practice the drills, and you will soon notice a difference in the rest of your golf shots. You will also see smaller numbers on your scorecard.

Record your point totals from each of the drills in this step, and add them together. If you scored at least 130 out of 223 points, you're ready for the next step. If you scored fewer than 130 points, review the drills that gave you the most trouble before you move on to the next step.

SCORING YOUR SUCCESS

Pitch Shot Drills

1.	String	___ out of 20
2.	See the Spot	___ out of 10
3.	Pitch Shot Appreciation Check	___ out of 25
4.	Target Towel	___ out of 30
5.	Pitch and Putt Practice	___ out of 20
6.	Pitch and Putt Stroke Play	___ out of 20
7.	Pitch and Putt Match Play	___ out of 18
8.	Hazard	___ out of 20

Pitching Strategy Drills

1.	Chip or Pitch?	___ out of 30
2.	Mission Impossible	___ out of 30
Total		**___ out of 223**

Almost 75 percent of all shots in a round of golf are fewer than 100 yards from the hole, so the success of your short game largely determines your success overall. With the completion of this step, you have learned the skills and strategies of the short game: putting, chipping, and pitching. When you find yourself within 100 yards of a golf hole, you now know what to do and how to do it. The next logical step is to get from the tee to the green. To successfully launch the ball off the tee or to hit an approach to the green from the fairway requires a single skill, the full golf swing.

Taking a Full Swing

For a proficient golfer, the full swing includes a wide variety of swings. For example, a golfer might execute a full swing with a driver or another wood to play the ball as far as possible. In another situation, the golfer might take a full swing with a sand iron or lob wedge to play the ball high in the air and stop it quickly on the green. In other words, the flight of the ball is grossly affected by the club that is used, but it is also affected by the speed of the swing (club head) and whether or not the ball is hit with the sweet spot of the club. Two main factors influence the direction of the shot: the path of the swing (club head) and the direction in which the club face is facing when hitting the ball. Consequently, a golfer can manipulate a shot in many ways and must be able to adapt to the situation at hand. The golfer also needs to determine what club and shot to hit (see step 6 for tips on choosing the right club).

During a round of golf, the ball is bound to end up in a number of different lies. Playing the game effectively means developing ways to deal with each and every one of those lies. Research shows that experts have more ways to execute a shot from a given lie than players who are less skilled. A good start is to develop a basic full swing that you can manipulate when needed.

On many of the oldest courses in England and Scotland, there are no driving ranges. Golf was and is a game played on a course; with no driving ranges, players have to spend all their time playing and practicing on the course. This means they learn golf skills in gamelike conditions. Since driving ranges, where the conditions are very unlike those in playing the game, are the place most players go to learn golf, the risk exists that the skills will not transfer to the course. Practicing only at the driving range, a player simply will not learn how to master all the various situations that occur when playing a course. If you practice only from a good lie on flat ground using a full swing, you will improve only under those conditions. In this step, you will not only learn the full swing, you will find ways to practice in conditions that better resemble those in which you will play. This real-life practice helps you become a better overall player.

EXECUTING THE FULL SWING

Preparation for the full swing includes many of the details mentioned in step 2. The grip should allow you to freely swing the club with your hands, arms, and body. You must hold the club with your fingers, not in the palm of your hand.

Choose from an overlap grip, interlocking grip, or 10-finger (baseball) grip (figure 5.1). In an overlap grip, the little finger of the right hand overlaps between the index and middle finger of the left hand. The overlap grip is also called the Vardon grip after its inventor, Harry Vardon. In an interlocking grip, the little finger of the right hand interlocks with the index finger of the left hand. In a baseball grip, the hands are separated a bit but close to each other. Experiment with all three to discover which grip works best for you. Remember to hold the club in the fingers of your hands rather than in the palms. See the first misstep in step 2.

The overlap grip is the most common grip. The baseball grip can be a good choice for juniors or players with small hands since having all 10 fingers on the grip may increase the feeling of strength. Small hands may be a disadvantage with the interlocking grip. The hands need to be able to come up on top of the grip (note the two knuckles as described in step 2).

The stance or address for a successful full swing contains a few vital elements (figure 5.2). The ball is placed somewhere from the middle of the stance and forward depending on the club that is used; a general rule is that when you are playing a 6-iron or higher, the ball should be in the middle of the stance. When playing a wedge, the ball can be even farther back if you feel this will give you cleaner contact with the ball. The ball may be forward in the stance toward the target-side foot if you are using a longer club such as a low iron or wood. With a 5-iron, you can move the ball slightly forward of center, and for each club lower, move the ball a bit more forward. However, the ball should never be ahead of the inside heel of the forward foot. Feet should be shoulder-width apart, and weight should be equally distributed between the right and left foot and between the toe and heel of each foot. The feet, hips, and shoulders are parallel with the target line. The knees are slightly bent, with the hips slightly flexed and the arms hanging freely in front of the body. The hands grip the club in a relaxed way.

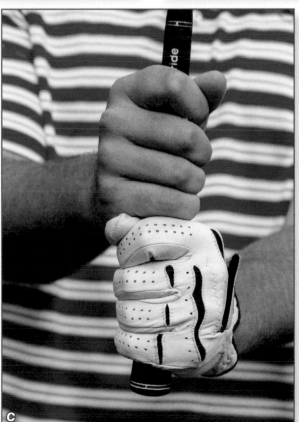

Figure 5.1 Grips: *(a)* overlap, *(b)* interlocking, and *(c)* 10-finger (baseball).

Figure 5.2 Correct address position, with knees slightly bent, feet shoulder-width apart, and weight equally distributed.

Once you have achieved the proper setup, the next step is the actual swing. Think of the swing in three phases:

1. Backswing, including the takeaway
2. Downswing, including contact with the ball
3. Follow-through

Some players start the backswing with a forward press (figure 5.3a). In a forward press, the hands, arms, and right knee act as a trigger to start the takeaway. For the most part, using a forward press is an individual preference. Say you are supposed to jump up from a position with your knees slightly bent. Will you feel more comfortable jumping by merely extending your legs? Or will you feel more comfortable if you quickly flex your legs before extending them? Most people find the latter option more comfortable, because it uses the stretch-shortening effect. They feel stronger when they flex slightly before jumping. Some players feel the same way about the golf swing and the forward press.

Another reason to try the forward press is that some players aren't certain when and how to start the backswing. With a forward press, the start of the backswing becomes more of a reaction to the forward movement caused by the forward press. However, some players feel more at ease starting the backswing by moving away from the ball. Try both options, and stick to what feels best for you.

The backswing (figure 5.3b) begins as the triangle of hands and shoulders move with the left hip and knee to bring the club head straight back. Weight shifts to the heel of the inside foot (right foot for a right-handed hitter). The right knee stays bent. The shoulders turn about 90 degrees until the left shoulder comes under the chin, allowing the club shaft to move into a position parallel with the ground. The left arm stays reasonably straight.

The start of the downswing (5.3c) is a crucial part of the full swing. The start of the downswing determines both the path the club will take and the position of the club-face through impact with the ball. The downswing is a movement that points downward and forward. As the club moves down toward the ball, the body weight moves forward toward the front foot (left foot for a right-handed golfer). This is called the magic move. If you are swinging with an iron, the club should hit the ball and then the ground, leaving a divot after the ball. Think about starting the downswing by letting the weight shift to the front foot and bringing the heel to the ground while at the same time bringing the right elbow back down toward the body.

One of the most common problems for golfers is that they try to keep too many swing thoughts in mind at the same time. Instruction books and magazines are often full of tips designed to help, but more is not always better. If too much thinking becomes a problem for you, perhaps the legendary British golf coach, John Jacobs' simple description of the swing will help: "two turns with a swish in the middle."

If the backswing and downswing work the way they should, the follow-through (figure 5.3d) is easy. If you have a good follow-through, chances are your backswing and downswing are good because the follow-through is a result of what has happened before. Body weight should now be on a flat left foot with the body in an erect position and the club resting on the left shoulder. The follow-through position should be comfortable to hold. The body should feel balanced, and you shouldn't feel like you are about to fall over.

MISSTEP

During the takeaway, you lift the club off the ball using your hands and arms.

CORRECTION

Make sure your hands and shoulders work together during the takeaway. Try the Belly-Button Backswing drill.

MISSTEP

At the top of the backswing, the body weight is on the left foot, making the body look like a backward C.

CORRECTION

This error occurs when you do not shift your weight to the right foot or straighten the right knee. Body weight should be on the inside right heel and the right knee should still be bent at the top of the backswing. Try the Back-Tapping drill.

Figure 5.3 **EXECUTING THE FULL SWING**

Forward Press

1. Use as a trigger to the take-away.
2. Press with the hands, arms, and right knee (right-handed golfer).

Backswing

1. Beginning with the triangle of hands and shoulders, take the club head away from the ball.
2. The left knee and hip should follow as the club head moves straight back the first few inches.
3. Shift your weight to the inside right heel.
4. Keep your right knee bent.
5. Turn the shoulders about 90 degrees until the left shoulder is under the chin.
6. Move the shaft so that it is parallel with ground as the left arm is straight.

Downswing

1. Shift your weight to the left foot while the right elbow comes back down to the body.
2. Use a smooth downswing to increase speed.
3. Allow the club head to release (this will be caused by the centrifugal force as long as you do not try to block it).
4. At impact, the club head should be square to the target.
5. Turn the back of the left hand to the target.
6. The club head should hit the ball and then cut a divot in the ground.

Follow-Through

1. Your weight should be on the flat left foot.
2. Keep the body erect, not bent.
3. Rest the club on the left shoulder and behind the back.
4. Make sure that the finishing position is comfortable and east to hold.

MISSTEP

You hit on top of the ball, resulting in no ball flight.

CORRECTION

This error can be the result of a number of faults: ending up on the wrong foot at impact, not shifting weight at the start of the downswing, or the misconception that the player should lift the ball up in the air (ball flight should instead be created by the loft of the club). Use Full-Swing Drills 4, 5, and 6 to reinforce the weight shift and attack on the ball.

MISSTEP

You find it difficult to stay in the follow-through position.

CORRECTION

You may be distributing your weight incorrectly at address or starting the backswing too quickly. Try the Finish drill, focusing on finding a comfortable follow-through.

Full-Swing Drill 1   Forward Press

Set up to a ball as if you are about to play a shot. Try a forward press, using the hands, arms, or right knee (right-handed golfer). Immediately start the backswing after the forward press. Try to start the backswing without a forward press on every second swing, and note which style feels most comfortable. Complete each start by swinging the club all the way back to the top of the backswing. Take a total of 20 swings, 10 with a forward press and 10 without, trying to complete the backswing with your weight shifting to your rear foot. Give yourself 1 point for each completed backswing with or without the forward press. Give yourself 2 points if you complete the backswing with your weight mostly on the rear foot (still on inside of rear foot, though).

TO DECREASE DIFFICULTY

- Swing the club only halfway through the backswing, focusing solely on the start of the swing.
- Stand in front of a mirror, and watch yourself as you perform the backswing.

TO INCREASE DIFFICULTY

- Slowly continue the swing, bringing the club down to the point at which the club would hit the ball. Stop and notice your position.
- Continue the swing through the downswing, and try to hit the ground with the club head.
- Complete the swing to the finish position.

Success Check

- Complete the forward press with the hands, arms, or right knee.
- Shift your weight to the rear foot during the backswing.

Score Your Success

0 to 6 points = 0 points

7 to 12 points = 1 point

13 to 19 points = 2 points

20 to 26 points = 3 points

27 to 33 points = 4 points

34 to 40 points = 5 points

Your score _____ (out of 5 possible points)

Full-Swing Drill 2   Belly-Button Backswing

Grip down the shaft of the club, taking a normal stance. Touch your belly button with the butt of the grip. Feel the one-piece takeaway as you start the backswing with the triangle of hands and shoulders. Let your body rotate, allowing the weight to shift to your rear foot. Start the swing, and go halfway back on the shoulder turn. Take 10 swings, scoring yourself based on the following criteria:

- Butt of grip loses contact with your belly button at the start of the backswing = 0 points
- Butt of grip loses contact with your belly button shortly after the start of the swing = 1 point
- Club stays in contact with your belly button as the shoulders turn halfway = 2 points
- Shoulders turn halfway, the club stays in contact with your belly button, and weight shifts to the rear foot = 3 points

TO DECREASE DIFFICULTY

- Focus only on the first few inches of the swing. Try to get a feel for how the backswing starts with the arms, hands, and shoulders moving together.

TO INCREASE DIFFICULTY

- Grip farther up the shaft, and do not let the butt of the grip contact your belly button; keep the grip pointing at your belly button as you start the swing.
- Grip the club as you normally would, take a normal stance, and try to execute the same kind of one-piece takeaway.

Success Check

- Slowly execute the takeaway with the arms, shoulders, and hands working as a triangle.
- Move your weight to the inside right heel.

Score Your Success

0 to 5 points = 0 points

6 to 10 points = 1 point

11 to 15 points = 2 points

16 to 20 points = 3 points

21 to 25 points = 4 points

26 to 30 points = 5 points

Your score _____ (out of 5 possible points)

Full-Swing Drill 3   **Back-Tapping**

Take a normal address position, execute a backswing (with or without a forward press, whatever feels right for you), and stop at the top of the backswing. With your eyes still focused on the ball, gently let go of the club and notice where it falls. The shaft of the club should hit your shoulder or right biceps (for a right-handed golfer). Take a total of 10 swings, and give yourself points based on the following criteria:

- Club doesn't come to the top of the backswing = 0 points
- Club comes to the top of the backswing, eyes lose focus on the ball = 1 point
- Club comes to the top of the backswing, eyes stay focused on the ball, club falls behind the body = 2 points
- Club comes to the top of the backswing, eyes stay focused on the ball, club hits the shoulder or right biceps = 3 points
- Club comes to the top of the backswing, eyes stay focused on the ball, club hits the shoulder or right biceps, weight is on the rear foot = 4 points

TO DECREASE DIFFICULTY

- Let your eyes follow the club back and adjust your position at the top of the backswing so that the club falls on your shoulder or right biceps.
- Stand in front of a mirror, and adjust to the image you see.

TO INCREASE DIFFICULTY

- Have a friend check your backswing position. Complete the full swing instead of stopping at the top of the backswing.
- Hit balls as a friend watches the top of your backswing position.

Success Check

- Set up in a normal stance that feels comfortable, and grip the club.
- Swing the club back while letting your weight shift to the inside heel of the rear foot.
- Keep your focus on the ball.

Score Your Success

0 to 6 points = 0 points

7 to 13 points = 1 point

14 to 20 points = 2 points

21 to 27 points = 3 points

28 to 34 points = 4 points

35 to 40 points = 5 points

Your score _____ (out of 5 possible points)

Full-Swing Drill 4   **The Magic Move**

Take a normal address position, but instead of using a ball put a tee in the ground where the ball would go. Swing the club back, and start the downswing by shifting your weight to the left foot as you bring the right elbow back down to your body (the magic move). Focus on the left foot, making sure you rest your heel firmly on the ground (right-handed golfer).

As you continue the downswing, keep in mind what the finish position feels and looks like; try to reach that position instead of thinking about swinging the club down to the ball. Focus on clipping the tee at impact. If you run into problems with your downswing, try to watch a good player at the club or on television. Pay attention to what the player does. Note especially how the club attacks the ball in a downward motion as the body weight shifts to the target-side foot.

The goal is to clip the tee at impact. Start with a lot of tee above the ground, then as you progress, press the tee deeper into the ground. Be sure to clip the tee before you hit the ground. Take a total of 10 swings, giving yourself points based on the following criteria:

- Swing back, start the downswing, but do not shift weight to the forward foot = 0 points
- Swing back, start the downswing with the magic move and right elbow = 1 point
- Swing with the magic move to the finish position but miss the tee = 2 points
- Swing correctly using the magic move and clip the tee = 3 points
- Swing correctly using the magic move, clip the tee, and hit the ground = 4 points

TO DECREASE DIFFICULTY

- Use a tall tee, and focus only on clipping the tee.
- Use a long club or a wood at first to make it easier to reach the tee.

TO INCREASE DIFFICULTY

- Press the tee deeper into the ground. Be sure to clip the tee and then hit the ground.
- Take away the tee, and use a ball instead. Hit the ball and then the ground (make a divot).

Success Check

- Set up comfortably to the tee in a relaxed position.
- Swing back and shift your weight to the rear foot.
- Start the downswing with the magic move, and complete the swing to the finish position.

Score Your Success

0 to 6 points = 0 points

7 to 13 points =1 point

14 to 20 points = 2 points

21 to 27 points = 3 points

28 to 34 points = 4 points

35 to 40 points = 5 points

Your score _____ (out of 5 possible points)

Full-Swing Drill 5   Right Foot, Left Foot

Set up in a normal address position. Without using a ball, swing back, simultaneously lifting the forward foot (left foot for a right-handed golfer) off the ground. Swing down and through as you return the forward foot to the ground and lift the rear foot off the ground. Place a ball in front of you, and hit it to a target using the same technique. Hit a total of 10, balls and give yourself points based on the following criteria:

- Swing back, lift the forward foot off the ground but lose balance = 0 points
- Swing back, lift the forward foot, swing through, lift the rear foot but lose balance = 1 point
- Swing back and forward, lift both feet, miss the ball = 2 points
- Swing back and forward in good balance and hit the ball = 3 points
- Swing back and forward in good balance and hit the ball to the target = 4 points

TO DECREASE DIFFICULTY

- Put the ball on a tee, and use a long club.
- Put the ball on a tee, and use a short club.

TO INCREASE DIFFICULTY

- Put two or more balls in a row, and hit them one after another. Take a short break between shots.
- Put up to five balls in a row, and hit them one after another without stopping between shots. Slowly move forward to hit the next ball in line.

Success Check

- Take a few practice swings to get a nice rhythm going. Move the rear foot and then the forward foot.
- Focus on your balance, and do not swing too hard.

Score Your Success

0 to 6 points = 0 points

7 to 13 points = 1 point

14 to 20 points = 2 points

21 to 27 points = 3 points

28 to 34 points = 4 points

35 to 40 points = 5 points

Your score _____ (out of 5 possible points)

Full-Swing Drill 6   **Finish**

Set up to play a shot, but don't use a ball. Instead of swinging the club back, swing it forward to your intended finish position. Be sure the club is in a position that feels comfortable. Your weight is on the left foot (for a right-handed golfer), and your body is erect. Check your balance, and allow your body to feel the position.

Take a swing, trying to finish in the position you just practiced. Compare the positions, adjust, and try again. When you feel you can get to the comfortable position without a ball, try the same thing with a ball. Hit a total of 10 shots, and give yourself points based on the following criteria:

- Difficult to find a balanced finish position = 0 points
- Balance comfortably in the finish position = 1 point
- Swing back, forward, and finish in balance = 2 points
- Swing back, hit the ball, and finish in balance = 3 points
- Swing back, hit the ball, and find the perfect finish = 4 points

TO DECREASE DIFFICULTY

- Take a practice swing or find the finish position without the ball between each shot.
- Take away the ball, and focus only on the swing. Try to hit the ground when swinging.

TO INCREASE DIFFICULTY

- Change clubs after each shot.
- Change clubs and lies, trying the drill from uphill, downhill, and sidehill lies.

Success Check

- In your mind draw a clear blueprint of the perfect finish position, and test yourself to see if you can recreate that finish position in reality. What does that feel and look like? Does it match the picture you had in your mind.
- Focus on reaching the balanced finish position during every shot. When you do, the rest will take care of itself.

Score Your Success

0 to 6 points = 0 points

7 to 13 points = 1 point

14 to 20 points = 2 points

21 to 27 points = 3 points

28 to 34 points = 4 points

35 to 40 points = 5 points

Your score _____ (out of 5 possible points)

FULL-SWING STRATEGY

Hitting shots with a full swing involves strategic thinking. First, ask yourself what you want to do with the shot. As you develop skill, strategic concerns such as ball flight, right or left turn, and high or low trajectory become more and more important.

New golfers spend most of their strategy time finding a target and picking a club simply because the number of ways they can hit a shot is limited. Professional players, on the other hand, take all aspects of the shot into account. Wind, lie, slopes, hazards, pin position, green firmness, individual preferences, and other factors all help the professional player decide on ball flight.

For example, PGA Tour player Jesper Parnevik was once faced with an interesting strategic decision while on his way to winning the Byron Nelson Golf Classic in Dallas. Jesper was standing on the 17th tee, a par-3 hole with the pin far back on the right-hand side of the green. To the right of the green was a water hazard, but to the left of the pin the green was wide open. All the external clues pointed to the conclusion that the best shot would move from left to right, stopping the ball left of the pin and completely avoiding the water. However, Jesper felt more comfortable hitting a shot that moved from right to left, a much more difficult shot under the circumstances. Even so, he hit the shot, put the ball on the green, and walked away with the tournament win.

As you develop as a player, the answer to the question of what to do with the ball will become a matter of adjusting to the conditions set by the golf course and by yourself. The better player you are, the more answers you will find and the more variety your shots will have.

Once you've decided what you want to do, consider how you will get it done, investigating your ability to perform the necessary shot. A good player is able to create the best shot for any given situation. Consider again the example of Jesper Parnevik. He probably knew that the best shot was not a high draw (moving right to left), but his confidence in hitting such a shot was so much greater, he decided to hit it anyway. Hitting a fade that moved left to right might have ended up in water and led to a disastrous finish. On the other hand, if Jesper wanted to become an even better player, he would learn to hit a fade shot even in pressure situations. There may come a time when that is the only shot to play.

Before you can reach Jesper Parnevik's level, the most important answer to the question *How?* is simply the technique you need to produce the shot. A straight forward shot may require your regular full swing. For softer ball flight, perhaps a smoother swing with a longer club could do the trick.

It isn't easy to practice strategic thinking for a full swing without playing on a golf course. A driving range or practice area usually looks different from the course. Practicing under gamelike conditions will help you transfer what you learn in practice to the golf course.

Full-Swing Strategy Drill 1   Hit the Target

On the driving range, pick a target for your shot, such as a sign, a different-colored spot on the ground, or a group of balls lying on the fairway. Your goal is to hit the target, but on every shot decide on an area around the target about the size of a green. Play at least 20 shots with different clubs, and give yourself 1 point every time you hit the green area.

TO DECREASE DIFFICULTY

- Make your visualized area of the green bigger.
- Use all clubs in the bag all the way up to the driver.

TO INCREASE DIFFICULTY

- Make your visualized area of the green smaller.
- Use only the 8-iron up to the wedge.

Success Check

- Focus on the target; let your swing take care of itself.

Score Your Success

0 to 2 greens hit = 0 points

3 to 5 greens hit = 1 point

6 to 8 greens hit = 2 points

9 to 11 greens hit = 3 points

12 to 14 greens hit = 4 points

15 to 20 greens hit = 5 points

Your score _____ (out of 5 possible points)

Full-Swing Strategy Drill 2   Curve Ball

When you play a game of golf you will find yourself in a variety of situations and lies. Every shot will have its own best solution in terms of ball flight, club selection, and the swing that is required for producing the desired shot. If you are able to work the ball in various ways, you are likely to increase your chances to have the required shot in your bag. The Curve Ball drill helps you find different ways of getting the ball to move in the air.

Pick a club that you feel comfortable hitting. Take 20 balls; your aim is to hit 10 shots using a draw and 10 shots using a fade. Score 1 point every time you manage to create to desired ball flight. At this stage it is all right to do this drill without a target.

TO DECREASE DIFFICULTY

- Hit all 20 balls with the same club and the same shape.

TO INCREASE DIFFICULTY

- Instead of hitting 10 of each shot before changing, try to change the type of shot each time.

(continued)

Full-Swing Strategy Drill 2 *(continued)*

Success Check

- Decide on whether you want to hit the shot moving right to left (draw if you are a right-handed player) or left to right (fade if you are a right-handed player).
- If a draw is your desired shot aim right (for a right-handed player) of where you want the ball to finish while aiming your club face to the desired finishing point (target).
- If your desired shot is a fade (for a right-handed player), do the opposite; in other words, aim left with the face of the club pointing toward an intended target.
- Make a normal swing, allowing the path of the swing to determine the initial direction of the ball flight and the club face to dictate the turn of the ball. A club face pointing left of the swing path at impact will cause the ball to turn right to left, and a club face pointing right will cause the ball to turn right.

Score Your Success

0 to 2 points = 0 points

3 to 5 points = 1 point

6 to 8 points = 2 points

9 to 11 points = 3 points

12 to 14 points = 4 points

15 to 20 points = 5 points

Your score _____ (out of 5 possible points)

Full-Swing Strategy Drill 3   The Improviser

Good players want to vary not only the shape of the ball flight (right to left or left to right) but other factors as well. Proficient players have a variety of ways to get the ball from point A to point B; they pick the shot taking into account every aspect of lie, wind, target, conditions around the target, their own preferences, and many other things. Experienced players also know that you can use the same club in many more ways than one. This drill helps you explore some of those ways.

Take 10 balls and pick two clubs out of your bag. Using five balls for each club, pick a target that will not require a full swing to get there. Choose a type of shot—high, low, fade, draw, or straight. Score 1 point for every time you hit your target and 1 point for the correct ball flight. Change target and distance after each shot.

TO DECREASE DIFFICULTY

- Use one club only, and hit all 10 shots with the same one.
- Use only one target and one club.

TO INCREASE DIFFICULTY

- Vary the lie as much as you can as well—longer grass, side hill, and so on.
- Compete with a friend.

Success Check

- Be clear in your mind about the type of shot you want to hit.
- Make a practice swing that you think will create the desired shot.
- Evaluate after each shot, and try to improve based on the previous shot.

Score Your Success

0 to 2 points = 0 points

3 to 5 points = 1 point

6 to 8 points = 2 points

9 to 11 points = 3 points

12 to 14 points = 4 points

15 to 20 points = 5 points

Your score _____ (out of 5 possible points)

Full-Swing Strategy Drill 4   Parnevik

Jesper likes to curve his shots. Fade, draw, high, and low are types of trajectories he uses all the time. Take 10 balls, and before each shot, decide on a target and the type of shot you want to hit. For example, try to hit the 100-yard (91-meter) marker with a fade shot. What club will do the job? How will you swing? Give yourself 1 point every time you hit the target (within what you think is an acceptable distance) and 2 points every time you get the ball flight and trajectory correct and hit the target.

TO DECREASE DIFFICULTY

- Use the same club for all 10 shots, and vary only the trajectory.
- Hit three draws in a row, then three fades, three high, and so on.

TO INCREASE DIFFICULTY

- Change clubs and targets for every shot.
- Vary the distances using long clubs to short clubs.

Success Check

- Make sure you have a clear idea of what to do and how to do it.

Score Your Success

0 to 2 points = 0 points

3 to 5 points = 1 point

6 to 8 points = 2 points

9 to 11 points = 3 points

12 to 14 points = 4 points

15 to 20 points = 5 points

Your score _____ (out of 5 possible points)

FULL SWING SUCCESS SUMMARY

Developing a sound full swing is fundamental to playing successful golf. A good player does not necessarily use the full swing as a straightforward shot during tournament play, but every swing is some sort of manipulation of the basic swing based on the conditions at hand.

The full swing has three phases: backswing, downswing, and follow-through. You can execute a full swing with nearly any club in the bag. Strategic thinking for the full swing involves understanding club selection, knowing how to hit many types of shots, and adjusting to the ever-changing conditions on a golf course.

Record your point totals from each of the drills in this step, and add them together. A score of 35 points or more indicates you have mastered this step and are ready to move on to the next. A score of 25 to 34 points is adequate, and you should be able to move to the next step after reviewing and practicing the drills in which you scored low. If you scored fewer than 25 points, review and practice the drills a few more times before you move on to the next step.

SCORING YOUR SUCCESS

Full-Swing Drills

1.	Forward Press	___ out of 5
2.	Belly-Button Backswing	___ out of 5
3.	Back-Tapping	___ out of 5
4.	The Magic Move	___ out of 5
5.	Right Foot, Left Foot	___ out of 5
6.	Finish	___ out of 5

Full-Swing Strategy Drills

1.	Hit the Target	___ out of 5
2.	Curve Ball	___ out of 5
3.	The Improviser	___ out of 5
4.	Parnevik	___ out of 5
Total		**___ out of 50**

A golf course is ever-changing with varying slopes, different lengths of grass, hazards, and trees to make the round more interesting and challenging. Now that you have mastered the full swing and have a basic understanding of how to strategically adjust to various conditions, you are ready to take your swing to the course, which will test your ability with a number of lies. Sidehill lies, uphill lies, downhill lies, and other types of bad lies are waiting for you in the next step, so move ahead to learn how to master those shots.

Ball Flight, Shot Patterns, and Club Selection

Steps 1 through 5 have focused on the specific physical skills needed for success in golf. Putting, chipping, pitching, setting up, and executing a full swing all require understanding of the physical components or technical aspects in order to efficiently and consistently perform them on a golf course. Each of those skills influences how a ball is going to get from where it is on the golf course to where you want it to be. Understanding the flight of a golf ball, the various patterns a shot can take, and how to select the proper club to execute your intended shot can help you to be a better player.

Because a golf ball travels such great distances in a game, a slight error in the launch of the ball can have disastrous effects on a golf course. A ball that flies too far away, too short, or too far to the left or to the right can land in a lake rather than on the green. To ensure your success in golf, it is helpful to understand the factors that influence ball flight and what you as a player can do to influence and that flight. In this step, you learn about the influence of the club face on the direction the ball takes during its flight, how to control the shape of the shot (forming an intended, predictable path the ball will take to the target), and how to select the appropriate club to make the ball go where you want it to go and in the way you want it to get there.

BALL FLIGHT

The flight of a golf ball is determined by only two factors. Both these factors are relative to the club face, and both occur at impact with the ball: club face angle and club face direction. Your execution of the golf swing determines both of these factors, so you have direct control over where the ball will fly and how. At impact a club face can have one of three angles—open, closed, or square. Also at impact, the club can be traveling at one of three directions—outside to inside, inside to outside, or inside to square. These directions are illustrated next.

The direction and angle of the club face at impact determines the direction the ball will travel in the air. The three positions for each factor offer six potential impact possibilities. Most players (and their instructors) strive to have the club face square to the target line with the direction of the club head coming from inside the target line to square to the target line at impact. This direction creates the straight shot. Many beginning players struggle to get the club face square at impact and therefore have it open at impact, causing the ball to slice to the right (for a right-handed golfer). If you are experiencing problems with ball flight, it may be helpful to inspect the direction of the club face and its angle at impact. Taking video is a helpful and efficient way to see the direction and angle so that you can make adjustments to the shot. This step offers several drills to improve the direction and angle of the club face at impact and consequently improve the quality of the ball flight.

SHOT PATTERNS

When you gain control over the direction and angle of the club face, you can begin to manipulate these factors to impart a spin that will cause an intended pattern to the ball flight. The three desirable shot patterns are

- straight shot (ball travels straight along the target line),
- draw (ball travels outside the target line and then curves back to the target line before landing), and
- fade (ball travels inside the target line and then curves back to the target line before landing).

When conditions are ideal, a straight shot is highly desirable. However, at times conditions are such that you may want to shape the shot to the hole. For example, this could be when playing in windy conditions where a shaped shot (i.e. the ball moving or wanting to move from left to right or right to left) could be a way to keep the ball flying fairly straight in the wind. Other occasions could be when the pin is placed towards the right or left hand edge of the green which would mean a proficient golfer could aim at the center of the green and shape the shot toward the pin.

There may be an obstacle along the target line between the ball and the target. Common obstacles include trees, bunkers, and water hazards. Successfully navigating around these obstacles may require the ball flight to curve left or right rather than fly straight. Wind can also affect ball flight, so if a strong wind is blowing left to right across the target line, you may want to stroke the ball as you would for a draw (for a right-handed golfer; for a left-handed golfer this would mean a fade, trying to move the ball right to left). In this way, the ball will turn against and resist the wind and fly straight along the target line. These skills are usually considered advanced, but with a little knowledge and practice, they are not difficult to master.

Two particular shot patterns represent radical deviations from the target line, and most golfers try to avoid them. They are the slice and the hook. A fade can turn into a slice when the ball flight takes a radical, unintended, and uncontrollable turn to the right (for a right-handed golfer). The opposite of a slice is a hook, which occurs when the ball turns sharply and uncontrollably to the left (for a right-handed golfer). These shots usually occur when both the club face and the club direction are not aligned to the target (e.g., an outside to inside club direction with an open club face usually results in a hard slice). The slice and the hook are undesirable shots, because they turn to such an extent that they land far from where the golfer intended.

Shot Pattern Drill 1   Parnevik

You will recognize this drill from step 5. Trying to hit different types of shots will develop your swing as well as your ability to actually play the shots. This time the focus is on shot patterns rather than on the swing. Rest assured though that your swing will improve at the same time!

PGA Tour champion Jesper Parnevik likes to creatively shape his golf shots. Fade, draw, high, and low are types of trajectories he uses as he golfs his ball around the course. For this drill, take 10 balls, and before each shot, decide on a target and the type of shot you want to hit. For example, try to hit the 100-yard (91-meter) marker with a fade shot. What club will do the job? How will you swing? Where do you want the angle and direction of the club face to be when the club impacts the ball? Give yourself 1 point every time you hit the target (within what you think is an acceptable distance) and 2 points every time you get the ball flight and trajectory right and hit the target.

TO DECREASE DIFFICULTY

- Use the same club for all 10 shots, and vary only the trajectory.
- Hit three draws in a row, then three fades, three high, and so on.

TO INCREASE DIFFICULTY

- Change clubs and targets for every shot.
- Vary the distances using long clubs to short clubs.

Success Check

- Make sure you have a clear idea of what to do and how to do it.

Score Your Success

0 to 2 points = 0 points

3 to 5 points = 1 point

6 to 8 points = 2 points

9 to 11 points = 3 points

12 to 14 points = 4 points

15 to 20 points = 5 points

Your score _____ (out of 5 possible points)

CLUB SELECTION

Once you have learned how to get the ball in the air, you will start noticing differences between clubs. That is, different clubs cause differences in the trajectory and distance of the ball flight. According to the rules of golf, a player is allowed to carry 14 clubs; which 14 clubs he or she decides to carry is completely up to the player. Good players usually carry the same clubs each week, but they also have a few clubs they change depending on the characteristics of the golf course or changes in the weather. A specific course or changes in wind conditions may lead a golfer to add an extra wedge, an extra hybrid or long iron, or an extra fairway metal such as a 5- or 7-wood. High-caliber players know that it pays off to spend some time finding the mix of clubs that will allow them to play the shots that the course requires. A new golfer's challenge when mastering club selection is to understand the ways different clubs affect the ball flight and distance.

For a new golfer it may seem a bit much to carry 14 clubs. It is a good idea to start out with a short set of two woods, four or five irons, and a putter. Still, it is important to find out as soon as possible how the different clubs influence the ball so that you can make a more informed decision about which 14 clubs to carry with you on a golf round.

A general rule is, the lower the number on the club, the lower the trajectory and the longer the ball will travel in the air. This concept applies to irons as well as woods. Wedges give the ball the highest trajectory and shortest flight as well as the most spin, which causes the ball to stop quickly as it lands. As you move to lower-numbered irons, ball flight will be lower and longer and the ball will spin less. A 5- or 7-wood can replace the lowest-numbered irons since the woods are usually easier to use. LPGA player Carin Koch says that ladies should not carry irons lower than 4 or 5 and can instead complete their sets of clubs with a 7-, 9-, or 11-wood. As you move to lower-numbered woods down to the driver (1), the ball will travel farther. The driver is used mostly off the tee box, but good players can also use it from the fairway if the lie is good and they want to hit the ball as far as possible.

Club Selection: On the Course

On-course club selection is done during the preparation phase for the shot. While preparing for the shot, stand behind the ball and gather as much information as possible regarding factors that will determine a quality golf shot. How far do you need to hit the ball to the target? Do you need to fly the ball a certain distance to avoid hazards or hit the green? Check the wind and determine the lie of the ball. Are you playing in dry or wet conditions? What is the landing area like? To choose the right club, you need to consider the circumstances.

The largest determining factor in on-course club selection will be how far you need to carry the ball to the target. Therefore, you should know how far you hit each club. If your target is 125 yards (114 meters) away, which club in your bag will carry the ball 125 yards with a full swing? Club manufacturers construct sets of golf clubs to differ each club's carry by approximately 10 yards (9 meters). While differential will vary by player, that means that if you hit your 9-iron 120 yards (110 meters), your 8-iron should carry the ball approximately 130 yards (119 meters), a 7-iron will carry the ball 140 yards (128 meters), and so on through the irons. The variation on the fairway metals differs a bit more. Usually there will be a variation of 15-25 yards (14-23 meters) between the fairway metals, depending on the club and player.

If you are playing into the wind, the ball will lose distance and you will need to play a longer club than you would without the wind. If you are playing with the wind, the wind will help the ball and you will need to select a shorter club. The same is true with elevation. If the target area is significantly uphill, you need to adjust your clubs down to increase the length, and if the target is considerably downhill, you need to adjust your clubs up to decrease the distance the ball will travel.

The lie also affects the distance of the ball and consequently affects club selection. When the ball is in thick grass, the shot is shorter, because the grass lowers the speed of the club head. This condition could also cause a so-called flyer, which even good players sometimes have problems with. Grass between the ball and the club decreases the spin on the ball, which can cause it to fly longer. A *flyer lie* usually occurs in deep rough when the ball rests on the ground. If the ball is resting in the long grass but not touching the ground, this is known as a *fluffy lie,* and the ball is likely to fly a shorter distance than usual due to the resistance of the long grass.

When hitting a downhill lie, try to keep the same club-head speed as in a normal lie so that the ball will come out lower and travel farther in the air. It probably will be difficult to maintain club-head speed, however, so the ball will go shorter. An uphill lie will increase the loft on the club and the ball will travel higher and shorter than from a normal lie. Because of lost club-head speed, a sidehill lie will probably cause the ball to travel shorter. These lies are described in greater detail in step 7.

Club selection is not only about picking a certain club. Variations in the way the ball travels can be created in more than one way, and good players have numerous ways to use every club in the bag. One of the first British instructors to go to Sweden was a man named John Cockin. He later became a highly respected chairman of the Swedish PGA. Cockin once said to me, "Think of a golfer as a table tennis player. A table tennis player only has one racket but think of the number of different shots he can hit with that racket. If a golfer can come anywhere close to that number of ways to use each one of his or her clubs there is enough to work on for a life in golf."

A good player is not stuck with only one way to swing a club. Depending on the circumstances (lie, wind, target, and so on), many variations exist for using the same club. Start on the driving range by hitting to a target with each club. Try to find out what modifications you need to get the ball to fly as you would like it to. What happens if you grip down on the club, if you swing slower or shorter, or if you move the ball back in your stance or forward? Finding out the effects of small or large alterations in setup, grip, and swing is a great way of practicing. Experiment with modifications on the driving range as well as on the course.

Iron Club Selection

The irons in a player's bag can range from a 1- or 2-iron to a 9-iron and a few wedges. Some options include a pitching wedge of 48 degrees, a gap wedge of 52 degrees, a sand wedge of 56 degrees, and a lob wedge of 60 degrees. Good players generally try to pick three or four wedges to eliminate gaps between clubs (distances for which they have no club with which to hit a comfortable shot). Irons are used anywhere from very close to the green for chipping or pitching (see steps 3 and 4 for ideas on choosing clubs for chipping and pitching) to off a tee on a par-3 hole, or any hole where you need more control than a wood provides. When selecting an iron (figure 6.1), consider the following factors:

- Lie—Will it cause the ball to go longer or shorter?
- Weather and wind—Will it cause the ball to go longer or shorter?
- Area where the ball will land—Do you need to put a lot of spin on the ball, or do you want the ball to run when it lands?
- Trajectory—Is a high or a low shot more favorable?
- Ball flight—Is there any need to curve the ball right or left?

With these factors in mind, you can make a decision based on the numbers on the clubs. As previously mentioned, a lower-numbered club will cause the ball to go longer and have a lower trajectory than a higher-numbered club. A higher-numbered club has a steep club-face angle and will give the ball more backspin, causing it to stop on the green more quickly. This is due to both spin and the height of the shot. A lower-numbered club has a more shallow face and does not create as much backspin, so it is easier to create sidespin with these clubs. The sidespin can often result in the previously mentioned hook or slice for unskilled golfers, beginners should use higher-numbered clubs. Even though the ball does not go as far, it allows players greater control over their golf shots.

Figure 6.1 **SELECTING AN IRON CLUB**

1. The lower the club number, the farther the ball will fly.

2. The lower the club number, the lower the trajectory.

3. The lower the club number, the more difficult it will be to control the shot because sidespin increases with lower-numbered clubs.

4. The lower the club number, the closer the ball should be positioned to the left heel (for right-handed golfers; for left-handed golfers this would be the right heel).

MISSTEP

You try to help the ball get up in the air, causing you to top the ball.

CORRECTION

When the club reaches the ball, it has already reached its lowest point. The golf swing is a downward movement, so only the loft of the club should help the ball up in the air. Hit down on the ball, catching the ball first and then the ground to take a shallow divot.

MISSTEP

You end up short of the target.

CORRECTION

The ball's flight will be short if you slightly miss the center of the club face. Hitting the toe or heel of the club will cause the ball to go shorter and it may also cause the ball to go sideways. It is often recommended to take one extra club so that even if you mis-hit the ball you will still reach your target.

Iron Club Drill 1   The Stepladder

Use the same swing tempo, and hit four balls each with a 9- or 8-iron, 6- or 5-iron, and 4- or 3-iron, for a total of 12 shots. Select three targets you think you can reach with the different shots. Alternate targets and clubs between shots. Give yourself points based on the following criteria:

- Mis-hit the ball so that it does not fly the way it should = 0 points
- Make solid contact with the ball, ball ends up nowhere near the target = 1 point
- Make solid contact with the ball, ball ends up somewhere around the target = 2 points
- Hit a good shot, ball ends up at the target = 3 points

TO DECREASE DIFFICULTY

- Hit all shots with the same club before you change club and target.
- Use a wedge, 9-iron, and 8-iron or other clubs close to each other.

TO INCREASE DIFFICULTY

- Hit only one shot with the same club, then change both club and target.
- Use a middle iron, a long iron, and a fairway metal.

Success Check

- Take a normal swing, and keep your attention focused on the target.
- Try to keep the same tempo with all clubs.

Score Your Success

0 to 4 points = 0 points

5 to 9 points = 1 point

10 to 14 points = 2 points

15 to 21 points = 3 points

22 to 27 points = 4 points

28 points or more = 5 points

Your score _____ (out of 5 possible points)

Iron Club Drill 2   The Triple

With a 7- or 8-iron, hit three balls to a 100-yard (91-meter) target, three balls to a 125-yard (114-meter) target, and three balls to a 150-yard (137-meter) target. If the distance is too far, choose three other distances as long as they allow you to play a shorter shot than normal, a normal shot, and a longer shot than normal with the selected club. After you have hit nine balls, work backward, starting with three shots to the 150-yard target, three to the 125-yard target, and three to the 100-yard target. Give yourself 1 point every time you hit the right distance or the right direction, and give yourself 2 points every time you hit the right distance and direction. Try to hit at least two shots out of three at each distance with the correct distance and direction.

TO DECREASE DIFFICULTY

- Start with a wedge and closer targets.
- Use only two distances, one normal and one shorter than normal, and hit four balls to each target.

TO INCREASE DIFFICULTY

- Use a club that will prevent you from hitting a normal shot to the target. Pick three targets that are all shorter or all longer than you would normally hit with the club you selected.
- Play only one shot to a target before you move to the next target.

Success Check

- Adjust your tempo to change the distance the ball flies.
- See what happens when you grip farther down the shaft of the club.

Score Your Success

0 to 4 points = 0 points

5 to 9 points = 1 point

10 to 14 points = 2 points

15 to 21 points = 3 points

22 to 27 points = 4 points

28 points or more = 5 points

Your score _____ (out of 5 possible points)

Iron Club Drill 3   High or Low

Use a 7-, 8-, and 9-iron for this drill. The trajectory of a golf shot can be controlled in part by the ball position in the setup. If the ball is forward (toward the target-side foot), the ball will have a higher trajectory. Conversely, if the ball is back in the stance (close to the nontarget-side foot) the trajectory will be lower. For each club, hit three shots with the ball forward in your stance, three shots in the middle of your stance, and three shots in the back of your stance. Begin with the 9-iron. Hit all nine shots, then nine shots with the 8-iron, and finish with nine shots with the 7-iron for a total of 27 shots. Concentrate on striking the ball solidly. Note what happens to the ball in terms of trajectory (lower, medium, or higher) when ball position changes in the stance.

TO DECREASE DIFFICULTY

- Hit each shot with a 3/4 swing or chip shot rather than a full swing.
- Use a pitching or sand wedge instead of a 7-iron.

TO INCREASE DIFFICULTY

- Use a different club for each shot, and score yourself compared to the normal trajectory for that club.
- Use a longer iron.

Success Check

- Make your normal preparations for each shot, and take aim at a target for every shot.
- Concentrate on the alteration you are about to make and letting the ball react to your swing.

Score Your Success

For each set of three shots for each club, use the following scores:

One shot out of three travels the desired trajectory (high, medium, low) = 1 point

Two shots out of three travels the desired trajectory (high, medium, low) = 2 points

Three shots out of three travels the desired trajectory (high, medium, low) = 3 points

Total:

7-iron ____

8-iron ____

9-iron ____

Your score ____ (out of 27 possible points)

Wood Club Selection

Depending on the number of irons you decide to carry in your bag, you will have room for a larger or smaller number of woods. These clubs are also referred to as fairway metals, because they now made from metal. However, because the club heads for these clubs were traditionally made from wood (persimmon in most cases), to many golfers the term *wood* remains. These clubs generally have longer shafts, have rounded heads, and are designed to hit the ball across greater distances. Most players carry at least two woods—a driver and a 3-wood—in their bags, and many players add a 5-wood and maybe a 7-wood if they decide to take out some of the longer irons.

A wood is typically used off the tee, because that is when you want the ball to travel as far as possible. Of course, it is equally important that the ball not only fly long, but fly straight as well. When a straight shot becomes more important, players reevaluate and choose a club they feel confident will put the ball on the fairway. For some players, that means using a higher-numbered wood than the driver. For others, it means selecting a lower-numbered iron instead.

As when choosing an iron, it is important to assess the conditions when choosing a wood. The lie, weather, landing area, and type of shot needed will guide your decision as to what wood to use (figure 6.2). However, when you are playing from the tee box, decisions about the lie are not critical, because you can place the ball on a tee rather than hit in on the ground. The farther you want the ball to fly, the lower the number of wood you should use. If the ball is in a good lie on the fairway, an experienced player could use a driver, but for most players using a 3-, 5-, or even a 7-wood is easier to hit due to the increased loft and backspin. Again, sometimes it is prudent to use a club that travels less distance but is more accurate.

Figure 6.2 **SELECTING A WOOD CLUB**

1. A longer shaft means a longer swing arc, which means faster club-head speed without increasing the speed of the swing.

2. Commonly used woods are 1 (driver), 3, and 5; also popular are 4, 7, and 9.

3. Address the ball opposite the forward heel with the feet a little farther apart.

4. The ball is toward the forward heel, so you will sweep the ball off the fairway or off the tee.

5. Swing just as in a regular swing. The club will carry the ball the requisite distance. Increasing your swing speed in attempt to generate more power generally has a disastrous outcome. Swing your driver with the same tempo you would use with your 9-iron. You change the club to change the distance. The swing remains the same regardless of the club.

MISSTEP

You top the ball when swinging at it with the wood.

CORRECTION

When the club reaches the ball, it has already reached its lowest point. If you top the ball, the ball is probably too far forward in the stance. Move the ball back toward the middle of the stance. A general rule is to keep the ball opposite the inside of the left heel. If that does not help, try moving the ball back a little more, but never move it farther back than the middle of the stance.

Wood Drill 1   The Wood Picker

Pick out all the woods in your bag except for the driver. Say you have 3-, 5-, and 7-woods. Select three targets on the driving range that are reasonable distances for the three clubs. Your goal is to hit three good shots in a row with each club (you decide on the definition of a good shot). After you have hit three good shots, that club is out. If you hit two good shots and then miss the third, you have to start over. Count how many total shots it takes you to hit three good shots in a row. Divide this number by the number of woods you have to get the average number of shots it takes per club. The best possible average is three shots per club. Your goal is to hit 3 good shots per club in no more than 12 total shots.

TO DECREASE DIFFICULTY

- Settle for two good shots in a row instead of three.
- Lower your standards for what makes a good shot.

TO INCREASE DIFFICULTY

- Try to hit four good shots in a row instead of three.
- Raise your standards for what makes a good shot.

Success Check

- Decide how to hit the shot before stepping up to the ball.
- Stick to your tempo.

Score Your Success

13 shots or more per club = 0 points

12 to 11 shots = 1 point

10 to 9 shots = 2 points

8 to 7 shots = 3 points

6 to 5 shots = 4 points

4 to 3 shots = 5 points

Your score _____ (out of 5 possible points)

Wood Drill 2   **The Transporter**

A wood is often used to move the ball along the fairway. For example, on a par-5 hole when the green cannot be reached a wood will carry the ball closer to the green than an iron. When you use a wood in this way, accuracy is more important than distance. The distance goal may be to get the ball as far as possible, but in terms of accuracy you definitely want to keep the ball on the fairway.

In this drill, think about a hole you played where you used a wood to move the ball on the fairway. Think of how wide the fairway was, and use that image to visualize the boundaries of a fairway on the driving range. Hit 10 balls on the driving range. Give yourself 3 points for hitting the correct spot on the imaginary fairway, 2 points for hitting the fairway but not on the right spot, and 1 point for hitting the first cut of the rough.

TO DECREASE DIFFICULTY

- Use a wider fairway.
- Use a higher-numbered wood.

TO INCREASE DIFFICULTY

- Use a narrower fairway.
- Find two different holes, and alternate between them.

Success Check

- Be specific when you decide how to hit the shot. Make sure you know what you want the ball to do and how you will make it do what you want.
- Execute the shot as planned.

Score Your Success

0 to 6 points = 1 point

7 to 12 points = 2 points

13 to 18 points = 3 points

19 to 24 points = 4 points

25 to 30 points = 5 points

Your score _____ (out of 5 possible points)

Hybrid Club Selection

In recent years, the hybrid, a relatively new golf club, has become common in many players' bags. The hybrid is a cross between an iron and a wood club. Specifically, it is designed to incorporate the easier swing characteristics of an iron and the forgiveness and distance of a wood club. Many golfers find long irons (iron numbers 1-4) difficult to hit well because of the small club face and amount of sidespin generated by the low-lofted clubs. Therefore, hybrids are designed to replace the long irons but supplement the woods. For example, you may replace a 3-iron with a 3-hybrid.

Hybrids are designed with a larger club face and consequently a larger sweet spot, but they have shorter shafts more similar to irons, making them easier to control. The shorter shaft of the hybrid also comes in handy in tight spots such as near bushes, in tall grass, or under trees. Hence, a common name for the hybrid is the "rescue club," because it can help you out of a difficult situation.

Hybrid Club Drill 1   Which Club?

This drill is designed to allow you to assess the differences between an iron, a hybrid and a wood in hitting a similar shot. For this drill, you will need a 3- or 4-iron, a 3-hybrid, and a 5-wood. Select a target between 150-200 yards (137-182 meters). First, hit three shots with the 3-iron, then three shots with the 3-hybrid, and finally three shots with the 5-wood. Repeat the drill three times. Each time you reach the target with a club, score 1 point. It is possible to earn a maximum of 9 points with each club in this drill. Which club produced the greatest number of points?

3-iron points____

3-hybrid points____

5-wood points_ __

Your score ____ (out of 27 possible points)

Tee Shot Club Selection

When you select a club for a tee shot, consider these factors:

- What is a good landing area for the tee shot?
- From where would you like to play your next shot?
- What is more important, distance or accuracy? How will this affect your choice of club?
- Are there hazards or other obstacles that you definitely want to avoid? Can you select a club that will avoid these hazards or obstacles?

The most common club to use off the tee is the driver (figure 6.3). The driver will get the ball to travel the farthest distance, so for many players it is the most logical choice off the tee. The driver's loft, usually between 8 and 11 degrees, will create the most sidespin in the ball. Loft is the angle between the club face and a line at a 90-degree angle from the surface. For some players, the 3-wood is a better choice, because they can be far more accurate with it, and the distance they give up over using a driver is minimal. Henrik Stenson, PGA and European Tour Champion, often uses a 3-wood rather than a driver off the tee for greater accuracy.

Figure 6.3   SELECTING A CLUB FOR THE TEE SHOT

1. Hit the tee shot with the driver unless hazards or other obstacles prevent it.
2. Tee the ball up high.
3. Place the ball toward the forward heel in the stance.
4. Use a normal swing, and sweep the ball off the tee.

MISSTEP

You keep missing fairways and hitting shots way off target.

CORRECTION

The best way to hit a long shot off the tee is not to muscle the ball to the fairway but to hit the ball with the sweet spot of the club. Reduce your tempo, and focus on making a solid swing and good ball contact.

Tee Club Drill 1   Last Golfer Standing

This drill is perfect for two or more people. Use a tee box on the driving range, and choose two markers on the field to use as an imaginary fairway (one on each side of the fairway). Using the driver, hit one ball at a time, then switch players. As long as you hit the fairway, you stay in the game. The last golfer standing is the winner of the game. If you are alone, simply count the number of fairways you hit in a row. Your goal should be to hit at least eight fairways in a row.

TO DECREASE DIFFICULTY

- Make the fairway wider.
- Use a 3-wood or an iron instead of the driver.

TO INCREASE DIFFICULTY

- Make the fairway narrower.
- Ask a friend to try to disturb your focus, such as by talking to you during the backswing.

Success Check

- Make a distinct decision on which shot to hit at which target.
- Trust your body during the swing, and keep your focus on the target.

Score Your Success

0 to 1 fairways = 0 points

2 to 3 fairways = 1 point

4 to 5 fairways = 2 points

6 to 7 fairways = 3 points

8 to 9 fairways = 4 points

10 or more fairways = 5 points

Your score _____ (out of 5 possible points)

Tee Club Drill 2   The Tee Shooter

Think back to your favorite course or any course you are familiar with. On the driving range, picture a par-4 or par-5 hole on the course as vividly as possible. Visualize where the hazards and the obstacles on the hole would be and where the fairway and your ideal landing area would be. Pick your club, and hit your shot. Your goal is to hit the visualized landing area on the driving range. Hit 10 balls. Give yourself 3 points each time you hit your intended landing area, 2 points if you miss your area but hit the fairway, 1 point if you miss the fairway but avoid obstacles such as trees or other hazards that would prevent you from hitting a normal second shot, and 0 points if you put the ball in a hazard.

TO DECREASE DIFFICULTY

- Pick an easy hole where you can hit a club that you feel comfortable with.
- Pick a hole with as few obstacles as possible.

TO INCREASE DIFFICULTY

- Use five different holes so that you hit to the same target, or visualized landing area, only twice.
- Hit a couple of iron shots in between every tee shot.

Success Check

- Be specific when you decide how to play the shot. Make sure you know what you want to do and how to do it.
- Execute the shot as planned.

Score Your Success

0 to 6 points = 1 point

7 to 12 points = 2 points

13 to 18 points = 3 points

19 to 24 points = 4 points

25 to 30 points = 5 points

Your score _____ (out of 5 possible points)

CLUB SELECTION STRATEGY

When it comes to club selection, strategic thinking is crucial. Good players have dozens of ways to use each club. The type of shot and club depend on the situation at hand and the conditions. Is there a need for a high shot, low shot, curved shot, bump and run (a shot that only briefly flies in the air and then runs on the ground), or shot that stops quickly after landing? Again, the answer to the question *what* lies in understanding what the present circumstances will do to the ball. Say that the pin is tucked in behind a bunker on the right side, the green is fairly firm, and a light breeze is blowing left to right. The ball is resting nicely on the fairway. A good player in this situation would most certainly try to hit a high shot with a club that would carry the ball over the bunker and at the same time give the ball enough spin for it to stop on the green. The player would aim left of the flag and let the wind or a smooth fade (curve from left to right) move the ball toward the pin. The player would much rather end up left of the pin than right of it with the risk of missing the green on the wrong side (with the pin on the right of the green, a shot from the green-side rough on the right would probably be much more difficult than from the left).

The next question, *how* to execute a shot like that, may require a bit of practice and training. You can accomplish any of these shots by changing clubs, but you can also execute them by changing the way you hit with various clubs. Ask yourself:

- What do I want to do with the shot?
- What shot is called for?
- How is the shot executed?
- Am I skilled at this shot?
- What club and what swing or technique do I need to use to hit this shot?

Club Selection Strategy Drill 1   Course Roulette

Play nine holes. Give yourself different shots and lies than those you usually have. For instance, on a 350-yard (320-meter) par-4 hole, hit the tee shot with a 7-iron to leave yourself a different approach shot. Every time you leave yourself a different shot within two clubs off your normal club and you still hit the green, give yourself 2 points. Give yourself 1 point for hitting to a chip lie or a green-side bunker.

Success Check

- Carefully plan and execute your shots even if you are not using the club and distance you would normally use.
- Evaluate each shot, and use that knowledge in your next shot.

Score Your Success

0 to 1 point = 0 points

2 to 4 points = 1 point

5 to 7 points = 2 points

8 to 11 points = 3 points

12 to 14 points = 4 points

15 points or more = 5 points

Your score _____ (out of 5 possible points)

Club Selection Strategy Drill 2   **Target and Club Me**

Team up with a partner who is at roughly the same skill level as you. On the driving range, take turns selecting a target and club for each other. Hit to the target your partner has selected with the club your partner has selected. Give yourself 3 points if you hit the target with what you think is a good shot, 2 points if you hit the target but do not feel you hit a good shot, 1 point if you miss the target with what you think is a good shot, and 0 points if you miss the target and hit a bad shot. Hit 10 shots each.

TO DECREASE DIFFICULTY

- Use only two different clubs for the 10 shots.
- Play with a partner who is equal to or not as skilled as you are.

TO INCREASE DIFFICULTY

- Put big gaps between the targets and clubs you use. For example, first use a wedge and then a 3-wood.
- Play with a partner who is more skilled than you are.

Success Check

- Figure out a way to take the ball to the target even if the club is not one you would normally use.
- Stick to your decision, and execute the shot according to the plan.

Score Your Success

0 to 6 points = 1 point

7 to 12 points = 2 points

13 to 18 points = 3 points

19 to 24 points = 4 points

25 to 30 points = 5 points

Your score ____ (out of 5 possible points)

SELECTING CLUBS SUCCESS SUMMARY

Selecting clubs is a matter of understanding two things: Different clubs do different things with the ball, and each club can be used many different ways. Selecting a club means not only responding to the conditions or the yardage at hand but also deciding the required ball flight and what type of shot to hit. The more ways you can use the clubs, the better prepared you will be for each lie.

Record your point totals from each of the drills in this step, and add them up. If you scored at least 30 points, you have mastered this step and are ready to move on to the next. If you scored 20 to 29 points, you should be able to move on to the next step after reviewing and practicing a bit more, focusing on the drills where you scored low. If you scored fewer than 20 points, review the step again and practice the drills a few more times before moving on to the next step.

SCORING YOUR SUCCESS

Shot Pattern Drill

    1. Parnevik   ___ out of 5

Iron Club Drills

    1. The Stepladder   ___ out of 5

    2. The Triple   ___ out of 5

    3. High or Low   ___ out of 27

Wood Drills

    1. The Wood Picker   ___ out of 5

    2. The Transporter   ___ out of 5

Hybrid Club Drill

    1. Which Club?   ___ out of 27

Tee Club Drills

    1. Last Golfer Standing   ___ out of 5

    2. The Tee Shooter   ___ out of 5

Club Selection Strategy Drills

    1. Course Roulette   ___ out of 5

    2. Target and Club Me   ___ out of 5

Total   ___ **out of 99**

Understanding club selection is a crucial part of golf. Why else would a player carry around as many as 14 clubs? As your golf game develops, you will find infinite ways to hit a golf ball and use a golf club. This is one of the reasons it takes quite a bit of practice to become an accomplished golfer. Now it is time to move on to using these different alternatives on the golf course. This is when course management becomes crucial. Read more on this in step 10, Managing the Course.

Overcoming Difficult Lies and Shots From the Rough

When you take your game from the practice tee to the golf course, a big difference you will notice is that your ball is often found in places that are not flat or consisting of evenly mowed grass. As you work your way around a golf course, you will probably never have two lies that are the same, except perhaps when playing from the tee box. When you find your ball in a lie that is not ideal, think of it as part of the challenge of golf rather than as misfortune. The good news is that with some knowledge and a bit of practice, you can learn to make the necessary adjustments in your swing to still strike the ball well and create a serviceable golf shot.

Unlike most sports, golf is usually practiced in a different environment from the one in which it is played. Practicing on a driving range usually means standing on a mat or a flat area of neatly mowed grass and hitting balls. While helpful in honing the technical aspects of golf skills, such conditions do not offer a realistic environment that makes a productive transition from practice to performance. In order for your practice to be transferable to your game on the course, you must practice the uneven lies you are likely to encounter on the course.

Good lies occur when the ball comes to rest on a flat, tightly mowed, grassy area, much like the driving range. The advantages of a good lie are many. Most important, it is easiest to get into a comfortable address position and to strike a golf ball solidly from a good lie. A solid strike means the ball is contacted first, and then the ground, which propels the ball straighter and farther. It also imparts the necessary spin so that the ball will stay on the green rather than bounce or roll off into the rough or perhaps a hazard.

A bad lie is more likely to occur than a good lie. A bad lie is anything where it is difficult to get the club head squarely or solidly on the ball. This may happen when the ball is lying on an uphill, downhill, or sidehill slope, in an old divot, in deep grass, behind a tree, in some shrubs, or in a hazard. Rather than developing a new set of skills, being able to hit a ball successfully from a difficult lie usually means adapting and modifying the skills you have already developed in the previous steps.

In what is generally considered the greatest shot in golf, Tom Watson had hit his ball over the green on the 17th hole of the 1982 U.S. Open Championship at Pebble Beach. Tied with Jack Nicklaus for the lead, it looked like Tom had all but lost the Open. But as he surveyed the ball on a downhill lie in deep rough, he considered carefully what he would have to do. He turned to his caddie, Bruce Edwards, knowing he had a fairly good lie in the rough, but Edwards knew that despite the lie the shot would be difficult to control and almost impossible to stop near the hole. The danger was in failing to hit the shot crisply enough, which would either leave the ball short and above the hole with a severe downhill putt to follow, or missing the hole and leaving a long uphill putt. Either scenario could lead to double bogey and wipe away any chance of victory. To remind Watson to, at all costs, give himself a chance to make another par putt, Edwards told Watson, "Get it close." Watson smiled and replied, "Get it close? Hell, I'm going to sink it."

With a confident swing and crisp contact the perfectly struck chip bounded into the flagstick and dropped into the hole. Because he overcame a difficult lie, Tom Watson went on to become a U.S. Open Champion.

One of the more common difficult lies on the course is caused by unevenness of the ground. When the pitch of the ground is anything but flat, the location of the ball relative to your feet when you set up to hit the ball defines the type of lie. In a sidehill lie, the ball is either above or below your feet (figure 7.1). In an uphill or downhill lie, the ball is even with your feet but the slope it is resting on puts your feet at different levels. The target-side foot is either higher (uphill) or lower (downhill) than the rear foot. The following section explains the swing adjustments necessary to hit successful shots from uneven lies.

Figure 7.1 Sidehill lies: *(a)* ball above feet and *(b)* ball below feet.

UNEVEN-LIE ADJUSTMENTS

You can adjust to an uneven lie in many ways. Ball position, weight distribution, grip, alignment, swing length, and club selection are important factors to consider when adjusting to the terrain. Hitting a 5-iron from a downhill, uphill, or sidehill lie is different than hitting it from a flat fairway. A good player automatically calculates risk and reward when faced with such a lie. Is it better to select a higher-numbered club to make a clean connection with the ball? Can you swing with full speed and still keep your balance and proper ball flight? Will the ball curve in any direction because of the slope? The best way to discover what works for you is to try different lies and observe what the ball does. However, a few guidelines can help. For an uneven lie, the preparation needs to allow for a free swing. With practice you will learn what slope does to the ball, but the suggestions here will help you manage uneven lies.

Uphill and Downhill Lies

When the ball is even with your feet but your feet are on different levels, the club must have a chance to come down to the ball on the same path as in a shot from flat ground. This means your shoulders must follow, or be parallel with, the level of the ground when you set up to the shot.

When playing from an uphill lie (figure 7.2), the target-side foot is higher than the rear foot, so the first thing to do is to get the shoulders parallel to the ground at setup. This stops the club from coming into the ball at too steep of an angle and still allows for clean contact between the club and the ball. The grip is the same as in a normal shot, although it may help to choke down on the grip a little to get your hands closer to the ball.

Figure 7.2 Uphill lie.

The ball can be a bit forward in the stance to make the club's angle of attack slightly shallower. It is a good idea to step away from the ball, take a couple of practice swings, and note where the club hits the ground relative to your feet; that is where the ball position should be. Since the ball will tend to draw from an uphill lie (i.e., move right to left for a right hand golfer), modify your alignment so that you aim to the right (figure 7.3*a*).

The swing should be no different than a normal swing. Take the club back, and let your weight shift to the rear side (figure 7.3*b*). You may want to shorten the backswing a fraction to maintain your balance. Because of the slope it will be much easier to shift weight in the backswing, but it will also be more difficult to shift weight to the target side in the downswing and follow-through. At the finish of the swing, moving all your weight to the forward foot is going to be more or less impossible, but you should be able to find a position in which you can maintain your balance (figure 7.3*c*).

Figure 7.3   HITTING AN UPHILL LIE

Preparation

1. Use the same grip as when hitting a normal full swing.
2. Choke up on the grip a little (hands closer to the ball).
3. Use a normal stance with the alignment slightly right of the target.
4. Make sure your shoulders are parallel with the slope.
5. Evenly distribute your weight on both feet or slightly more on the lower foot.
6. Lean into the hill.
7. Position the ball slightly toward the target foot.

Backswing

1. Start the swing and backswing as in a normal full swing.
2. Shorten the backswing a little to maintain balance.
3. Shift your weight to the rear side during the backswing.

Impact and Follow-Through

1. Start the downswing as in a normal swing.
2. Shift your weight to the target side.
3. Swing through as in a normal swing.
4. Balance at the end with your weight on the target foot.

MISSTEP

When you hit from an uphill or downhill lie, the ball ends up either right or left of the target.

CORRECTION

You are most likely aiming directly at the target. The slope, however, causes the ball to curve, so you need to adjust your aim. If you are a right-handed golfer, aim to the right of the target on uphill shots and to the left on downhill shots.

When playing from a downhill lie (figure 7.4), the rear foot is higher than the target foot. Making the shoulders parallel to the ground at setup requires the opposite adjustment of that for an uphill lie. You may feel the weight leans a bit more to the target-side foot, which will help the club achieve a steeper angle of attack. The grip is the same as in a normal shot, but choke down closer to the shaft. Because the ball can be a bit farther back in the stance, gripping down on the club will allow a steeper angle of attack into the ball and prevent you from planting the club head into the ground behind the ball.

Figure 7.4 Downhill lie.

Step away from the ball, take a couple of practice swings, and note where the club hits the ground relative to your feet. Use that mark for your ball position. Your alignment should be slightly left of the target, since the ball tends to fade (figure 7.5*a*).

When playing a downhill lie, the swing should be no different than a normal swing. Take the club back, and let your weight shift to the rear side, which will be more difficult than in a normal shot (figure 7.5*b*). Similar to the uphill lie, you may want to shorten the backswing a fraction to maintain your balance. As you swing through it will be easy to shift weight to the target-side foot. With the ball a bit back in the stance you should be able to make clean contact. A good visual to have in mind on contact is to chase the ball down the hill; in other words, continue moving the club head downhill along the ground until well after contact. At the finish of the swing, find a position where you can maintain your balance with weight on the target-side foot (figure 7.5*c*).

Figure 7.5 **HITTING A DOWNHILL LIE**

Preparation

1. Use the same grip as for a normal full swing.
2. Choke down a bit on the grip (hands closer to the ball).
3. Use a normal stance with the alignment slightly left of the target.
4. Make sure your shoulders are parallel with the slope.
5. Evenly distribute your weight between both feet.
6. Position the ball slightly back in your stance (toward the nontarget-side foot).

Backswing

1. Start the swing as in a normal full swing.
2. Shorten the backswing a little to maintain your balance.
3. Shift your weight to the rear side during the backswing.

Impact and Follow-Through

1. Start the downswing as in a normal swing.
2. Shift your weight to the target-side foot.
3. Swing through as in a normal swing.
4. Continue moving the club head downhill, along the ground to insure clean contact.
5. Balance at the end with your weight on the target-side foot.

MISSTEP

You hit the top of the ball when hitting from a downhill lie, or you hit the ground before you hit the ball (hit the ball fat).

CORRECTION

You probably have too much weight on the high foot, or the ball is too close to the low foot. Be sure to finish with your weight on the low foot. Move the ball toward the high foot when you set up.

Sidehill Lies

Like uphill and downhill lies, sidehill lies will also be easier to hit with some slight modifications in the swing. In a sidehill lie, the ball is either above or below your feet when you address it. When you hit a shot from a sidehill lie, the ball is likely to curve in the downward direction of the slope. That is, for a right-handed golfer, an uphill lie will produce a shot that curves to the left, and a downhill lie will result in the shot curving to the right. Compensations in the setup will allow you to better control the direction of your shot as well as increase the likelihood of better contact with the ball.

When you set up to a sidehill shot with the ball above your feet (figure 7.6a), you may not need to make many changes. Since the ball is above your feet you may want to choke down on the grip a bit so that you don't hit the ground before you hit the ball. Also, the slope may make you put more weight on the heels than in a normal shot, so bend your knees a bit more to evenly distribute your weight on your feet. When the ball is above your feet, it will tend to draw or hook as you play the shot. To adjust for that, simply aim slightly to the right. The longer the shot, the more you will need to compensate to the right. The actual swing is basically a normal swing (figure 7.6b), though it may be a fraction shorter so that you can maintain balance and you will need to pay attention to the finish of the swing (figure 7.6c). Balance can be hard to find on a sidehill slope.

Figure 7.6   **HITTING A SIDEHILL LIE, BALL ABOVE FEET**

Preparation

1. Use the normal grip, but choke down a little on the club.
2. Use the normal setup, but aim slightly right of the target.
3. Distribute your weight evenly between both feet.
4. Position the ball in the center of the stance or slightly forward, especially when using a longer club.

Backswing

1. Start the swing and backswing as in a normal full swing.
2. Shorten the backswing a little to maintain balance.
3. Shift your weight to the rear side during the backswing.

Impact and Follow-Through

1. Start the downswing as in a normal swing.
2. Shift your weight to the target side.
3. Swing through as in a normal swing.
4. End in balance with your weight on the target-side foot.

MISSTEP

You hit the ground before you hit the ball (also known in golf terms as hitting the ball "fat") when the ball is above your feet.

CORRECTION

You need to make more of an adjustment to the slope. Choke down on the club, move a bit further from the ball, and check the ball position to insure it is in the middle of your stance and not too far forward.

Setting up to a sidehill shot where the ball is below your feet (figure 7.7a) also does not require many changes. Because the ball is below your feet, you may want to use the full length of the grip to prevent you from hitting the ball thin (i.e., hitting the middle or lower half of the ball, but not hitting the ground. This makes it difficult to control both direction and length of the shot). So take your grip a bit closer to the end of the handle. Bending your knees more than in a normal swing will also allow you to get closer to the ball and lessen the risk of hitting a thin shot. Putting a little more weight on the toes will also help you hit the ball cleanly. When the ball is below your feet, it will tend to fade or slice as you play the shot, so simply aim to the left. The actual swing is basically a normal swing (figure 7.7b), except it may be a fraction shorter to help you maintain your balance, and you will need to pay attention to the finish of the swing (figure 7.7c).

Figure 7.7   HITTING A SIDEHILL LIE, BALL BELOW FEET

Preparation

1. Use the normal grip, using the full length of the club.
2. Use the normal setup, but aim slightly left of the target.
3. Bend the knees to allow you to get closer to the ball.
4. Distribute your weight evenly between both feet or slightly toward the toes.
5. Position the ball in the center of the stance.
6. Position the ball slightly forward if hitting a wood.

(continued)

Figure 7.7 (continued)

Backswing

1. Start the swing and backswing as in a normal full swing.
2. Shorten the backswing a little to maintain balance.
3. Shift your weight to the rear side during the backswing.

Impact and Follow-Through

1. Start the downswing as in a normal swing.
2. Shift your weight to the target side.
3. Swing through as in a normal swing.
4. End in balance with your weight on the target-side foot.

MISSTEP

With the ball below your feet on a sidehill lie, you hit the top of the ball.

CORRECTION

You need to make more of an adjustment to the slope. Use the full length of the club, and bend your knees more than normal. Maintain your posture over the ball, making sure you are not sitting back too much on your heels.

MISSTEP

When you hit a ball from a sidehill lie, the ball ends up right or left of the target.

CORRECTION

You are probably aiming at the target. Since the slope will cause the ball to curve, you need to adjust your aim. Aim left of the target for a sidehill lie with the ball below your feet, and aim right of the target for a sidehill lie with the ball above your feet.

Uneven Lie Drill 1   Find the Ground, Uphill and Downhill Lies

Driving ranges can be difficult places to practice hitting from uneven lies. They are traditionally flat, and consequently they do no accurately represent what you will find on most golf courses. However, if you look around the range you can usually find a slope where you can set up to hit uphill and downhill lies. These may be at the ends of the range or even near the short game practice area. Since you will not hit balls at first, you can use the same slope and face the opposite way without causing danger. Set up to hit a shot, but don't use a ball. Use a 5- or 6-iron. The goal is to hit the ground where the imaginary ball is positioned and to maintain balance throughout the full swing. This drill will work on balance and allow you to see where the sole of the club strikes the ground when playing from uneven lies. Take 10 swings—5 uphill and 5 downhill—varying the type of shot as much as you can (for example, uphill lie followed by a downhill lie followed by an uphill lie).

Your goal is to complete 10 swings—5 uphill and 5 downhill—hitting the ground in the correct spot and maintaining balance throughout each swing.

TO DECREASE DIFFICULTY

- Hit all five uphill lies before hitting the five downhill lies.
- Use a longer club, such as a 3- or 4-iron, instead of the 5- or 6-iron.

TO INCREASE DIFFICULTY

- Use a shorter club, such as a 9-iron or pitching wedge, instead of the 5- or 6-iron.
- Use a different club for each shot.

Success Check

- Adjust your setup and grip to the lie.
- Take a couple of practice swings if you feel uncomfortable. Try to find your balance.

Score Your Success

Lose your balance and miss the ground = 0 points

Maintain your balance but miss the ground = 1 point

Hit the ground but lose your balance = 2 points

Maintain your balance and hit the ground = 3 points

Your score after 10 swings ____ (out of 30 possible points)

Uneven Lie Drill 2   Clip the Tee, Uphill and Downhill Lies

This drill is the same as uneven lie drill 1 (Find the Ground, Uphill and Downhill Lies), but instead of simply using the ground, you firmly press a tee into the ground where your imaginary ball would be. The goal is to break or knock the tee out of the ground while maintaining your balance throughout each swing. Take 10 swings—5 uphill and 5 downhill—varying the type of shot as much as you can (uphill lie followed by a downhill lie followed by an uphill lie, for example).

Your goal is to complete 10 swings—5 uphill and 5 downhill—clipping the tee and maintaining balance throughout each swing.

TO DECREASE DIFFICULTY

- Hit all five uphill lies before hitting the five downhill lies.
- Use a longer club, such as a 3- or 4-iron, instead of the 5- or 6-iron.

TO INCREASE DIFFICULTY

- Use a shorter club, such as a 9-iron, instead of the 5- or 6-iron.
- Use a different club for each shot.

Success Check

- Adjust your setup and grip to the lie.
- Take a couple of practice swings if you feel uncomfortable. Try to find your balance.

Score Your Success

Give yourself points for each swing based on the following criteria:

Lose your balance and miss the tee = 0 points

Maintain your balance but miss the tee = 1 point

Hit the tee but lose your balance = 2 points

Maintain your balance and hit the tee = 3 points

Your score after 10 swings _____ (out of 30 possible points)

Uneven Lie Drill 3   Find the Ground, Sidehill Lies

Find a slope where you can set up for sidehill lies both with the ball below your feet and above your feet. You will not hit balls, so you can use a slope facing the opposite way without causing danger. Set up as if to hit a shot, but without a ball. Use a 5- or 6-iron. The goal is to hit the ground where the imaginary ball is positioned and to maintain your balance throughout the swing. Complete 10 swings—5 with the imaginary ball above your feet and 5 with it below— varying the type of shot as much as you can (for example, sidehill lie with the ball below the feet followed by a sidehill lie with the ball above the feet).

ALTERNATIVE DRILL SETUP

If you cannot find a sidehill lie in your practice area (either on the range or in the short game practice area), try these alternatives:

- To simulate a sidehill lie with the ball below your feet, stand on two small range buckets or on a wooden board as you take your swings. The imaginary ball will be below your feet, thus allowing you to practice swinging in these conditions.
- To simulate a sidehill lie with the ball above your feet, place an extra plastic practice mat in front of you, imagining a ball on the mat as you take your swings. Your goal is to complete 10 swings—5 with the imaginary ball above your feet and 5 with it below—hitting the ground in the correct spot and maintaining balance throughout each swing.

TO DECREASE DIFFICULTY

- Hit all five sidehill lies with the ball below your feet before you hit the five sidehill lies with the ball above your feet.
- Use a longer club, such as a 3- or 4-iron, instead of the 5- or 6-iron.

TO INCREASE DIFFICULTY

- Press a tee into the ground so that only the top shows where the imaginary ball is. Hit the tee when you hit the ground.
- Use a shorter club, such as a 9-iron, instead of the 5- or 6-iron.

Success Check

- Adjust your setup and grip to the lie.
- Take a couple of practice swings if you feel uncomfortable. Try to find your balance.

Score Your Success

Give yourself points for each swing based on the following criteria:

Lose your balance and miss the ground = 0 points

Maintain your balance but miss the ground = 1 point

Hit the ground but lose your balance = 2 points

Maintain your balance and hit the ground = 3 points

Your score after 10 swings _____ (out of 30 possible points)

Uneven Lie Drill 4   Clip the Tee, Sidehill Lies

This drill is the same as drill 3, Find the Ground, but instead of simply trying to find the ground, you press a tee firmly into the ground where the imaginary ball is. Try to clip the tee on each shot. Your goal is to hit the tee where the imaginary ball is positioned and to maintain your balance throughout the swing. Complete 10 swings—5 with the imaginary ball above your feet and 5 with it below—varying the type of shot as much as you can (for example, sidehill lie with the ball below the feet followed by sidehill lie with the ball above the feet).

ALTERNATIVE DRILL SETUP

If you cannot find a sidehill lie in your practice area (either on the range, or in the short game practice area), try these alternatives:

- To simulate a sidehill lie with the ball below your feet, stand on two small range buckets or a wooden board as you take your swings. Because you can do it on the practice range, use a golf ball instead of a tee, and attempt to hit the ball below your feet as you would from such a lie on the golf course.
- To simulate a sidehill lie with the ball above your feet, place an extra plastic practice mat in front of you, and place a ball on the mat and attempt to hit a clean strike of the ball.

Your goal is to complete 10 swings—5 with the tee or ball above your feet and 5 with the tee or ball below your feet. Hitting the tee or ball in the correct spot and maintaining balance throughout each swing is your goal.

TO DECREASE DIFFICULTY

- Hit all five sidehill lies with the ball below your feet before you hit the five sidehill lies with the ball above your feet.
- Use a longer club, such as a 3- or 4-iron, instead of the 5- or 6-iron.

TO INCREASE DIFFICULTY

- Use a shorter club, such as a 9-iron, instead of the 5- or 6-iron.
- Use a different club on every shot.

Success Check

- Adjust your setup and grip to the lie.
- Take a couple of practice swings if you feel uncomfortable. Try to find your balance.

Score Your Success

Give yourself points for each swing based on the following criteria:

Lose your balance and miss the tee = 0 points

Maintain your balance but miss the tee = 1 point

Hit the tee but lose your balance = 2 points

Maintain your balance and hit the tee = 3 points

Your score after 10 swings _____ (out of 30 possible points)

Uneven Lie Drill 5   Uneven Game

A round of golf provides a number of uneven lies, and you will seldom face two similar lies in a row. To play well, you need to be able to adjust to every shot. The best way to prepare for this uncertainty is to practice a variety of lies. For this drill, find a place where you can hit uphill, downhill, and sidehill shots to various targets. Some driving ranges have areas like this, but if you cannot find one perhaps you can find a place in the short game practice area or on the golf course itself. (Note that some courses prohibit on-course practice.) Take 12 balls, and hit shots from 12 different lies (uphill, downhill, and sidehill) to 12 different targets. Be sure to vary your shots, such as uphill lie with the ball below the feet followed by downhill lie with the ball above the feet. Pick a different target for every shot. Your goal is to put all 12 shots within 10 percent of the total distance to the target. For example, if you play from 100 yards (91 meters) the ball must come to rest within 10 yards (9 meters) of the target.

TO DECREASE DIFFICULTY

- Use more of the same lies and less variation.
- Increase the limit to 20 percent and 30 percent of the distance for 2 and 3 points.

TO INCREASE DIFFICULTY

- Vary the distance between the long clubs (3- to 5-irons) down to the wedges.
- Decrease the limit to 10 percent and 5 percent of the distance for 2 and 3 points.

Success Check

- You adjust to the slope for each lie.
- Take a practice swing before each shot to get a feel for each lie.

Score Your Success

Give yourself points for each swing based on the following criteria:

Hit the ball but miss the target = 1 point each shot

Land the ball within 20 percent of the distance to the target = 2 points each shot

Land the ball within 10 percent of the distance to the target = 3 points each shot

Your score after 12 shots ____ (out of 36 possible points)

STRATEGY FOR PLAYING DIFFICULT LIES

The questions of what to do and how to do it apply to difficult lies as well as they do when playing shots from good lies. What shot is in front of you, and what are the demands of the hole? Let's say you have a downhill lie with water between you and the green. The green is firm and surrounded by bunkers. This would be a challenging shot even if you were hitting from a good lie on the fairway, but with a downhill lie, it is a greater challenge. The lie will affect the flight of the ball, so your challenge is to apply backspin so that the ball stops on the green quickly rather than bouncing away. If you still think you can get the flight necessary to stop the ball on the green, the answer to the question of *how* will be different than the answer for a flat fairway lie. To get the same trajectory, you will need to hit a higher-numbered club, causing the ball to fly shorter. If you still think you can make the green, fire away! At other times, the only answer may be to lay up short of the water and try to chip or pitch the ball up close enough to the hole to get into the hole in one putt.

A good rule of thumb in situations like this is to ask the question *If I hit this shot 10 times, how often would I be successful?* If you don't believe you would be successful 8 out of 10 times, take the more conservative choice. It is always better to take a safe bogey than risk a big number on a hole due to poor decision making.

The number of difficult lies a golfer can face during a round are countless. Slopes and uneven lies are only a small part of what you can expect; thick rough and trees will also get in your way. Only by playing a lot of golf can you learn to make appropriate decisions when facing different lies. When asked how he knew what club to hit when he was behind a tree, Ryder Cup player Niclas Fasth answered, "Experience. There is no general rule for that because the lies will make the ball fly differently every time. I can also affect the ball flight in different ways with the same club so the answer may be different from one time to another."

A classic story in golf is Jean Van de Velde's 18th hole of the British Open at Carnoustie in 1999. He was in what looked like a safe lead as he teed off from the 18th tee. A bad drive and a bold iron shot later, he was in the creek short of the green. When he decided to take off his shoes and step into the creek to play the shot, he was really in deep trouble. It took him a triple bogey to hole out, and he lost the championship to Paul Lawrie in a playoff. In retrospect, it is easy to say that Van de Velde made a couple of bad decisions and hit a couple of bad shots. Would he have made the same decisions in a smaller tournament or during an earlier round of the championship? Would he have played the shots better? Golf is about constantly considering the task at hand, weighing the risk and reward involved, and reacting to all the different lies you face.

Difficult Lies Strategy Drill 1   Difficult Lie Challenge Game

This drill is done on the driving range with a playing opponent. Both of you begin by playing your ball from the same spot of the driving range. Take turns picking the lie and the target. Visualize trees and other obstacles in your way. For example, for the first shot you might have hit a shot that carries 100 yards (91 meters) in the air over an imaginary water hazard and lands on a small green. For your second shot, imagine having to hit under branches that are no higher than the first flag on a driving range so the ball stops on a target that is 150 yards (137 meters) away. Continue until you have played 10 balls each.

TO DECREASE DIFFICULTY

- Use the same club but vary the targets.
- Hit two shots with the same task, and see if the second one goes better.

TO INCREASE DIFFICULTY

- Vary targets and clubs for each shot.
- Hit from an area with rough, slopes, and other difficult lies.

Score Your Success

Give yourself points for each swing based on the following criteria:

Wrong trajectory and miss the target = 0 points

Accurate trajectory but way off target = 1 point

Good trajectory and hit the target = 2 points

Your score _____ (out of 20 possible points)

Difficult Lies Strategy Drill 2   Bad Throw

When playing a round of nine holes on the golf course with a friend, make a rule that you can throw each other's ball once on every hole with your nondominant throwing hand. The ball cannot be thrown into a hazard and it must be possible to find and play without penalty. Play from the lie where the ball ends up. Replace a ball where the original would have been and continue play from there, but also play the thrown ball.

TO DECREASE DIFFICULTY

- Only use the throw in the short game.
- Throw the ball no more than 15 yards (14 meters).

TO INCREASE DIFFICULTY

- Use the drill for 18 holes.
- Set no limits on where the ball can be thrown.

Success Check

- Always calculate risks and rewards when deciding what shot to play.
- Think one shot ahead of the shot at hand. From where do you want to hit your next shot?

Score Your Success

Give yourself points for each swing based on the following criteria:

Return the ball to fairway or putting green in 3 or more strokes = 0 points

Return the ball to fairway or putting green in 2 strokes = 1 point

Return the ball to fairway or putting green in 1 stroke = 2 points

Your score _____ (out of 18 possible points)

SHOTS FROM THE ROUGH

Ideally you would like every shot to hit the fairway or green, but that is just not going to happen. Occassionally, you will find your ball in the rough. Even the best players in the game miss a fairway or green and must play from the rough. One of the reasons these people are considered great players is they know the techniques that allow them to hit successful shots despite less-than-ideal conditions.

There are times when a golf course superintendent, the person in charge of the course setup and maintenance, wants to make the course more difficult. One way to do this is known as *growing the rough*. Because the quality of both golfers and golf equipment has improved over the years, tournament directors and course superintendents are looking for ways to make courses more challenging. One of the fastest and least expensive ways of doing this is to grow the rough. For players, this means we will see more rough on more courses as time goes on.

The rough can be grown in two ways. First the superintendent can mow less of the fairway, increasing the amount of tall grass defining the sides and both ends of the fairway. This is known as *narrowing the fairway*. There are times they let the grass grow around the green, and this can be among the most challenging of rough as it becomes difficult to hit a precise or delicately placed shot from the rough. This rough is known as *greenside rough*.

A second way of growing the rough is by letting the grass along the fairway grow taller so there are different levels of rough. For example, a superintendent may let the first 3 or 4 yards of grass on the sides of a fairway grow an inch or two taller than the fairway. This is known as the *first cut of rough*. After 3 or 4 yards, the grass may be grown to 4 to 6 inches. This is known as the *second cut of rough*. In some circumstances, there may be a *third cut of rough* in which the grass is not cut at all. Depending on the type of grass, you may find yourself looking for your ball in grass that is knee or perhaps waist high. The United States Golf Association (USGA) is notorious for growing the rough to make a course very difficult when they set up for the United States Open Championship. The rough is a fact of life on a golf course, and to be a successful golfer you must learn to play from it.

Hitting shots from the rough is much like hitting a shot from the fairway, but with two adjustments. These adjustments apply whether you are attempting a full swing from fairway rough or a partial swing pitch shot from greenside rough. First as you take your stance and address the ball, open the clubface slightly (figure 7.8*a*). The tall grass has a tendency to catch the club around the hosel, twisting the clubface shut and sending the shot left for a right-handed player or right for a left-handed player. Opening the clubface slightly at address compensates for this.

Second, during the takeaway, break your wrists slightly so that you take the club up more abruptly (figure 7.8*b*). The tall grass will slow the clubhead down before it reaches the ball, so you must get as much clubhead on the ball while catching as little grass as possible on the downswing. Lifting the clubhead abruptly on the takeaway allows you to bring the clubhead back to the ball at a steeper angle and minimize the amount of grass you catch before contacting the ball (figure 7.8*c*). Playing the ball slightly back in your stance, particularly on shots from greenside rough, will also help you make cleaner contact with the ball. Make sure the club follows the ball toward the target on the follow-through and that you finish with a balanced stance (figure 7.8*d*).

If you are playing the ball from moderate to deep rough, tighten your grip a bit. This will help minimize the effect the grass has on your golf club. If you a pitching the ball less than 50 yards to a green, open the clubface and swing about 50% harder than you think is necessary. The clubhead will slide under the ball and pop it out. If you are chipping the ball onto the green from deep rough, exaggerate the wrist break on take away and be aggressive on the downswing in order to get the clubhead through the grass. For shorter shots, take a shorter backswing. These shots must be hit aggressively to get the clubhead through the tall grass.

The more you practice shots from the rough, the more you will both improve your technique as well as understand the effect rough has on the ball once it comes out. Few golf courses, however, intentionally grow rough in their practice areas. You may, however, find a bit of rough to practice in at either end of the driving range.

Figure 7.8 **EXECUTING A SHOT FROM THE ROUGH**

Preparation

1. Open clubface slightly at address.
2. Play ball back in stance.
3. Take a firm grip.

Execution

1. Break wrists on the take away and bring club up at a steep angle.
2. Arms, hands, and club naturally follow the turn of the shoulders.
3. Downswing begins with weight shift from back to front foot.
4. Pull down sharply on the club handle to maintain a steep angle of decent into the ball.
5. Minimize contact with the grass and maximize contact with the ball.

(continued)

Figure 7.8 *(continued)*

Follow-Through

1. Club follows ball toward target.
2. Finish on balance with body weight on target side foot.

MISSTEP

You hit behind the ball, catching more grass than ball.

CORRECTION

Play the ball further back in your stance. Break the wrists on your takeaway to abruptly lift the club. On the downswing, shift your weight forward and pull down on the handle to maintain an up-and-down steep angle of decent into the ball. Make sure your weight is forward on the target-side foot when you make contact.

MISSTEP

The ball is pulled off the target line.

CORRECTION

Maintain an open clubface. Tall grass grabs the hosel of the club and closes the clubface. Compensate by opening the clubface at address and maintaining a firm grip—especially with the hand on the top of the grip.

Shots From the Rough Drill 1   Angle of Attack

To successfully play a shot from the rough, you must bring the clubhead into the ball with a steep angle of attack, taking a minimum of grass as you swing. This drill will help you develop a steeper angle of descent in your swing. You do not need to hit shots from the rough for this drill.

On a driving range, place a board or foam roll one yard behind a golf ball (figure 7.9). Use a 9-iron or pitching wedge. First, assume a normal stance with the ball in the middle of your stance. Begin the takeaway by breaking your wrists and lifting the clubhead straight back and directly into the air over the board. Repeat 10 times. Give yourself 1 point every time you clear the board on your takeaway, for a maximum of 10 points.

Second, repeat the drill but only complete your backswing. Repeat 10 times. Give yourself 1 point every time you clear the board on your takeaway and backswing, for a maximum of 10 points.

Finally, repeat the drill, executing the takeaway and backswing, and finish the drill by completing the swing and striking the ball. On the downswing, pull the handle of the club down sharply to

Figure 7.9 Angle of Attack drill.

(continued)

Shots From the Rough Drill 1 *(continued)*

maintain a steep angle of descent into the ball. The swing should feel controlled and the ball should be crisply contacted. Repeat 10 times. Give yourself 1 point for clearing the board on your takeaway and backswing, and 1 point for crisp contact with the ball (you strike the ball before you strike the ground). Maximum of 20 points.

TO DECREASE DIFFICULTY

- Hit three-quarter swing shots rather than full swing shots.
- Move the board 1 inch further (2 inches total) from your golf ball.

TO INCREASE DIFFICULTY

- Execute the drill using a wedge, iron, and fairway metal.

Success Check

- Begin the backswing by lifting the club abruptly and breaking the wrists.
- Maintain a steep angle of decent throughout the shot.
- Maintain a firm grip throughout the swing.
- Play the ball back in your stance.

Score Your Success

Take-away only ____ (out of 10 points)

Complete backswing ____ (out of 10 points)

Complete downswing ____ (out of 10 points)

Your score ____ (out of 30 possible points)

Shots From the Rough Drill 2 In the Rough

To become familiar with playing the ball out of the rough, you may have to do some searching to find a place where you can practice taking partial or full swings at a golf ball from the rough.

From medium rough (2 to 4 inches), chip a golf ball to a target. Emphasize a steep angle of attack, maximum contact with the ball, and minimum contact with the grass. The chip should be no more than a three-quarter swing. Hit five chip shots to a target 10 yards away, five chip shots to a target 15 yards away, and five chip shots to a target 20 yards away. Give yourself 2 points for every chip shot that travels at least 5 yards in the air, for a maximum of 30 points.

From medium rough, pitch a golf ball to a target. This should be a full swing with an emphasis on lifting the club abruptly on the takeaway and striking the ball using a steep angle of attack. Hit five pitch shots from the rough to a target 25 yards away, five pitch shots to a target 35 yards away, and five pitch shots to a target 45 yards away. Give yourself 2 points for every pitch shot that travels at least 10 yards in the air and 5 points for each pitch shot that travels at least 20 yards, for a maximum of 75 points.

TO DECREASE DIFFICULTY

- Hit shots from light or less dense rough.

TO INCREASE DIFFICULTY

- Execute the drill from rough where the ball is buried deep.
- Execute the drill while changing the depth of rough with each shot.

Success Check

- Maintain a firm grip throughout the swing.
- Use a steep angle of attack minimizing contact with the grass and maximizing ball contact.
- Keep the club face open at address.

Score Your Success

Chips shots from the rough ____ (out of 30 points)

Pitch shots from the rough ____ (out of 75 points)

Your score ____ (out of 105 points)

Shots From the Rough Drill 3   Short but Deadly

When a golf ball is surrounded, or partially covered, by grass, it is difficult to get the clubhead cleanly on the ball, which makes it difficult to control the shot. This can be a particular problem when the rough is around the green and the shot requires a bit of touch to get it close to the hole. From a lie in medium rough (no higher than the tops of your shoes), chip a golf ball to a hole that is less than 10 yards away with a sand wedge. Repeat ten times.

TO DECREASE DIFFICULTY

- Hit shots from light rough (midway up your shoes)
- Hit shots to a hole 20-30 yards or 18-27 meters away (the more green you have to work with, the easier these shots are to make as the ball has a tendency to roll more when coming out of the rough).

TO INCREASE DIFFICULTY

- Execute the drill from rough where only the very top of the ball is visible.

Success Check

- Bring the clubhead up sharply at takeaway.
- Use a steep angle of decent to contact more ball and less grass.
- Maintain a firm grip on the club throughout the swing.

Score Your Success

Ball lands on the green = 1 point

Ball stops within 3 feet of the hole = 2 points

Your score ____ (out of 20 possible points)

Shots From the Rough Drill 4   Pitching From the Rough

From a lie in medium rough (no higher than the tops of your shoes) using a sand wedge, pitch a golf ball to a hole on a green that is between 20 to 30 yards away. Repeat ten times. Remember, open the clubface, swing aggressively, and the ball will roll more as it will have less spin coming out of the rough. This shot is executed more like a bunker shot, but instead of taking sand with your shot, you take grass.

TO DECREASE DIFFICULTY

- Hit shots from light rough (midway up your shoes).

TO INCREASE DIFFICULTY

- Aim for a hole that is within 5 yards of the edge of the green nearest to you.
- Execute this shot so the ball must carry a sand bunker before landing on the green.

Success Check

- Club face remains open through the swing.
- Swing aggressively.
- Grip firmly with the left hand to keep the club from turning in the tall grass.
- Body remains in balance throughout the swing.

Score Your Success

Ball lands on the green = 2 points

Ball stops within 3 feet of the hole = 3 points

Your score _____ (out of 30 possible points)

ROUGH PLAY STRATEGY

Golfing a ball from the rough is a bit more challenging than playing from the fairway. Planning strategically helps insure the shot comes off with greater success. In this section, we cover the major points to consider and offer several suggestions for making the best from a difficult situation.

Begin by determining the sort of grass you are in. Is the grass thick or sparse? How high is it? Is the ball sitting down or up in the grass or somewhere in between? Finally, how far does the ball have to travel to get back to the fairway or onto the green? Remember, when playing from a difficult lie, the first consideration is to get the ball back into reasonable play and not compound the problem with unnecessary strokes and creating more difficult lies. Play within your skill set and play safe. Don't be greedy or feel you have to make up for mistakes. In golf, the conservative strategy is generally the smarter strategy. Do not make a bad situation worse.

Once you know what sort of grass you are playing from, decide what shot you want to hit. For example, if the ball is 180 yards from the green and buried deep into the rough with little of the ball showing, you will have to dig deep into the rough to extract the ball. With so much grass covering the ball, there is slim hope that you will reach the green, so you may decide simply to advance the ball 30 yards and back onto the fairway. If the ball is sitting up on thick greenside rough 3 yards from the green, you should have no problem contacting the ball cleanly with minimal interference from the grass. Therefore you may decide to attempt to hole the ball with a chip shot.

Once you decide on the shot to make, you need to select a club that will best serve you in executing that shot. Because the clubhead will, in all likelihood, catch the grass first and then the ball, the rough will slow the clubhead down and influence its direction in unpredictable ways. Therefore select a club that will minimize the effect of the rough on your shot. For average golfers, a 5 iron is the iron with the least loft they can effectively play from any rough. If using a fairway wood, a 5 wood is about the limit of effective loft. Any less loft and you will have difficulty getting the clubhead to make reasonable contact with the ball. A better choice for long shots (shots over 100 yards) from the rough are hybrid clubs, also known as rescue clubs (for the very reason that they are effective from rough and other difficult lies). Again, with a hybrid club, it is important to make the same adjustments when hitting from the rough as any other club (i.e., steeper angle of approach, ball back in your stance, and firm grip).

If the ball is sitting in a nest of light or moderate rough, neither perched nor buried with most of the ball showing, this is known as a *flyer lie* (figure 7.10). When a ball is in a flyer lie, the clubhead will make contact with the grass before the ball. The

Figure 7.10 Flyer lie.

Figure 7.11   A buried lie.

Figure 7.12   With a ball sitting on top of thick rough, choose a club that plays more like a tee shot.

grass will not reduce the club-head speed because it is not that thick, but some grass will come between the clubhead and the ball. This will reduce the back-spin on the ball and the shot will be virtually spinless. The ball will come out faster, fly lower, and bounce and run longer. A ball struck well from a flyer lie will roll a long way. When hitting from a flyer lie, take one less club that you normally would to account for the greater ball roll. For example, if you normally hit a 7 iron 140 yards, take an 8 iron for the same distance with this lie.

When the ball is buried in heavy rough (figure 7.11), your goal must be to simply get the ball out and back to the short grass. Don't run up your score by trying for too much distance with this shot. Given the amount of grass the clubhead must fight through to reach the ball, you are not likely to make sufficient contact to gain much length from this shot. Usually a wedge is a good choice. Play the ball back in your stance, break your wrists on the takeaway, and use a steep up-and-down swing to extract the ball. A general rule of thumb is the deeper the lie, the steeper the descent.

When most golfers find their ball perched on top of thick rough, they consider themselves lucky. But don't think you've got an easy shot. It is easy to whiff this shot or pop the ball straight in the air by getting the clubhead too far under the ball. This shot should be hit more like a tee shot—a low, driving shot rather than a steep downward approach—just the opposite of the shot for a ball buried in heavy rough. Select a club that will send the ball the required distance as no grass should inhibit this shot (figure 7.12). To promote the necessary shallow, sweeping action needed for this shot, take the club back long and low.

Strategic Play From the Rough Drill 1   **High, Medium, or Low**

Use a practice green that has deep rough within 20 yards. Place 10 balls deep into the rough (step on them, figure 7.13*a*), 10 balls at a medium distance in the rough (drop them from shoulder or hip height, figure 7.13*b*), and 10 balls perched on top of the rough (place them, figure 7.13*c*). Pick a target in the middle of the green 15 to 20 yards away and pitch the 30 balls to this target. For each of the three lies, find the club that best helps you get the ball consistently closest to the target.

Figure 7.13   High, Medium, or Low drill.

(continued)

Strategic Play From the Rough Drill 1 *(continued)*

TO DECREASE DIFFICULTY

- Play five balls from each lie, and place the balls within 10 yards of the practice green.

TO INCREASE DIFFICULTY

- Vary the distance to the green for each of the 10 balls in the 3 different lies.

Success Check

- Adjust the angle of the clubhead descent for the particular lie you are playing.

Score Your Success

For each shot, give yourself 2 points if the ball lands on the green and 3 points if the ball stops within 5 yards of the target hole, for a maximum of 150 points.

10 shots from deep rough ____

10 shots from medium rough ____

10 shots from light rough ____

Your score ____ (out of 150 possible points)

Strategic Play From the Rough Drill 2   Perched Shot

Using a sand wedge, perch 10 balls on top of thick rough approximately 20 yards from the practice green. Alternate pitching the balls to two holes at different distances on the practice green. Repeat twice.

TO DECREASE DIFFICULTY

- Play shots from 10 yards from practice green.
- Play shots to the same hole.

TO INCREASE DIFFICULTY

- Vary the distance to the green for each shot.
- Play each shot to a different hole.

Success Check

- Take the club back long and low to promote a shallow, sweeping action.

Score Your Success

For every shot that lands and remains on green = 1 point

For every shot that comes to rest within 6 feet of hole = 2 points

For every shot that comes to rest within 3 feet or less of the hole = 3 points

Your score ____ (out of 30 possible points)

DIFFICULT LIES AND ROUGH SHOTS SUCCESS SUMMARY

The key to mastering difficult lies is adjusting to the ground on which the ball rests. When the ball is below your feet, adjust the grip to give yourself a longer club to work with. When the ball is above your feet, shorten the club. Try to align your shoulders parallel with the ground.

When playing from an uphill or downhill lie, adjust the ball position. Move the ball forward in the stance for an uphill lie and back in the stance for a downhill lie. If you notice that good shots end up left or right of the target, keep in mind that the slope will usually cause the ball to curve. Aim left for a downhill lie or a lie with the ball below your feet. Aim right for an uphill lie or a lie with the ball above your feet.

Additionally, developing the ability to play the ball successfully from the rough will provide a significant boost to your advancement in becoming a successful golfer. A few simple adjustments to your swing and a reduction in your expectations for your shot will minimize the penalty of finding your ball in the rough. Make no mistake: Playing from the rough is difficult. But it is a reality for every golfer, even the very best. But players who hone their skills by practicing these shots and thinking strategically will feel less frustration when finding their balls in the rough because they will know the what and how for getting out of trouble.

Record your point totals from each of the drills in this step and total them. If you scored at least 300 out of 559 points, you're ready for the next step. If you scored at least 250 points but fewer than 300, you are almost there. Move on after reviewing the sections you feel you can improve the most. If you scored below 250 points, review the techniques and practice the drills again to raise your scores.

SCORING YOUR SUCCESS

Uneven Lie Drills

1. Find the Ground, Uphill and Downhill Lies   ___ out of 30
2. Clip the Tee, Uphill and Downhill Lies   ___ out of 30
3. Find the Ground, Sidehill Lies   ___ out of 30
4. Clip the Tee, Sidehill Lies   ___ out of 30
5. Uneven Game   ___ out of 36

Difficult Lies Strategy Drills

1. Difficult Lie Challenge Game   ___ out of 20
2. Bad Throw   ___ out of 18

Shots From the Rough Drills

1. Angle of Attack   ___ out of 30
2. In the Rough   ___ out of 105
3. Short but Deadly   ___ out of 20
4. Pitching From the Rough   ___ out of 30

Strategic Play From the Rough Drills

1. High, Medium, or Low   ___ out of 150
2. Perched Shot   ___ out of 30

Total   **___ out of 559**

The term difficult lies may say more about the player than the actual lie itself. A lie that a new golfer would view as difficult or impossible may be no problem at all to an experienced player. It is also common for beginner golfers to underestimate the challenge of hitting a shot from the rough or an uneven lie. Becoming a better golfer is about finding more ways to execute the shots you face. If you master difficult lies on the grass, you will soon be able to master the next step, hitting shots from a sand bunker. Move on to the next step!

Bunker Play

A golf ball coming to rest in a bunker strikes fear into the hearts of most amateur golfers, yet professional golfers much prefer the bunker over being in the rough. Who is right? The professionals. While often perceived as a difficult shot, the bunker shot is actually one of the easiest. As with most shots in golf, a little knowledge and practice will turn this shot into a potent force in your arsenal of golf shots. What makes the bunker shot truly unique is that you don't hit the ball, you hit the sand. By hitting the sand under the ball, you send the ball out of the bunker with the sand. Because there is a lot more sand than golf ball to hit, it is easier to hit the sand rather than a golf ball. With practice, therefore, a bunker shot can become an easy shot to execute.

Sand bunkers are placed in strategic locations where players are likely to hit shots. Bunkers are also used by architects to distract you from the real target, such as the green or the flag on the green. At times you may find it difficult to concentrate on hitting the ball to the green when the biggest object in your vision is a large, gaping bunker that looks eager to swallow even a slightly mis-hit shot. While the white sand can provide a visually pleasing contrast to the green, most players find sand bunkers more intimidating than pleasing. One of the more famous bunkers at the Old Course in St. Andrews, Scotland, has earned the name Hell Bunker for the centuries of agony it has caused some players. The intimidation factor is intended to enhance the challenge and test your skill. You will, however, greatly diminish the intimidation factor by practicing and perfecting your bunker play. Again, these shots are among the easiest in golf, but they do require some knowledge and more than a little practice. In this step, you will learn to rise to the challenge by developing the skill to hit bunker shots from greenside and fairway bunkers.

BUNKER RULES AND ETIQUETTE

The bunker is a unique feature on a golf course, so rules and etiquette exist that apply specifically to the sand. Not knowing or not abiding by the rules will cost you penalty strokes, so you must learn them. The rule specific to bunker play is rule 13.4 of the USGA rule book (*USGA 2012 Rules of Golf*). According to the rule, the club may not touch the sand before the downswing motion made in executing the shot. If you touch the sand prior to executing your swing, the result is a two-stroke penalty. You can avoid this severe penalty simply by being careful with your club while in the bunker.

A bunker is considered a hazard. Therefore, you may not remove any natural objects such as stones, sticks, or clumps of sand that may impede your swing or contact with the ball. However, you may remove any man-made objects such as rakes, bottles, or paper if they obstruct your swing. If the ball moves as you remove a man-made object, you must replace the ball in its original position.

If your ball has come to rest in standing water in the hazard, you may remove the ball from the water, and take a drop at the nearest point of complete relief without a penalty being assessed. However, you must drop the ball within the hazard. If it rolls outside the hazard on the drop, you must drop it again so that it remains within the hazard.

As a matter of etiquette, carry a rake into the bunker, and place it out of your way as you set up and execute the shot. Before leaving the bunker, rake away any disturbances you created in the sand while hitting the shot or walking in the bunker (figure 8.1). Leave the bunker looking the way you would like it to look if your ball were to land there again. When leaving the bunker, place the rake with the teeth down outside or just inside the bunker.

Figure 8.1 Rake the bunker after your shot.

GREENSIDE BUNKER SHOTS

The sand wedge (figure 8.2) is specifically designed for use in greenside bunkers. It is now common for players to carry several wedges of varying lofts that can be used for bunker play. Although the sand wedge can be effective with other shots, the heavier bottom of the club, also known as the bounce, makes it particularly effective in sand. Because sand is heavier than grass, the bounce allows the club to slide easily through the sand. The high loft of a sand wedge helps the club lift the ball into the air without a player having to hit down on the ball as is required when playing shots on grass.

Figure 8.2   Sand wedge.

Preparation for the bunker shot will vary depending on the lie. Like other parts of the golf course, a bunker can have undulations that affect your stance as you set up for your shot. Uneven lies (uphill, downhill, and sidehill) are common in bunkers. Stance adjustments that ensure your body is balanced and your swing follows the contours of a lie (see step 7, Overcoming Difficult Lies and Shots from the Rough) are the same in the bunker as they are in other parts of the course. If your ball sits directly on top of the sand in a greenside bunker, you have a regular or normal lie (figure 8.3a). A ball that is plugged in the sand and resembles a fried egg is known as a buried lie (figure 8.3b). There are several differences between playing shots from regular and buried lies.

Figure 8.3 Bunker lies: *(a)* regular lie and *(b)* buried lie.

Regular Lie

A greenside bunker shot is similar to a full swing except for slight modifications in the setup. To make full use of a sand wedge's bounce, open the club face so that the face points directly skyward, then take your grip on the club (figure 8.4a). You will notice that this causes the club face to point away from the target. To correct the club face alignment, open your stance by moving the target-side foot back from the target line, and adjust the hips and shoulders to align with the feet. The club head should now be facing the target line.

To keep from sliding in the soft sand, shuffle your feet down into the sand an inch or two. Digging into the sand also gives you a feel for the depth and texture of the sand, which is a tip as to how the club head will react once it strikes the sand. If the sand feels dry and fluffy, the club will slide easily. If the sand is damp and packed, you will need more effort to get the club through the sand. Having the feet below the ball will also help you contact the sand before the ball.

To encourage the correct swing and follow-through, grip the sand wedge high on the handle as in a normal shot. Grip the handle tightly with the fingers of the left hand (for a right-handed golfer) so that the club head doesn't get caught in the sand and twist. The shaft should point to the zipper of your pants, and your hands should be slightly forward of the club head. Play the ball in the middle of the stance or slightly forward in the stance. With the club face open and aimed at the target, take a normal swing along the line of the shoulders, hips, and feet (figure 8.4b). Strike the sand 2 to 4 inches (5 to 10 centimeters) behind the ball, making a shallow divot in the sand about the size of a United States dollar bill. Let the ball splash on a blanket of sand out of the bunker and onto the green.

The key to distance control in a greenside bunker shot is the follow-through. Swing through to a complete finish for long bunker shots (up to 20 yards/18 meters), but shorten the follow-through when the pin is closer. The follow-through should finish with the hips and shoulders square to the target, the body in balance, and the weight primarily on the target-side foot (figure 8.4c). It takes practice to develop a sense of touch and distance control in a bunker shot.

Figure 8.4 EXECUTING A GREENSIDE BUNKER SHOT FROM A REGULAR LIE

Setup

1. Open the club face, aim toward the target, and take a normal grip.
2. Grip the club firmly with the fingers of the left hand to control the club.
3. Point the shaft at your zipper, hands slightly forward of the club head.
4. Use an open stance by pulling the target-side foot away from the target line and aligning the hips and shoulders with the feet.
5. Dig your feet into the sand.

Execution

1. Take a normal swing along the line of the shoulders, hips, and feet.
2. Strike the sand 2 to 4 inches (5 to 10 centimeters) behind the ball, taking a shallow divot of sand.
3. To improve control, keep the lower body still during the swing.

(continued)

Figure 8.4 *(continued)*

Follow-Through

1. Complete a full swing with high follow-through for long bunker shots.

2. Shorten the follow-through if the hole is close to the bunker.

3. Finish with the hips and shoulders square to the target.

4. Finish on balance with your weight primarily on the target-side foot.

MISSTEP

When hitting a bunker shot from a regular lie, you contact the ball instead of the sand behind the ball.

CORRECTION

First, check your ball position to see if it's too far back in your stance. Move the ball to the middle or slightly to the target side of your stance. Second, check your downswing. You may be watching the ball rather than a spot 2 to 3 inches (5 to 10 centimeters) behind the ball. Focus on where you want the club to enter the sand.

MISSTEP

When hitting a bunker shot from a regular lie, you take too much sand and the ball remains in the bunker.

CORRECTION

First, check your ball position to see if the ball is too far forward in your stance; if it is, move the ball back to the middle of your stance. Second, insure that the club face is facing skyward to allow the club to slide through the sand rather than dig into it. Finally, check your downswing. The angle of the club head is probably too steep, driving the club head into the sand. Take a shallower swing, attempting to skim the sand out from under the ball.

Buried Lie

You walk into the bunker and see your ball sitting down in the sand rather than resting on top of it. Playing a buried lie is similar to playing a regular lie except for a few modifications in the setup, execution, and follow-through. This shot appears to be even more challenging than a bunker shot from a regular lie. However, like most golf shots, with a little insight and practice you'll soon hit it like a pro; it's easier than it looks.

For the setup, play the ball in the back of your stance (figure 8.5*a*). Unlike a bunker shot from a normal lie, for a plugged lie you must close the club face so that it is turned squarely toward the target. Take a normal stance rather than an open stance. As when playing a regular lie, dig down into the sand with your feet, but place a bit more weight on the target-side foot.

On the takeaway, break the wrists (quickly bend the wrists) a bit so that the club cocks upward (figure 8.5*b*). This will allow you to come into the ball at a very steep angle. The secret to the shot is this: With the hands leading the club head, drive the club down behind the ball, between the ball and the sand. In other words, a buried lie usually features a small space between the ball and the sand, and you should aim for this target or just behind it. Driving the club head down into this area will cause the ball to climb up the clubface and pop out of the bunker. Unlike a normal lie where you try to splash the ball out of the bunker on a blanket of sand, with a buried lie you are attempting to pop the ball out, driving the club head down behind the ball, with a minimum amount of sand coming between the ball and the club head. Even a small amount of sand between the ball and the club head can kill any spin on the ball. Therefore the ball will come out lower and roll farther than a shot from a regular lie. If you can drive the club head behind the ball firmly, it will pop out and come to rest on the green.

Because you are driving the club head down, the sand will naturally restrict the follow-through. Your body should remain balanced throughout the shot and you should finish with the hips and shoulders angled toward the target (figure 8.5*c*).

Figure 8.5   **EXECUTING A GREENSIDE BUNKER SHOT FROM A BURIED LIE**

Setup

1. Place the club face square to the target using a normal grip.
2. Grip the club firmly with the fingers of the left hand (for a right-handed player).
3. Point the shaft toward the target-side thigh, the hands ahead of the club head.
4. Position your weight on the target-side foot with the ball in the back of the stance.
5. Dig your feet into the sand.

Execution

1. Cock ("break") the wrists during the takeaway.
2. Swing along the line of the shoulders, hips, and feet.
3. Drive the club head into the small space between the sand and the ball.
4. To insure accurate contact, keep the lower body still during the swing.

Follow-Through

1. The follow-through is abbreviated due to the club digging into the sand.
2. Turn the hips and shoulders toward the target.
3. The body should be balanced with your weight primarily on the target-side foot.

MISSTEP

When hitting a bunker shot from a buried lie, you take too much sand and the ball fails to come out of the bunker.

CORRECTION

Check your downswing. Contact the spot just behind the ball, driving the club head into the sand. If your swing is too shallow, you will take too much sand. Moving the ball back in your stance on the setup will also help promote a steeper angle into the ball.

MISSTEP

The ball shoots out of the bunker sideways rather than straight.

CORRECTION

First, check your grip. If your grip is too light, the sand will twist the club head. Grip the club more tightly with the three fingers on the top hand of the grip. Second, check your hand position. If the club head is ahead of the hands on the shot, the sand will deflect the club head. Keep your hands in front of the club head throughout the swing.

Greenside Bunker Drill 1   Sand Shots

First, select three targets on the green at 10, 15 and 20 feet (3, 4.5, and 6 meters). If there are holes on the green, they might make good targets, or you can use cones, towels, or clubs placed on the green at these distances. With a sand wedge, take a full stroke, strike the sand, and hit a shallow divot of sand onto the green at each target. Now just use your normal bunker technique, hitting the sand so that it reaches the target. Hit first to the target closest to you, then to 15 feet, and then to 20 feet. Repeat this drill two more times for a total of nine bunker shots. Score 1 point every time sand hits the intended target. Where the sand lands is where your ball would land if you were using a ball. The purpose of this drill is to help you judge distance and give you the correct feeling of how hard you need to hit the sand just to get the ball to specific distances on the green.

TO DECREASE DIFFICULTY

- Place the targets at 3, 6, and 9 feet (about 1, 2, and 3 meters).

TO INCREASE DIFFICULTY

- Repeat the drill using a pitching wedge and a 9-iron.
- Repeat the drill with your eyes closed.
- Use a ball, and attempt to land the ball and sand on the target.

Success Check

- Focus on using an open club head.
- Execute a smooth, fluid swing with a balanced finish position.

Score Your Success

Sand lands on the intended target = 1 point

Your score after 9 swings _____ (out of 9 possible points)

Greenside Bunker Drill 2 *Parallel Line Progression*

Success in greenside bunker shots directly depends on your ability to move the club head through the sand. Striking the sand in the same place and taking a shallow, consistent divot each time helps you develop confidence and skill in making the ball fly out of the bunker and onto the green. Practice this drill to develop feel and consistency when playing out of the sand.

Draw two parallel lines in the sand approximately 4 feet (100 centimeters) long and 6 inches (15 centimeters) apart (figure 8.6). Straddle the lines as you take your setup, and place the middle point between the two lines in the middle of your stance. Take practice swings without a ball, moving up the line after each stroke. Attempt to enter the sand on the nontarget-side line and exit the sand just before the target-side line, throwing a small amount of sand onto the green. Pay particular attention to the feel of the club head as it spanks the sand, taking a shallow divot. Accelerating the swing on contact with the sand will help you move the club head through the sand. Take 10 swings. Give yourself 1 point for each swing that enters the sand on the nontarget-side line and exits just before the target-side line (10 points maximum).

Figure 8.6 Parallel Line Progression drill.

Score Your Success

Fail to enter the sand prior to the non-target-side line or exit after the target-side line = 0 points

Enter the sand prior to the nontarget-side line and exit after the target-side line = 1 point

Your score after 10 swings _____ (out of 10 possible points)

(continued)

Greenside Bunker Drill 2 *(continued)*

Repeat the drill, placing 10 golf balls midway between the two parallel lines. Concentrate on entering and exiting the sand, taking a shallow divot, and using the lines as a guide. You will find greater success if you concentrate on striking the sand rather than focusing on the ball. Take 10 swings. Give yourself 1 point for each swing that enters and exits the sand at the lines. You will need to strike the sand more aggressively than in a shot hit from the green as the clubhead must pass through the resistance of the sand. Therefore, give yourself 1 bonus point for each ball that reaches the green (20 points maximum).

TO DECREASE DIFFICULTY

- Take half swings, concentrating on entering the sand on the back line.
- Draw a single line, straddling the line in your setup so that it is at the midpoint of your stance. Enter the sand on one side of the line, and exit on the other side, throwing a shallow divot of sand onto the green.

TO INCREASE DIFFICULTY

- Repeat all three parts of the drill using a pitching wedge and a 9-iron.
- Repeat the first part of the drill with your eyes closed.
- Repeat the drill from a downhill, uphill, or sidehill lie.

Success Check

- Focus on using an open club head and entering and exiting the sand on the lines.
- Execute a smooth, fluid swing, and finish in a balanced position.
- Play the ball at the midpoint of your stance.

Score Your Success

Fail to enter the sand prior to the non-target-side line or exit after the target-side line = 0 points

Enter the sand prior to the nontarget-side line and exit after the target-side line = 1 point

Enter the sand prior to the nontarget side line and exit after the target-side line and ball reaches green = 2 points

Your score after 10 swings _____ (out of 10 points; 20 possible points for drill)

Greenside Bunker Drill 3   Buried Lie

Place 10 golf balls on the sand, and step on them until they are buried halfway in the sand. Focus on driving the club head between the line and the ball. Take 10 swings. Give yourself 1 point for each swing that enters the sand just behind the ball, making contact with both the sand and the ball. Give yourself 2 bonus points for each ball that reaches the green (30 points maximum).

TO DECREASE DIFFICULTY

- Repeat the drill without golf balls. Draw a line in the sand, and concentrate on hitting that line and driving the club head into the sand.
- Repeat the drill with golf balls, but roll your foot over the balls as you step on the sand to create a larger space between the ball and the sand.

TO INCREASE DIFFICULTY

- Repeat the drill using a pitching wedge and a 9-iron.
- Step on the ball until 3/4 of the ball is buried in the sand.
- Move up the bunker until you are near the front edge. Place 10 balls in this area, step on them, and repeat the drill.

Success Check

- Focus on using a closed club head and driving the club head between the ball and sand.
- Break the wrists on takeaway to promote a steep angle into the ball.
- Play the ball at the back of your stance.
- Finish with hips and shoulders facing the target.

Score Your Success

Fail to make contact with the ball = 0 points

Enter the sand behind the ball, and make contact with the ball = 1 point

Enter the sand behind the ball, make contact with the ball, and ball reaches green = 3 points

Your score after 10 swings _____ (out of 30 possible points)

Greenside Bunker Drill 4   Rapid Fire

This drill helps you develop a natural rhythm in hitting bunker shots. Place five golf balls 3 feet (.9 meter) apart in a bunker in a line running away from you and parallel to the practice green. Step up to the first ball, dig your feet into the sand, select a target on the green, and execute a shot with a full swing. Immediately step up to the next ball, and repeat the process. Continue until you have hit all five balls. Give yourself 2 points each time you hit the green. Set up to each ball quickly and do not hesitate in executing the shot, but do not increase your swing speed. Repeat the drill three times for a total of 15 shots (and a maximum of 30 points).

TO DECREASE DIFFICULTY

- Take half swings to increase control.

TO INCREASE DIFFICULTY

- Alternate hitting shots from regular and buried lies.
- Choose targets at different distances for each shot.

(continued)

Greenside Bunker Drill 4 *(continued)*

Success Check

- Contact the sand an inch or two behind the ball so that the ball rides to the green on a blanket of sand.
- Make sure you remain balanced throughout the swing.

Score Your Success

Ball lands on the green = 2 points

Your score after 15 swings ____ (out of 30 possible points)

Greenside Bunker Drill 5   Ladder

With 11 balls, hit one ball out of the bunker from a normal lie. Hit the next shot so that it lands just beyond the last shot until you hit all 11 balls. The drill represents a ladder in that each shot is a little farther than the last. This is a good drill for working on both shot technique and distance control. If you hit your ball passed your previous ball, score 1 point. If the shot is no further than a club length from the previous ball, score 2 points.

TO DECREASE DIFFICULTY

- Use only six shots and hit each shot past the last shot.

TO INCREASE DIFFICULTY

- Hit each shot just past and 1 yard (.9 meters) to the right or left of the last shot.
- Hit each shot so that it lands in front of and then rolls past the last shot.

Success Check

- Keep the lower body still throughout the shot.
- Use the length of the backswing, not the speed of the swing, to control distance.

Score Your Success

Shot lands past the previous shot = 1 point

Shot lands past, but within one club length of the previous shot = 2 points

Your score on 10 shots ____ (out of 20 possible points)

Greenside Bunker Drill 6   Distance Control

Place three targets on the green 5, 10, and 15 yards (4.5, 9, and 14 meters) from the edge of the green closest to the bunker. Towels, tees, or cones make good targets. Practice adjusting the length of your swing to hit bunker shots that land on or near the targets. First, hit a ball to each of the three targets, working closest to farthest.

Repeat two more times for a total of nine shots. Second, repeat the entire drill with buried lies for a total of nine shots. Try to get balls to land as close to the targets as possible. Note the roll produced by each shot.

TO DECREASE DIFFICULTY

- Hit shots from only good lies.
- Hit shots only to 5- and 10-yard (4.5- and .9-meter) targets.

TO INCREASE DIFFICULTY

- Alternate distances and lies with each shot.
- Use a pitching wedge and 9-iron, and increase the target distance.
- Use different ball flight trajectories with each shot.

Success Check

- Use follow-through length to control shot distance.
- Make sure the ball comes out of the bunker on a blanket of sand.

Score Your Success

Shot lands on the green = 1 point

Shot lands one club length from the target = 2 points

Shot hits the target on the roll = 3 points

Shot lands on the target = 5 points

Your score after 18 shots _____ (out of 54 possible points)

Greenside Bunker Drill 7   Uneven Lie

In a bunker, place five balls on a downhill lie, five on a level lie, and five on an uphill lie. You do not need to bury the balls for this drill. Place a landing target on the green, such as a towel or flag, and hit one ball from each lie to the target. Repeat until you have played all 15 balls. Give yourself 1 point for every ball that lands on the green and 3 points for every time you land on the target (ball does not have to remain on target to score point), for a maximum of 45 points.

TO DECREASE DIFFICULTY

- Select moderate slopes for uphill and downhill lies.
- Place a large target on the green.

TO INCREASE DIFFICULTY

- Hit each ball to a different target.
- Increase the steepest of the slopes for uphill and downhill lies.
- Use smaller targets such as a club, golf balls, or tees.
- Place the balls close to the lip of the bunker.

(continued)

Greenside Bunker Drill 7 *(continued)*

Success Check

- On uphill lies, the club should travel through the sand along the same angle as the slope.
- On downhill lies, the club should travel through the sand along the same angle as the slope.

Score Your Success

Shot lands on the green = 1 point

Shot lands on the target = 3 points

Your score after 15 shots ____ (out of a possible 45 points)

FAIRWAY BUNKER SHOTS

Golf course architects often place fairway bunkers to improve both the challenge and the beauty of the course. Therefore, it is common to find fairway bunkers located where tee shots or layup shots are likely to land, thus increasing the difficulty of the course. In contrast to greenside bunker shots, shots from fairway bunkers can represent a considerable challenge for the average golfer. Because a fairway bunker shot requires you to hit the ball so that it travels accurately for some distance, you need to make solid contact with the club. Unlike the greenside bunker shot, the fairway bunker shot requires the club head to directly meet the ball, and therein lies the challenge. To promote this contact, you will need to make several adjustments to the setup and execution of a normal shot hit from the fairway.

Begin your setup to the shot by digging down into the sand with your feet when taking your stance (figure 8.7a). This gives you a feel for the firmness of the sand, but even more important is that it stabilizes your lower body. A stable body allows you to more easily bring the club head directly back to the ball. Your weight should be evenly distributed between both feet.

A key factor in this shot is striking the ball before the sand, so ball position in the setup is an important consideration. The sand will slow the club-head speed and potentially misdirect the shot. You can use any club, from a fairway metal to a sand wedge, for this shot. (The section titled Bunker Play Strategy provides more information on club selection for this shot.) For setup purposes, the club and lie determine ball position. If you choose a fairway metal, the ball should be just to the target side of the center. As shaft length decreases with the irons, progressively move the ball back in your stance. For example, play the ball just in front of your nontarget-side foot if you are using a pitching wedge.

If you have an uphill lie, play the ball farther up in your stance (closer to your target-side foot). If you have a downhill lie, play the ball a little closer to your nontarget-side foot. When playing from an uphill or downhill lie, your hips and shoulders should be parallel with the slope of the bunker, and your weight should be distributed between both feet as evenly as possible. Again, these adjustments will give you the best chance of making clean contact with the ball.

Do not rush a fairway bunker shot. Because most golfers have a bit of fear when executing this shot, they tend to rush the swing and consequently overswing—with disastrous results. Be aware of this tendency, and calm yourself before taking the shot. Control is more important than power, because solid ball contact is the key to this shot. Stand tall to the ball to ensure clean contact. Loosen your grip to promote a smooth, controlled swing. Be careful to keep the club head above the sand; touching your club to the ground in a hazard is a two-stroke penalty (*USGA 2012 Rules of Golf*, rule 13.4).

Because hitting the ball first and then the sand is critical for this shot, a shallow angle (the club head comes more from around the body than from the top down) helps to make clean contact. To promote a shallow angle into the ball, keep the club head low and slow on the takeaway. The club head, hands, arms, and shoulders move away from the ball in one piece, just as they do in a normal full swing (figure 8.7b). The lower body remains set; no weight transfer occurs. The less the lower body moves, the greater the chance the club head will return directly to the ball. On the downswing, focus on the front of the ball. This will help you get the club head through the ball before you contact any sand.

The follow-through is the same as in the full swing. The club head fully extends through the ball, the weight is naturally carried onto the target side of the body, and the nontarget shoulder drives under and past the chin. The body finishes in balance (figure 8.7c).

Figure 8.7 EXECUTING A FAIRWAY BUNKER SHOT

Setup

1. Dig your feet into the sand.
2. Use a light grip to promote a relaxed, controlled swing.
3. Use a normal stance, evenly distributing weight between both feet.
4. Position the ball in the middle to back of the stance for a normal lie.
5. Keep the club head above the sand.

Execution

1. Use a normal swing along the line of the shoulders, hips, and feet.
2. Strike the ball cleanly, attempting to sweep the ball off the sand.
3. Keep the lower body still during the swing.

(continued)

157

Figure 8.7 *(continued)*

Follow-Through

1. Complete the full swing with a high follow-through for long bunker shots.
2. The weight should move naturally to the target side of the body.
3. Keep the body balanced throughout the swing.

MISSTEP

You strike the sand before hitting the ball.

CORRECTION

Check your ball position, weight distribution, and grip. If the ball is too far forward, you will have difficulty getting the club on the ball before hitting the sand, so move the ball back in your stance. If you have more weight on your rear foot during the downswing, the club will strike the sand first. Therefore, you should evenly distribute the weight between both feet and attempt to keep lower body still during the swing, thus making it easier to return the club head to the ball. A tight grip will produce tension, making it difficult to hit through the ball, so relax your grip, particularly your fingers.

Fairway Bunker Drill 1   Trench

This drill will help you develop the steep angle necessary to make clean contact with the ball first and then the sand. Select a pitching wedge or 9-iron for this drill. Using the club head, draw a trench in the sand about 3 to 4 feet (.9-1.2 meters) long. The trench should be at least two inches (5 centimeters) wide and deep enough so that there are walls on each side of the trench—a front wall on the target side and a back wall away from the target. Next, take a swing (without a golf ball), attempting to hit the front wall without hitting the back wall. Repeat the swing, moving down the trench until you have made 10 swings. Give yourself 1 point each time you hit only the front wall on the swing, for a maximum of 10 points.

TO DECREASE DIFFICULTY

- Dig a wide trench (i.e., more space between the front and back walls).

TO INCREASE DIFFICULTY

- Increase the steepest of the slopes for uphill and downhill lies.
- Use smaller targets such as a club, golf balls, or tees.
- Place the balls close to the lip of the bunker.

Score Your Success

You hit both the front and back walls = 0 points

You hit only the front wall on the swing = 1 point

Your score after 10 swings _____ (out of 10 possible points)

Fairway Bunker Drill 2   Progressive Clubs

From a practice fairway bunker, stroke five balls with a 9-iron, five with a 7-iron, and five with a high-lofted fairway metal (5-, 7-, or 9-metal). The point of the drill is to make clean contact with the ball before hitting the sand. Do not use a target for this drill; simply concentrate on making solid ball contact.

TO DECREASE DIFFICULTY

- Use a pitching wedge, 9-iron, and 8-iron for the drill. A higher-lofted club makes ball contact easier.
- Use half shots. Swing back to a 3-o'clock position, then downswing to a 9-o'clock position.

TO INCREASE DIFFICULTY

- Play from a medium- or high-lipped bunker.
- Use a 5-iron, 3-iron, and 3-metal for the drill.

Score Your Success

You hit the sand first, and the ball remains in the bunker = 0 points

You hit the ball cleanly first and then strike the sand, but the ball remains in the bunker = 1 point

You hit the sand first, then the ball, and the ball gets out of the bunker = 1 point

You cleanly strike the ball first and then the sand, and the ball gets out of the bunker = 2 points

Your score after 15 shots _____ (out of 30 possible points)

Fairway Bunker Drill 3　Varied Lie

In a practice fairway bunker using a 9-iron, stroke five balls from a level lie, five from a downhill lie, five from an uphill lie, five from a sidehill lie with the ball above your feet, and five from a sidehill lie with the ball below your feet, taking 25 total shots. The purpose of the drill is to make solid contact with the ball on each swing.

TO DECREASE DIFFICULTY

- Use a pitching wedge.
- Use half shots. Swing back to a 3-o'clock position, then downswing to a 9-o'clock position.

TO INCREASE DIFFICULTY

- Use a 5-iron or fairway metal.
- Play from a medium- or high-lipped bunker.

Success Check

- Keep the lower body still throughout the swing.
- Generate power for the shot with the shoulder turn.
- Your stroke should be controlled and smooth rather than rushed and quick.

Score Your Success

You hit the sand first, and the ball remains in bunker = 0 points

You hit the ball cleanly first and then strike the sand, but the ball remains in the bunker = 1 point

You hit the sand first, then the ball, and the ball gets out of the bunker = 1 point

You cleanly strike the ball first and then the sand, and the ball gets out of the bunker = 2 points

Your score after 25 shots ____ (out of 50 possible points)

BUNKER PLAY STRATEGY

The first strategic decision when playing a greenside bunker shot is to determine the target landing spot. Consider the lie when making this decision. A normal lie will permit you to land the ball on the green with moderate roll, while a shot from a buried lie will cause the ball to roll more. Consider where you want the ball to land so that it will roll near or perhaps even into the hole. The tighter you focus on your target, the greater the chance you have of hitting that target.

Getting the ball out of the bunker is your first order of business. Therefore, your first strategic decision when playing a ball from a fairway bunker is to determine which club will allow you to clear the lip of the bunker. Some fairway bunkers, like those at the Old Course in St. Andrews, have very steep walls. In these situations, a high-lofted club or sand wedge are the only options for escaping the bunker. Even then, the ball has to be played out sideways or backward if there is to be any hope of finding the fairway. Getting out of the bunker is the first priority. Do not be too greedy. Select a club that you are confident will get the ball in the air high enough to clear the bunker.

MISSTEP

The ball hits the side of the bunker.

CORRECTION

If the club has insufficient loft, the ball will not fly high enough to clear the bunker. Choose a club that you are confident will safely clear the bunker.

The second strategic decision when playing a ball from a fairway bunker is distance. Do you have a reasonable chance of reaching the green from the bunker, or will you need to hit a layup shot? In either case, you need to select the club that will allow you to put the ball in your target area. Because a fairway bunker shot demands a smooth, controlled swing rather than power, select a slightly stronger club than you would ordinarily use for the selected distance. For example, if the green is 140 yards (128 meters) away and your normal 140-yard club is a 7-iron, consider using a 6-iron if a 6-iron will safely clear the bunker lip.

MISSTEP

The ball lands short of the target.

CORRECTION

The fairway bunker shot requires a smooth, relaxed swing to ensure solid contact. Take one more club than usual for the desired distance.

BUNKER SHOT SUCCESS SUMMARY

Shots played from the bunker need not be difficult. Just remember to assess the lie (normal, uneven, or buried), plan the appropriate shot for the lie and distance (greenside or fairway bunker), and make the appropriate modifications to your setup and swing. Be sure you are developing the appropriate technique for these shots. Practice the drills to refine your skills and gain the confidence necessary to successfully play these shots on the course.

Record your point totals from each of the drills in this step, and add them together. If you scored at least 175 out of 298 points, you're ready for the next step. If you scored at least 150 points but fewer than 175, you are almost there. Move on after reviewing the sections that you feel you need to improve the most. If you scored fewer than 150 points, review the techniques and practice the drills again to raise your scores before moving on to the next step.

SCORING YOUR SUCCESS

Greenside Bunker Drills

1.	Sand Shots	___ out of 9
2.	Parallel Line Progression	___ out of 20
3.	Buried Lie	___ out of 30
4.	Rapid Fire	___ out of 30
5.	Ladder	___ out of 20
6.	Distance Control	___ out of 54
7.	Uneven Lie	___ out of 45

Fairway Bunker Drills

1.	Trench	___ out of 10
2.	Progressive Clubs	___ out of 30
3.	Varied Lie	___ out of 50
Total		**___ out of 298**

Gary Player, one of the few individuals to win all four of golf's major championships (British Open, U.S. Open, Masters, and PGA Championship) had this to say about escaping from bunkers: "No bunker shot has ever scared me, and none ever will. The key to this bravado is practice. There are no shortcuts; you must practice" (Freeman, *The Golfer's Book of Wisdom*, 27). The point is that escaping from bunkers is not a matter of luck, it is a matter of practice. In this step, you have learned and practiced the fundamentals of effective bunker play. Continued practice is synonymous with continued improvement in bunker play.

While few players intend to put the ball in the bunker, it eventually finds its way there if you play enough golf. Practice prepares you to play the shot you get, and that will keep you in the game. This theme will follow you into step 9, Practice to Improve Performance. Step 9 reviews fundamentals of practice and describe the activities necessary to make you a competent golfer who enjoys this great game.

Practice to Improve Performance

In most things you do in life, your ability to improve is directly related to the amount and the quality of the practice that you put in. In other words, if you want to make specific improvements, the practice you engage in needs to be specific. For example, if you want to be a good sprinter, it makes little sense to train marathons. Applying this principle to golf, you need to practice golf as closely as possible to the way a game of golf is played. This could be easier said than done; very often the practice area is quite different from the golf course, and people tend to have a lot more successful shots when practicing than in game play. Anyone familiar with the term "a bucket of balls" will know this. (A range balls are often delivered in a bucket, and the players' practice thereby often ends when the bucket is empty.) In order for practice to be efficient, you also need to think about what specific part you want to improve and how to best go about addressing it. Just putting the time in will not necessarily make you better.

GAMES FOR UNDERSTANDING

In a way the principle described earlier was exactly what was behind the creating of *Games For Understanding* by David Bunker and Rod Thorpe in 1982. They had noticed that a traditional approach to teaching physical education, which mostly involved the technical aspects of the game played, did not necessarily improve performance, often due to strategic shortcomings or badly made decisions. In golf, this concept translates into an improved golf swing but a score that is not getting any lower. So how would Bunker and Thorpe's model apply to golf?

Game Form

Golf is a target game. As is reinforced often throughout the steps in this book, the fundamental goal of golf is to stroke the ball with a club into the cup (target) in the fewest strokes possible. In order to do this, individuals make decisions regarding strategic ball placement, equipment selection, skills to be executed, playing conditions, psychological characteristics to be embraced, and the like. Every shot played in golf is played to a target, even if that target is not the cup or the flag.

Game Appreciation

Rules are what define games. They constrain the time and space in which a game is played, dictate scoring and penalty procedures, specify equipment, and determine requisite skills. Golf has a rather extensive rules book and even if the player must not know all of them, the basic rules need to be understood and applied. The more you understand the rules, the more options you have while playing the game and the less chance you have to inadvertently violate the rules and incur penalties.

Tactical Awareness

Determining the tactics to use in the game is crucial to most sports. In golf, the decisions relate to how, on the course at hand using skills and knowledge, a player can place the ball into the hole in the fewest possible strokes while avoiding penalties. Risk and reward become significant factors in making these decisions as does a player's characteristics. A beginner's tactics will look very different to those of a tour player.

Decision Making

In making decisions to execute the desired strategy as determined by the player, two questions must be answered:

1. *What do I do?* While there are common strategies in golf (for example, hit the ball into the fairway as long and straight as possible), conditions continually change (for example, there is a strong wind blowing left to right across a short, narrow fairway with water on the right). In deciding what to do, each situation needs to be assessed. So, being able to recognize situational cues and predict possible outcomes is very important in playing golf.
2. *How do I do it?* Once you have decided what to do, you need to decide the best way to do it. A good player in the situation described earlier would probably try to hit a right to left shot that would keep the ball from drifting out to the right, in danger of the water hazard.

Skill Execution

Skill execution is the actual production of the required movement to meet the decisions made. Skill execution includes both the mechanical efficiency of the movement, its relevance to the particular game situation, and the player's ability. Most players would realize that an appropriate shot for Tiger Woods in a given situation would be completely in appropriate for the rest of us; we simply are not able to perform the shot. The more skills you can develop under more situations, the better you are able to meet the final phase of this model.

Performance

Performance is the observed outcome: *Does the shot meet the needs?* Every shot put together makes the actual game or tournament round. Only when putting all these factors together a player can be determined as strong or weak. Golf is a measure of both the appropriateness of your responses (tactical decisions) and efficiency of your technique (skill level).

Based on this model, becoming a better golfer is a process that you can approach from many angles. Remember this when climbing your steps to success.

SETTING AND REACHING GOALS

Successful performers in any endeavor share one common approach to getting better: They set and achieve realistic, meaningful goals.

Simply swinging a golf club or banging balls time and again does not guarantee improvement in performance. Merely repeating a performance is not practice. To perfect a skill, you must practice with a purpose—a goal. Think of your handwriting. Has it improved in the last 10 years? Probably the answer is no. Even if today you handwrite less because you use technology more for communication, it is not the lack of doing it that prevents you from improving. If you want to improve your handwriting, it must become a priority to do so; you must clearly identify it as a goal, then work to meet that goal. Few people go through that process with handwriting and consequently are not really improving; some may even get worse. Stepping up your success in golf requires a goal-setting process.

Setting practice goals and planning improvement begins with selecting the skills that will make the biggest difference in your performance. Later in this step, you will learn how to identify these skills. For now it is enough to realize that improvement begins with the setting of a goal. Good practice goals are both meaningful and achievable.

A meaningful practice goal is one that you believe will lead you to increased success. You want to spend most of your practice time working on goals that will lower your scores. For example, you may think you cannot stroke the ball with consistent contact to find the fairway, so you set a goal of developing an efficient, repetitive swing.

Full swings account for 35 to 40 percent of the strokes in a round, while the other 60 to 65 percent are partial swings or putts. If you want to make a difference in your game, for every 3 hours of practice you should devote 2 hours to the short game. But when you go to most practice facilities, where do you see the majority of golfers? Banging away at the full swing. If that is what you enjoy doing with your practice time, fine. But don't think that your game is going to dramatically improve if you never make it to the short game.

When determining meaningful goals, you must have an accurate assessment of your skills prioritized in terms of your success on a golf course. For example, you may not be a particularly good bunker player and still score reasonably well, because you don't have to hit that shot very often in a round. However, if your putting is suspect, you should make it a priority, because no one finds success in golf without finding success in putting. Becoming a better putter is a meaningful goal for almost every player.

Making your goals achievable means you are able to reach them. Consider two things when identifying achievable goals. First, the goal must be realistic given your ability and physical conditioning. While all players would like to drive a golf ball more than 300 yards (274 meters), few have the ability to do so no matter how much they practice. Second, the goal should be measurable so that you will know when you have reached it. Becoming a better putter is a meaningful goal, but how will you know when you have improved? Setting a standard of comparison is helpful. For example, you may be able to make 5 out of 10 putts from 3 feet (.9 meter). Set a goal of making 8 out of 10 putts and practice for a week or two, then measure whether your goal of becoming a better putter has been achieved.

One of the best examples of how to identify areas to improve, setting goals for that improvement, and having ways to track the progress is former World Number 1 player Annika Sörenstam. When you are the best player in the world, how do you find your own next steps or your keys to further development? Benchmarking others in this instance may prove one thing only—that you are better than everybody else.

Annika was cleverer than this, though. She had her own way of keeping stats where she tracked the parts of the game that were most important to her. For example, she had a measure of how many times she would get the ball up and down from within a certain yardage. She set a goal for what she thought was a realistic figure, then designed practice activities that would help her improve. Continuing to use this statistical analysis, she was able to follow her progress and eventually reach her goal.

Because it is critical to achieve the goals you set, set no more than three goals at a time. Too many goals make it difficult to focus during practice, which makes it difficult to reach your goals. Pick out only the most meaningful goals that will increase your golfing success.

The next section discusses benchmarks of success—ways to determine how much progress you are making—then suggests ways these benchmarks can help you reach your goals faster.

MISSTEP
You set goals but never seem to reach them.

CORRECTION
Make sure your goals target specific skills and are measurable. It is difficult to improve with a vague goal such as *I want to shoot lower scores.* That kind of goal does not identify a skill that will lead to a lower score. A goal such as *I want to have more one-putt holes* will help you find appropriate practice activities that lead to achievement.

Goal-Setting Drill 1   Priority Goals

Identify the shots you need to improve the most, and design two practice goals that specifically state how you will know you have achieved success. For example, you might state, "My goal is to be able to chip 8 out of 10 balls to within 3 feet (.9 meter) of a hole that is 10 yards (9 meters) away on a practice green." Identifying three goals (two for short games and putting and one for the longer game) is probably a good idea.

Success Check

- Make sure goals are measurable and achievable.

Score Your Success

For each goal, give yourself 1 point if you identify a specific skill and 1 point if you identify the level of success you hope to achieve.

Your score _____ (out of 4 possible points)

DEVELOPING SKILLS

Few people enjoy doing anything poorly, and golfers seem to be particularly passionate perfectionists. While it is sometimes difficult to see immediate results from practice and learning on the golf course, there are many benchmarks of success that are achievable and rewarding. Many professional and amateur golfers set skill development goals and then craft effective practice regimens to meet those goals. Professionals in particular use on-course performance information to analyze strengths and weaknesses in their games and then set practice goals based on this information. This is an effective strategy that works for golfers of all levels.

First, keep a record of vital statistics while you play a round of golf (figure 9.1). This is rather easy to do if you simply record a little extra information on your scorecard. Basic performance statistics focus on four areas: fairways hit, greens in regulation, putts, and short-game skills. The first two statistics provide an indication of full-swing mechanics; the last two identify player skill within the crucial area of 100 yards (91 meters) from the green—the touch shots. Identifying the strongest and weakest areas in your game will allow you to take the second step: setting goals.

The importance of goal setting has already been explained; now it's time to apply those principles. If you don't hit the fairway very often, it is difficult to get the ball on the green and give yourself a chance to make a putt for a good score. Missing the fairway means finding your ball in the rough, in the trees, in a hazard, or out of bounds. If your game analysis shows that you hit a low percentage of fairways, then this may be an area where you can construct a practice goal. Once a practice goal is set, you are ready for the third step: practice.

	Hole									
	1	*2*	*3*	*4*	*5*	*6*	*7*	*8*	*9*	*Out*
Par	*4*	*4*	*4*	*5*	*4*	*3*	*4*	*4*	*3*	*35*
Yards to green	*360*	*386*	*307*	*451*	*423*	*174*	*316*	*415*	*141*	*2,973*
Handicap	*11*	*3*	*13*	*5*	*1*	*15*	*9*	*7*	*17*	
Score	*5*	*5*	*4*	*5*	*6*	*4*	*4*	*4*	*3*	*41*
Fairway hit		*X*		*X*	*X*		*X*			*4/7*
Green hit in regulation			*X*	*X*			*X*		*X*	*4/9*
Putts	*2*	*2*	*2*	*2*	*2*	*2*	*2*	*1*	*2*	*17*
Up and down, sand save	*NUD*	*NUD*			*NSS*	*NUD*		*NUD*		*1/5*

NUD: no up and down; NSS: no sand save

Analysis: Fairways hit: 4/7, 57%   Greens hit in regulation: 4/9, 44%
Putts: 17 (par = 18, 1 under par)   Up-downs, sand saves: 1/5, 20%

Based on the information from this round of golf, the golfer could most quickly improve his score by increasing his percentage of up-downs and sand saves. He should practice chipping, pitching, bunker shots, and putting—short-game skills.

Figure 9.1   Sample nine-hole scorecard with vital performance statistics.

USING ONLINE TOOLS AND APPLICATIONS

A number of tools are available to help you analyze your game and keep track of your statistics. There are websites and rather advanced systems used by tour professionals and National Teams.

With today's technology, you probably have a number of useful tools at your fingertips. If you are using a smartphone or a tablet, try doing an application search using the words *golf* or *golf stats* to get you started. Many smartphones also have a GPS rangefinder system that can help you with the yardage once you know the distance you hit with your respective clubs. Just make sure that using such an aid is allowed within the rules of the tournament you play.

OTHER WAYS TO EVALUATE PERFORMANCE

There are many ways to evaluate your performance and different players have different preferences. When Pia Nilsson, co-founder of Vision54, was head coach of the Swedish golf team, she introduced a very simple and yet very effective way to evaluate just about any activity. It evolved around three questions:

- What was good?
- What could be better?
- How do I improve?

The following chart (figure 9.2) asks the most basic questions all players should ask themselves in order to quantify successes and places where improvement is needed. For every hole played, mark with a "1" every time you can answer the questions with "yes". The goal is to get as many ones as possible.

Hole	1	2	3	4	5	6	7	8	9	10	11	12	13	14	15	16	17	18	TOT
Par	4	3	4	5	4	4	4	3	5	5	4	3	4	4	4	4	3	5	72
Did you play this hole well?																			0
If not, what could have been better?																			
Hole management and strategy																			
Decision making (what to do?)																			
Deciding on "How to do it"																			
Executing decisions																			
Other issues																			
Score																			

Did you play this hole well? Mark 1 for yes. This is a subjective judgment. Try not to let the result influence your judgment. If you did not play the hole well, put a 1 for the factor(s) you think influenced this (you can mark as many as you want).

1. **Hole management and strategy**—Did you play the hole the smartest way based on your skills today?

2. **Decision making**—Did you make clear and positive decisions for what to do with your shots? For example, start the ball at the left edge of the right fairway bunker and play a draw that comes into the center of the fairway.

3. **Deciding on "How to do it"**—Did you make clear decisions on how to execute your shots (including club selection)? For example, aim at the left edge of the bunker, close the blade slightly and swing the club a little bit inside out.

4. **Executing decisions**—Did you execute your shots the way you intended to?

5. What can you improve on for next time? _____

_____

_____

Figure 9.2 Player evaluation scorecard.

Perhaps it is a natural thing for human beings but it seems many golfers find it hard to identify the good things in a round. Players often skip that first question and move straight into the things that were not so good. Building on your strengths however is important so having a way to systematically identify the good parts is probably not a bad idea. Questions are often a powerful way to turn attention to what is important. In a study on different ways of analyzing golf performance that involved players on the England National Team a format developed using the Games For Understanding model discussed earlier. In very simple terms this evaluation included answering the question *Did I play this hole well?* on each hole. If the answer was no, follow-up questions helped to determine what could have been better. Was it strategy, decision-making regarding what to do or how to do it, the ability to execute decisions, or any other issues that were behind a perceived not-so-well-played hole? Finally, players were asked to identify what they thought they could improve until next time.

When asked which method they preferred, many liked the TGFU method but wished to also have some hard facts such as fairways hit, greens in regulation, and putts.

USING PRACTICE TO IMPROVE PERFORMANCE

Golf practice involves knowledge, commitment, and assessment. In other words, you must know what you are working toward and how you are working toward it, you must be committed to achieving that goal and be willing to put in the necessary time, and you must monitor your progress so that once you achieve that goal, you can set and pursue the next goal.

If a performance goal such as hitting 50 percent of fairways was accompanied by the practice goal of hitting 12 out of 20 practice fairways, you could establish a practice routine and monitor your progress. In this case, it might serve you well to review step 5 to remind yourself of proper mechanics and drills to ingrain the techniques of the full swing. You might also want to review step 6 to make sure you are using the club that will give you the greatest accuracy.

Next, commit to a regular practice time throughout the week. This can be as simple as taking practice swings in your living room to review your mechanics, but even better, plan on spending an hour or two several evenings a week at the practice range, working on drills from the preceding steps in this book. Practice with a goal in mind, because practice without purpose achieves nothing. Perhaps the former touring pro Tony Lema put it best in *The Golfer's Book of Wisdom*: "The most common practice error is to drift aimlessly to the range and start banging balls at random. This isn't practice. This is a waste of time. The worst thing you can do is practice your mistakes" (Freeman 1995). Finally, have a mechanism in place to monitor your progress. To see whether you can hit 12 out of 20 practice fairways, go to the practice range, take 20 golf balls, and see how many you can stroke into a fairway, imagining the fairway on the practice range based on landscape characteristics or target flags at a distance and width that represents your normal driving distance. The more often you practice and the more often you check your progress, the more quickly you will reach your goal.

Skill development does not always need to be tightly tied to performance, especially for beginners. Setting and reaching practice goals on the practice putting green, such as making 10 3-foot (.9-meter) putts in a row, will speed your progress toward becoming an accomplished putter. Improving skills such as chipping, pitching, or hitting bunker shots or increasing your knowledge of rules or etiquette will make you more successful and the game more enjoyable.

A frequently asked question is how much practice is needed to become a successful golfer. This question has no absolute answer, but there are several ways to judge how much practice you need. Goal setting is the easiest and most efficient way to gauge how long to practice. If you predetermine the standard of performance you wish to achieve in a given practice session, simply practice until you reach that standard. This was how six-time Masters champion Jack Nicklaus determined the length of his practices. He would set a specific goal, such as hit a target green five consecutive times with a 3-wood, and as soon as he reached the goal, that portion of the practice was over. If his only goal that day was to be more accurate with his 3-wood, it might be a short practice day.

Short, frequent practice sessions are more effective than a few marathon practices. If you have 3 hours a week for practice, it's better to schedule three 1-hour practices than a single 3-hour practice. Practicing while tired is not effective, and the briefer period ensures that you remain fresh during the entire practice. Practicing more frequently helps your muscles gain and retain the memory of the skill pattern you are attempting to ingrain. For this reason, frequently using a practice station at home to work on short-game skills, putting, or even a few slow-motion full swings every night will speed your progress much more than spending long hours once or twice a month at a fancy practice range.

If you can't get to a practice facility on a regular basis, it doesn't mean you can't practice. The good news is that the skills that usually need the most practice can be practiced at home. Anyone with a flat floor can practice putting. Jack Adler, former golf coach at the University of Oregon, likes to set up a little putting course in his house. He assigns each hole a par score as he sets up holes that go around doorways, move from the carpet to tile, and even go down stairs. If you have even a small patch of grass near your home, you can set up a chipping and pitching station. It is also possible to practice these skills by chipping from small carpet samples to towels or pillows. Ben Hogan practiced pitching for hours in his hotel room while he traveled from tournament to tournament. It can be both fun and easy to set up a small practice station, and a few hours of practice per week will pay off handsomely on the golf course.

Improving Practice Drill 1   Public Practice Facilities

Use the Internet or a telephone book to locate several practice areas that are accessible. Call or visit to see the skills that you can practice there. Place a checkmark next to each practice station available at the facility:

- Driving range for full swing (grass hitting stations) ____
- Driving range for full swing (artificial mat stations) ____
- Short-game area (chipping and pitching green) ____
- Short-game area (sand bunkers) ____
- Putting green ____

Visit one facility, and take your clubs with you. Score yourself based on the shots you were able to practice at the facility.

Score Your Success

Hit at least 10 balls at the driving range = 3 points

Hit at least 10 chip shots and 10 pitch shots = 5 points

Hit at least 20 putts = 10 points

Your score ____ (out of 18 possible points)

Improving Practice Drill 2   Personal Practice Station

Select a practice goal for a skill you would like to improve. Design a practice station in your home or office. In a one-week period, conduct at least three 20-minute practice sessions.

 TO INCREASE DIFFICULTY

- Devise a practice station where you may practice two or more skills.

Score Your Success

Conduct one 20-minute practice session in a week = 2 points

Conduct three 20-minute practice sessions in a week = 5 points

Conduct five 20-minute practice sessions in a week = 10 points

Your score ____ (out of 10 possible points)

Improving Practice Drill 3   Game Improvement Plan

Identify two skills you would like to improve and set two goals to improve them. You may use the goals established in the Priority Goals drill, or you may set new goals. Refer to the drills in the appropriate step in this book and select two drills for each goal, then identify where and when you will practice these goals for a two-week period. Record the goals, drills, and practice schedule in figure 9.3.

Goal 1 _____ _____

_____

Drill 1 _____ _____

Drill 2 _____

Goal 2 _____

_____

Drill 1 _____

Drill 2 _____

Practice location _____ _____

_____

Practice days and times

Day 1 _____ _____ **Time** _____ _____

Day 2 _____ ____ **Time** _____

Day 3 _____ **Time** _____

Figure 9.3   Game improvement plan: goals, drills, and practice schedule.

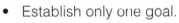 **TO DECREASE DIFFICULTY**

- Establish only one goal.
- Limit practice time to 10 minutes for each drill.

TO INCREASE DIFFICULTY

- Establish three goals.
- Increase the number of drills per goal to four.
- Increase the number of practice days to 4 or 5.

Score Your Success

Set a goal = 1 point per goal

Identify a drill to go with the goal = 2 points per drill

Identify an accessible practice facility = 5 points

Follow game improvement plan for two weeks = 20 points

Your score _____ (out of 35 possible points)

Improving Practice Drill 4   **The Pin Ball**

On your approach shot you get two shots, a pin ball and a green ball. The pin ball always goes for the pin, and the green ball only tries to hit the green. Count your lowest score, and indicate whether you made it with a pin ball or a green ball.

TO DECREASE DIFFICULTY

- Instead of playing your green ball as an approach shot, drop the green ball on the green once it's there, and putt into the hole. Count your score, and determine what your score would have been if you were able to hit every green in regulation.
- Do this drill for only three holes at a time, then play a normal game for three holes.

TO INCREASE DIFFICULTY

- Switch clubs for the green ball, and hit either a longer or shorter club than with the pin ball.
- Play the green ball with either a left-to-right or right-to-left shot.

Score Your Success

Lowest or equal score with the green ball on every hole = 5 points

Lowest or equal score with the green ball on at least 2/3 of the holes played = 10 points

Lowest or equal score with the green ball on at least 1/3 of the holes played = 15 points

Lowest or equal score with the pin ball on every hole played = 20 points

Your score _____ (out of 20 possible points)

Improving Practice Drill 5   **Carl Petersson**

Swedish PGA Tour player Carl Petersson presented this drill. He has used it frequently throughout his career. Play your normal game, but as you hit your approach shot (tee shot on par-3, second shot on par-4, third shot on par-5) you cannot hit the green. Instead try to hit it in a place where you will have the best chance for an up and down. If you hit the green, your partner gets to throw your ball into a greenside bunker, in the greenside rough, or just off the green. Hole out, and count your score.

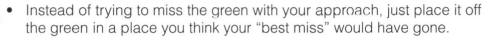

TO DECREASE DIFFICULTY

- Instead of trying to miss the green with your approach, just place it off the green in a place you think your "best miss" would have gone.
- Only do this drill on every second hole.

TO INCREASE DIFFICULTY

- Rather than trying to miss the green with your approach, throw the ball into the most difficult position (a "worst miss" scenario) you think you can find off the green.
- Do what was previously mentioned, but always choose a bunker.

Score Your Success

You manage to scramble (walk away with a par or hcp par) on 20 percent of the holes = 5 points

You manage to scramble (walk away with a par or hcp par) on 40 percent of the holes – 10 points

You manage to scramble (walk away with a par or hcp par) on 60 percent of the holes = 15 points

You manage to scramble (walk away with a par or hcp par) on more than 65 percent of the holes (this would give you a top 10 position in this quality on the PGA Tour!) = 20 points

Your score _____ (out of 20 possible points)

Improving Practice Drill 6   **Two Serves**

When playing a round, you get to have a second serve every time you hit the green in regulation. This means you get to putt a second time from the position your ball ended up in when hitting the green. See how this second serve affects your score!

Score Your Success

Score at least one birdie on the holes you played = 5 points

Score at least two birdies on the holes you played = 10 points

Score at least three birdies on the holes you played = 15 points

Score at least four birdies on the holes you played = 20 points

Score five birdies or more on the holes you played = 25 points

Your score _____ (out of 25 possible points)

PRACTICE TO IMPROVE PERFORMANCE
SUCCESS SUMMARY

Record your point totals from each of the drills in this step, and add them together. If you scored at least 80 out of 132 points, you are able to plan and execute effective practice sessions that will allow you to improve your performance. If you scored 50 to 79 points, you are almost there. Move on after reviewing the sections you feel you can improve the most. If you scored fewer than 50 points, review the information and go through the drills again to raise your scores. Understanding how to set goals, tailor drills to meet your goals, and arrange a functional practice schedule with effective activities are keys to your continued success as a golfer.

SCORING YOUR SUCCESS

Goal-Setting Drill
1. Priority Goals ___ out of 4

Improving Practice Drills
1. Public Practice Facilities ___ out of 18
2. Personal Practice Station ___ out of 10
3. Game Improvement Plan ___ out of 35
4. The Pin Ball ___ out of 20
5. Carl Petersson ___ out of 20
6. Two Serves ___ out of 25

Total ___ **out of 132**

Many golfers live by the belief that practice makes perfect. And in many ways it definitely does – we become good at what we practice However, the strongest opponent in golf is the golf course that needs to be overcome in order to produce a strong performance. You are now ready to move on to step 10 and learn more about how to Manage the Course.

Managing the Course

Success in golf depends a lot on learning the requisite skills as described in steps 1 through 8. However, at some point you will find yourself on a golf course rather than in a practice area. It is then that you will execute those skills to navigate your way around the course rather than to just improve your skills. At that time, your success in golf will be measured in the number of shots you take to play 18 holes. In other words, the scores you shoot will determine your success.

Success in golf takes more than a good set of skills. You must learn to manage the golf course as well. Each course is different, with varying challenges, terrain, and features. Consequently, each course requires the development of a sound strategy for playing the course successfully. Developing and implementing such a strategy is often referred to as managing the course. In this step, you will learn how to fit your skills to a course by developing a plan to guide your decision making on each hole.

Good course management lets you use your skills to move the ball from tee into the hole in the fewest strokes no matter what par the hole is. Good course management also lets you successfully navigate any challenges presented by the course designer—doglegs, water hazards, bunkers, hilly fairways, or fast greens.

KNOW YOUR GAME

Good course management begins not with the course but with knowing your game. Course management requires that you match your game to the golf course you are playing in order to shoot the lowest scores possible. Therefore, you must know both your game and the course well. The better you know both, the better you will be able to match your game to the course. While each course you play may differ, the skill set you bring to each of those courses largely remains that same. Therefore, it is imperative that you know the game you bring.

Knowing your game begins with knowing which of your skills are strengths and which are limitations. First, know the distance you hit with each club. You can assess your skills on a driving range by hitting 10 balls with each club in your bag. Record where each of the 10 balls land, then take the average distance by adding the yardages and dividing the sum by 10 (table 10.1). If you hit a shot so poorly that it would drastically misrepresent the yardage if included, then hit another shot and don't count the poor shot. You should not do this more than 2 or 3 times in calculating your yardage for a particular club. If you cannot hit a club reasonably well a majority of the time, perhaps you need to think about taking that club out of your bag until you can hit it successfully with greater consistency. Once you establish the average yardage you hit each of your clubs, you can use this knowledge on the course. For example, you will know which club to use to carry a ball 140 yards (128 meters) over water to a green.

Table 10.1 Club Yardage and Success Ratings

Club	1	2	3	4	5	6	7	8	9	10	Average	Success rating
Lob wedge												
Sand wedge												
Pitching wedge												
9-iron												
8-iron												
7-iron												
6-iron												
5-iron												
4-iron												
3-iron												
Fairway wood												
Driver												
Other												

Second, look at every club in your bag, and gauge your success with each one. Success is determined by your ability to land the ball on an intended target 75 percent of the time. Some players use a scale of 1 to 10, with 10 meaning they can hit the target 10 out of 10 times with that club. Record this information in table 10.1. The clubs with the highest rates of success should be used whenever possible in your round, and those with the lowest rates of success should receive the most attention during practice. For example, if your success with a driver is rated 3 but your 3-metal is rated 5, the 3-metal should be the club of choice for most tee shots.

Next, review the shots you have practiced in steps 1 through 8. Rate your success with these shots. Look at your scoring summaries in previous steps to find strengths and weaknesses, or use the same scale of 1 to 10 that you used for assessing clubs. Understanding your skills in putting, chipping, pitching, iron and wood play, and bunker play, helps you determine which shots to hit in a given situation. For example, if you are a better putter than a chipper and your ball is 5 to 10 yards (4.5 to 9 meters) off the green but not in the rough, you may choose to putt the ball rather than chip it to the hole. Honest assessments can often be hard on one's ego. Golf is, after all, a difficult game. An honest and objective appraisal of your skill is imperative to gaining success on the golf course. Accurately assessing your skills allows you to set realistic expectations for your shots and your game, play successfully within your limitations, and know when to be conservative and when to get aggressive on the golf course. Only when you have a firm and accurate knowledge of your golf skills are you ready to manage a golf course.

Know Your Game Drill 1 Yardage Guide

This drill helps you assess your skill with each iron and metal club. It is an important exercise for effectively managing your game. For best results, this exercise should be completed when there is no wind or rain. On a flat driving range, identify an imaginary line running from you out through the driving range. You will need at least three yardage markers on the range to help you gauge the distance of each shot. If there are no markers to determine yardage on the range, use a range finder to determine the distances you hit each shot. It is important that you learn the distances you hit each club you carry. Begin with your highest-lofted wedge, and finish with your lowest-lofted metal club. Hit 10 balls with each club. For each club, note the average distance the ball traveled in the air, the average distance the ball finished left or right of the line (dispersion), and your tendency to hit fade (left of the line) or draw (right of the line) shots. Record the data in table 10.2. Don't worry about how far your ball rolls forward. Many factors influence ball roll, such as ground moisture, grass type and length, elevation, and ball spin, and most of these factors are beyond your control. It is much more important to know how far in the air each of your clubs carries the ball.

Score Your Success

Give yourself 2 points for every club for which you calculate an average air yardage.

Your score _____ (out of 26 possible points)

(continued)

Know Your Game Drill 1 *(continued)*

Table 10.2   Yardage Guide

Club	Average air distance	Average dispersion	Fade or draw
Lob wedge			
Sand wedge			
Pitching wedge			
9-iron			
8-iron			
7-iron			
6-iron			
5-iron			
4-iron			
3-iron			
Fairway wood			
Driver			
Other			

Know Your Game Drill 2   My Success Clubs

Knowing which clubs you use with the greatest success will help you play to your strengths and allow you to practice your weaknesses. In this exercise, first picture an imaginary line running from your golf ball straight down the range. Next, hit 10 shots with each club. Note how far to the left or right of that line the ball lands. You can estimate this distance or use a range finder to get an accurate reading. After you hit the 10 shots, estimate the average dispersion (left or right) that each shot lands from the imaginary line. This information will give you an idea of your accuracy with this club. Next, count the number of shots you hit solidly out of the 10 shots, and record those shots in the appropriate column. Finally, rank your success with each club from 1 to 8, with 1 being the club with which you experienced the most success and 8 being the least successful. Record the information in table 10.1.

Score Your Success

Give yourself 1 point for each club you rated.

Your score _____ (out of 8 possible points)

KNOW THE COURSE

With an accurate assessment of your skill with your golf clubs, you are ready to take your game to the course. Golf is played one hole at a time, one stroke at a time. Keep that in mind when planning your course strategy.

The best way to plan a course strategy is by starting backward. In other words, begin with the hole, and work back to the tee. Ask yourself where on the green would be the best place for a putt (usually you want a straight, uphill putt). This will tell you where to land your approach shot on the green. Once you know that spot, ask yourself where on the fairway would be the best place to hit that approach shot. The answer to this question will help you get past hazards or high rough and land your tee shot where you would like it to be on the green. For example, on a par-4 hole with the hole cut behind a bunker on the left side of the green, you will want to place the tee shot on the right side of the fairway. This placement will give you a better angle to the green so that you don't have to hit a shot over the bunker (figure 10.1).

In addition to your skills, course strategy will be influenced by target distance, hole features such as hazards and hills, and weather.

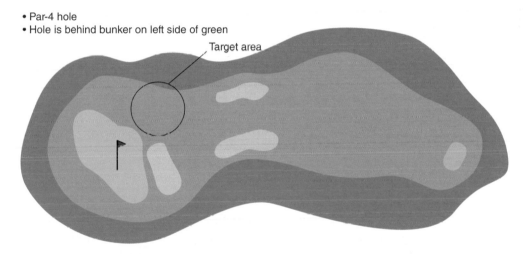

Figure 10.1 For this par-4 hole, put the tee shot on the right side of the fairway.

Target Distance

The best way to play a hole is very much influenced by the distance to the hole. In some cases, it is wise to ignore the par rating for the hole and simply calculate your chance of success based on the overall distance. For example, a par-3 hole may be 210 yards (192 meters) long and surrounded by deep bunkers (figure 10.2). Do you have a club that will reliably and accurately carry the ball that distance? Or, would it be better to hit a tee shot 150 yards (137 meters) to a landing area and then attempt to pitch the ball 60 yards close enough to the hole to have a reasonable putt for 3 (par), or take 2 putts for a 4 (bogey)? If the par-3 hole has deep bunkers, rough, or a water hazard around the hole, the second option may result in the lower score. You will avoid making a high score by hitting the ball into a hazard or mis-hitting a club that gives you difficulty under the best of circumstances. You may even have a chance for par on a difficult par-3 hole if you play it strategically. This was precisely the strategy Billy Casper used on the longest par-3 hole of the 1959 U.S. Open Championship. Rather than trying to blast the ball to the hole 216 yards (198 meters) away, he hit it accurately but short of the green. He then struck a well-practiced chip shot and putted in for par on the third hole at Winged Foot. He used this strategy all four days of the tournament, and he won the championship.

The same strategy will work equally well on par-4 or par-5 holes. If you hit only those shots that are within your comfort range you will experience greater success than attempting shots that you are not comfortable or confident in making. It does little good to hit a drive 300 yards (274 meters) if the ball comes to rest deep in the woods, a hazard or worse—out of bounds. It is always better to find your next shot a slightly longer shot to the green but safely in the fairway rather than a shorter shot from behind a tree, from the rough, out of the water, or in the case of being out of bounds, from exactly the same place but now having to record a penalty stroke on your card.

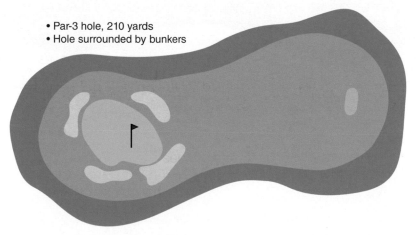

- Par-3 hole, 210 yards
- Hole surrounded by bunkers

Figure 10.2 On a par-3 hole that is 210 yards long, are you better off trying to hit the ball 210 yards from the tee or hitting it 150 yards from the tee and then pitching it 60 yards to the hole?

When standing on the tee box, consider the total distance to the hole and then decide which series of clubs will give you the greatest chance of success. For example, on a 400-yard (366-meter) par-4 hole, it may make more sense to hit a 150-yard (137-meter) tee shot, a second 150-yard shot, and then a 100-yard (91-meter) shot to the green (figure 10.3). If one of those three shots (or even all of them) veers a little left or right, the ball most likely will not find serious danger and you will still be on the green in three shots with a chance to make a putt for par.

Playing for a comfortable distance has the added advantage of letting you play in a comfort zone. That is, you will swing more freely and with more control when attempting a shot you think you can easily make. Attempting to hit the ball a great distance to a small target makes most amateur golfers swing too hard, which has an adverse effect on timing and control. In other words, it is more difficult to make a good shot when attempting to hit a ball too far. Play a comfortable game.

All golf courses have yardage markers, which are measured from the middle of the green to specific places in the fairway and from the tee box. Standard markers on most courses are placed at 100, 150, 200 yards (91, 137, and 183 meters) and at the tee box from the middle of the green for that particular hole. On many golf courses, the yardages to the middle of the green are also marked on the sprinkler heads. Sprinkler heads will also have the yard to the front and back of the green as well

When your ball is in the fairway and you intend your next shot to reach the green, you need to know the precise yardage to reach the green in order to know which club to select. To determine how far your ball lies from the middle of the green, a common practice is to step off your yardage; that is, find the closest yardage marker to your ball, and count the number of steps from there to your ball. If you can take a step of approximately 1 yard (.9 meter), simply add or subtract the number of paces to the yardage marker distance to determine the distance your ball lies from the middle of the green. This information is invaluable for knowing which club to choose for your next shot. The Step Off drill helps you practice this skill and establish the length of stride you will need to step off yardage.

Professional golfers begin their strategic decisions by first considering where on the green they would like their approaches to land. Next they determine the location in the fairway that will give them the best chance for making that shot. Finally, they choose the club for their tee shot that will get them to that spot in the fairway. That strategy helps them make a living at this game, and this way will work for you, too.

- Par-4 hole, 400 yards
- 150 yards off tee
- 150 yards from fairway
- 100 yards from green

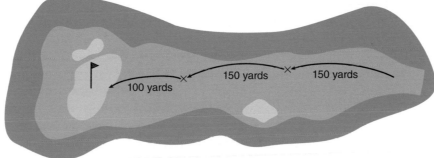

Figure 10.3   For a 400-yard par-4 hole, this golfer chose to hit a 150-yard shot off the tee, a 150-yard shot from the fairway, and a 100-yard shot to the green.

A final thought on distance as a factor in course management is this: Take a strong enough club. Most golfers overestimate both the distance they can carry a ball in the air with a particular club and their consistency in making shots with that club. Unless you consistently drive the ball through the fairway or hit over the green, err on the side of a stronger club (club with a lower number). In other words, choose a club you are confident will make the ball travel the distance it needs to go and perhaps even a bit farther.

MISSTEP
You don't take enough club, causing the shot to fall short of the target.

CORRECTION
Underclubbing is one of the most common mistakes golfers make. Know the yardage you can hit each club, and always be sure you have a strong enough club to reach the target landing area

MISSTEP
You take too much club off the tee, and your find your ball in trouble rather than in the fairway or on the green.

CORRECTION
The most important goal from the teeing ground is to put the ball in play by hitting the green or fairway. Use the club that will get the ball to the green or in the fairway rather than the club that will hit the ball the farthest.

Hole Features

Golf course designers structure the hole with a variety of features, including hills; water such as ponds, lakes, or the ocean; sand or grass bunkers; trees; sand waste areas; and grass to give definition, challenge, and beauty to a hole. The designer can also vary the routing patterns that turn the hole left or right from the teeing ground. These features are called doglegs; from an aerial view, the fairway appears to be shaped like a dog's leg.

While most designers prefer to use the natural characteristics of the land when designing a course, they often add a few additional features to each hole to make it both more visually appealing and more challenging. When planning your strategy and managing the course, you need to consider the features you find on each hole. The next section discusses these features in terms of the greatest effect they can have on your score, because it determines the feature's importance in your decision making.

White stakes on a golf course demand particular attention, because they mark the out-of-bounds areas. If you hit the ball to or past these stakes, you incur a one-stroke penalty in addition to the stroke you took to hit the ball out of bounds. You must replay the shot from the original position, so you lose both a stroke and distance. When choosing a landing area on the hole, make sure you are well clear of the out-of-bounds area. Out of bounds represents the severest of penalties on a golf course, so avoiding these areas is paramount to recording a good score.

After white stakes, consider areas on the hole where you might lose your ball or find yourself with an unplayable lie. These areas may be covered with heavy brush, bushes, or tall grass. The penalty for losing a ball is the same as the penalty for going out of bounds. An unplayable lie occurs when you cannot effectively get your club head on the ball in a manner to move the ball sufficiently forward and away from trouble. If it is not possible to play your ball, you can declare an unplayable lie. An unplayable lie results in a one-stroke penalty and a drop two club lengths from where the ball lies or a return to the original spot where the ball was played. Hitting a ball to these areas will increase your score, so play away from them if possible.

There is perhaps no other feature on a golf course that causes players more stress and consternation than water. Because water hazards (figure 10.4) cause players such anxiety, it is natural to attempt to avoid these areas. Water hazards are marked with yellow stakes, and lateral water hazards are marked with red stakes. If you hit your ball into a water hazard, you can drop your ball behind the water hazard or next to a lateral hazard so that you don't lose distance that you would with a lost or out-of-bounds ball. If forced to choose between hitting close to white stakes or red stakes, red stakes will hurt you less.

Although it is best to avoid severe rough, woods, or waste areas such as sandy or rocky areas not maintained by course personnel, if your ball does land in one of these areas you can play your next shot without penalty as long as you do not have an unplayable lie. However, it will not be easy to make these shots, because the conditions make it difficult to have an unobstructed shot to the green or fairway. When playing from one of these areas, your first priority should be to get the ball back in play, which usually means playing it back to the fairway with a pitch or chip shot. Realize that you have made an error, but don't compound the error by demanding too much of your next shot. Just get yourself out of trouble so that you can play the next shot without hindrances.

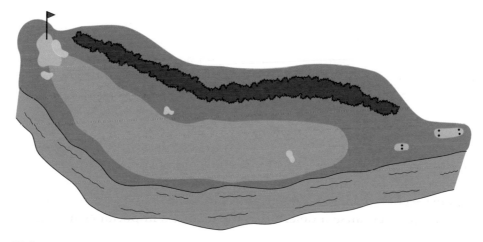

Figure 10.4 Don't fear water hazards. Hitting into a water hazard is less harmful to your score than hitting the ball out of bounds or losing a ball in the rough.

MISSTEP

You hit your ball out of bounds, into a hazard, or into a bad lie.

CORRECTION

You are most likely to be upset and anxious about the difficulty you are encountering. Take a moment to realize that this is just a part of the game and that all golfers face these situations. When you have collected yourself, consider your options and select the one you believe gives you the greatest chance for success.

MISSTEP

You consistently land in bunkers and other hazards.

CORRECTION

Study the holes carefully in order to play away from trouble. This may mean taking less club and landing your shot short of the bunker, even if it means being a little farther from the hole on your next shot.

Bunkers are the next feature to consider. A bunker will permit a good stance and a clean strike at the ball, so better players generally prefer playing out of a bunker over playing from deep rough (figure 10.5). While you will not be penalized for having to play out of a bunker, it is better to be on the fairway or the green if possible. Because of their size and color contrast as well as the fear most players have of being in the bunker, course designers place bunkers in strategic locations to add challenge and character to a hole. Perhaps it is stating the obvious to advise you to play away from bunkers, but on a very difficult hole a bunker may be a better option than risking running into other course features such as out of bounds or heavy rough.

Course designers use slopes, hills, and mounds for strategic and aesthetic purposes on a golf hole. Many players have difficulty hitting the ball from anything other than a flat lie, so consider the best place to land on the fairway or green. Look for flat lies in the fairways. When hitting to the green, leave yourself either a straight putt or one that is slightly uphill.

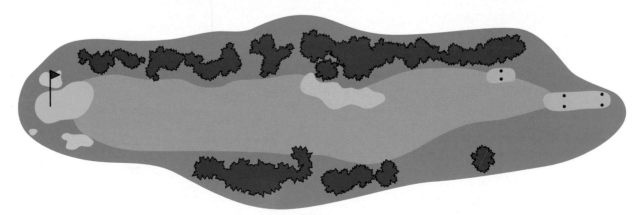

Figure 10.5   You can hit out of a bunker without penalty, so it is an acceptable option if you are concerned about hitting the ball out of bounds or into heavy rough.

MISSTEP

You miss the green close to the hole and have little room to land or roll the ball before it reaches the hole. This is known as missing the green on the wrong side or short-siding yourself.

CORRECTION

If a hole is cut close to the edge of a green, play to the middle of the green rather than to the flag. It is always better to be on the green with a putter in your hand, no matter how long the putt, than to be off the green with an iron or wedge in your hand.

Finally, course designers use the width and angle of the holes to provide definition and character. You should take into account the width of the fairway or green when choosing a club. A narrow fairway usually means a shorter hole, so perhaps a fairway wood or even an iron off the tee is called for to insure accuracy over distance. A fairway that is generously wide is probably longer and will require a club that can carry the ball farther even if you hit the club with less accuracy. Narrow greens require shots that are more accurate, usually with a higher trajectory so that the ball will stop sooner on the green. When planning your approach shot to the green, choose a club that will accomplish these two purposes: accuracy and trajectory.

If the fairway turns to the left or right, making the green invisible from the tee box, the hole is a dogleg (figure 10.6). When facing a dogleg, consider risk and reward. The closer you can put the ball to the turn in the fairway, the closer you will be to the hole; however, often you will also be closer to danger because course designers usually place bunkers, trees, water or waste areas near the turn. Determine your comfort zone when playing a shot near to or away from the turn. If the risk appears greater than the reward, play conservatively. If the risk appears minimal—you can drive the ball over the bunker or shape your shot around the trees—the reward may make the risk worth taking. In general, a conservative strategy is better for avoiding high scores.

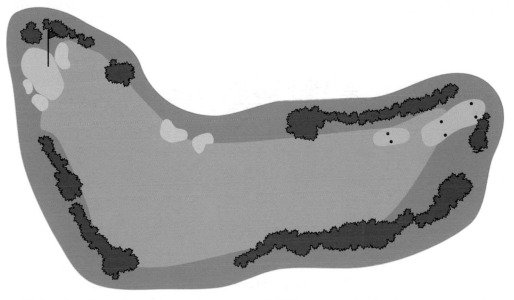

Figure 10.6 Consider the risks and rewards of hitting close to the turn on a doglegged fairway.

STRATEGIC IMPORTANCE OF HOLE FEATURES

- Out of bounds
- Lost ball and unplayable lie
- Water hazards
- Severe rough, waste areas, woods
- Bunkers
- Hills, slopes, mounds
- Shape of the fairway and green

Weather

Golf is an outdoor sport, consequently weather will affect your game. The only weather condition that halts play is lightning, so weather needs to be factored into your course strategy. In general, wind affects the flight of the ball more than any other weather condition. A gusty day can make for a long, challenging day on the golf course. Wind affects both the distance a ball will carry as well as the direction the ball flies. Shots hit into the wind will not carry as far as they would without wind. When hitting downwind, particularly with a club that lofts the ball high into the air, the ball will carry much farther. When selecting a club for a shot, consider the strength of the wind and its direction. For example, a 150-yard (137-meter) shot may actually play more like a 170-yard (155-meter) shot if you are hitting into a strong wind (figure 10.7).

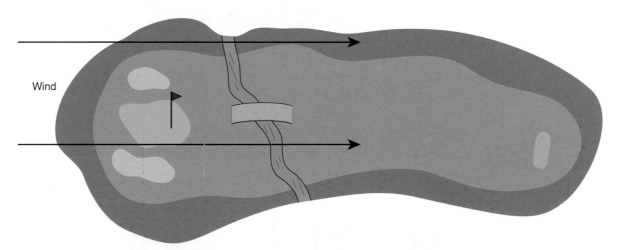

Figure 10.7 Hitting into a strong wind can make a 150-yard shot feel like a 170-yard shot.

Because the direction of the ball is affected by the wind, you will need to adjust your club and shot to compensate. A left-to-right wind can send a well-struck tee shot from the middle of the fairway into the middle of a lake (figure 10.8). Determining precisely how much effect the wind has on the ball is part experience and part guesswork. In general, wind will affect the ball more than you think, so play for it. Look at the tops of the trees or the flag on the green or toss some grass into the air to gauge the speed and direction of the wind.

A golf ball doesn't travel as far in cold weather or in rainy conditions. These elements will also affect your grip. A hand warmer on a cold day and a dry towel on a rainy day are good accessories to have in your golf bag. Conversely, on hot, dry days the ball will travel farther. If the fairway or green have baked in the hot sun for several days, the ball will roll much more than usual. Although it is not a weather condition, elevation also will affect a golf ball. The higher the elevation, the farther the golf ball will travel. Make adjustments for these conditions before striking the ball.

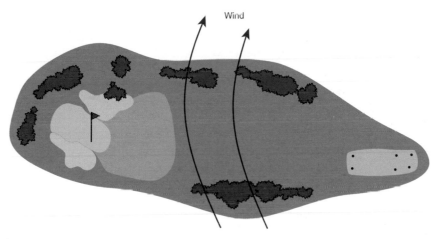

Figure 10.8 A good tee shot may go awry if it is hit into a strong wind blowing left to right.

Know the Course Drill 1   Hole Strategy

The golf hole in figure 10.9 is a relatively short 340-yard par-4 hole, but it has several hazards. Plan your strategy for this hole. Place a T where you would like your tee shot to stop, and in parentheses identify the club you would use to hit that shot. Next, place an A where you would like your approach shot to land on the green, and in parentheses identify the club you would use to hit that shot.

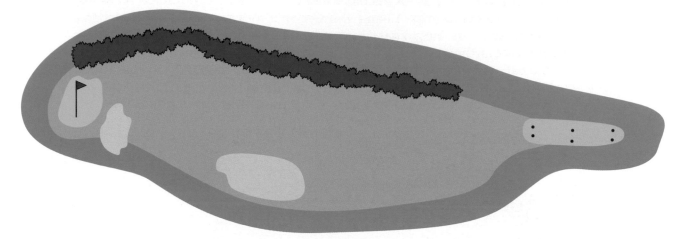

Figure 10.9   For this par-4 hole, place a *T* where you would like your tee shot to land and an *A* where you would like your approach shot to land on the green.

Score Your Success

Using your distance chart in table 10.2 , give yourself 2 points for each shot that avoided going over the hazards and 2 points for each shot that used the club that would get your ball to that spot.

Your score ___ (out of 8 possible points)

Know the Course Drill 2   Step Off

Take a tape measure, and extend it for 5 yards (4.5 meters) on a flat surface. Straddle the tape measure, and take steps so that your strides are as close to 1 yard (.9 meter) in length as possible (measured from the middle of your feet). In five steps, you should be at 5 yards. This often takes practice, so repeat it 10 times.

Next, pick a hole on a practice green, and step off distances from that hole to 5, 10, and 20 yards (4.5, 9.1, and 18.2 meters). Use golf balls to mark the distances as you step them off, then use the tape measure to check your accuracy. Repeat the drill three times from three different holes for a total of 9 yardage stepoffs.

Score Your Success

Give yourself 1 point for each measure that is within 24 inches (.61 meters) of the stepped-off distance and 2 points for each measure within 18 inches (.46 meters). For example, if you have stepped off a distance of 10 yards (30 feet) and it measures 31 feet, you score 2 points.

Your score ____ (out of 38 possible points)

Know the Course Drill 3   **Phantom Threesome**

On the practice range, imagine a par-4 hole with a fairway hazard such as water on the left or a bunker on the right and a green-side hazard such as a bunker or deep rough. Use objects such as flags or mounds on the driving range to shape your hole. Play the hole as an imaginary threesome, portraying three different players using three different strategies. Imagine you are a long hitter, then a shot maker (someone who can shape the flight path of their golf ball), and then a short-hitting, conservative player. Tee off as the long hitter first, then the shot maker, and then the conservative player. Play each ball onto the imaginary green from the practice tee as if you were actually playing the course as a threesome. After completing the first hole, imagine a par-5 hole with hazards and play that hole. Repeat until you complete nine holes. For each shot, give yourself 3 points for determining the distance the shot will travel, 1 point for considering the hazards on the imaginary hole, and 1 point for taking into account the wind and other weather conditions, for a maximum of 5 points per shot and 15 points per hole.

TO DECREASE DIFFICULTY

- Play the round as a single player.
- Design imaginary golf holes with wide fairways and no hazards.
- Play all holes as if they were par-3 holes.

TO INCREASE DIFFICULTY

- Include two fairway hazards on each hole.
- Imagine the holes as you would find them on your favorite golf course.

Success Check

- For each shot, consider shot distance, hole features, and weather conditions.

Score Your Success

_____ Score on Hole 1

_____ Score on Hole 2

_____ Score on Hole 3

_____ Score on Hole 4

_____ Score on Hole 5

_____ Score on Hole 6

_____ Score on Hole 7

_____ Score on Hole 8

_____ Score on Hole 9

_____ Your score (out of 135 possible points)

Know the Course Drill 4   Identify the Trouble

List the trouble areas of the hole shown in figure 10.10. Rank the trouble spots from 1 to 5, with 1 being the area most likely to result in a higher score. Give yourself 1 point for each correct ranking. (Answers appear at the end of the chapter.)

1. _____

2. _____

3. _____

4. _____

5. _____

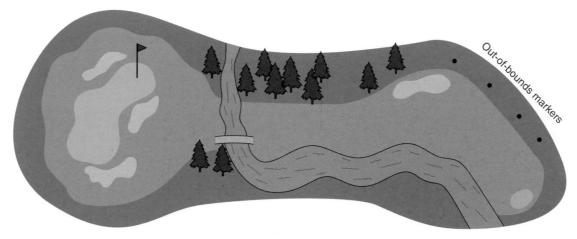

Figure 10.10   Rank the trouble spots for this hole in order from most to least dangerous.

Score Your Success

Give yourself 1 point for each correct answer.

Your score _____ (out of 5 possible points)

Know the Course Drill 5   Manage the Entire Hole

Good course management requires you to match your playing strengths to the hole's weaknesses. For each of the holes shown in the following figures, mark an X on an appropriate target landing area for each shot. Identify the club you would use to hit the ball to the target by placing a symbol beside the X such as 8i for an 8-iron, 5m for a 5-metal, SW for a sand wedge, or D for a driver. Figure 10.11 shows a sample hole already filled in. (Answers for figures 10.12, 10.13, and 10.14 appear at the end of the chapter.)

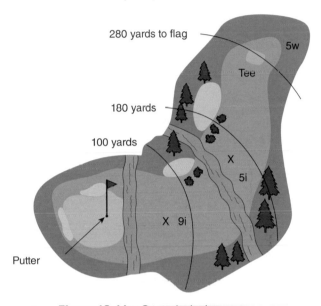

Figure 10.11   Sample hole.

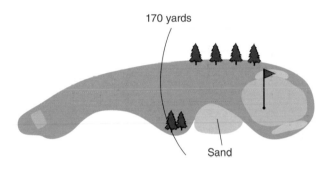

Figure 10.12   Hole 1, 341 yards (312 meters), par 4.

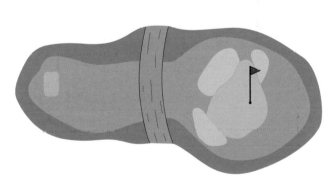

Figure 10.13   Hole 2, 168 yards (154 meters), par 3.

Figure 10.14   Hole 3, 502 yards (459 meters), par 5.

Score Your Success

Give yourself 1 point for each landing area you identified and 1 point for each club you correctly chose to get the ball to that point.

Your score _____ (out of 6 possible points)

Know the Course Drill 6   Managing Your Round

The better you can manage the course you are playing, the greater your chance of success. In figure 10.15, plot your strategy for each hole as you did in the previous drill, indicating the landing area and the club you would use for each shot. After completing this exercise, get a scorecard or yardage book from your favorite course and repeat the drill. Then go play a round, and compare your plan with your actual play.

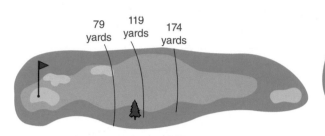

Figure 10.15a   Hole 1, 254 yards (232 meters), par 4.

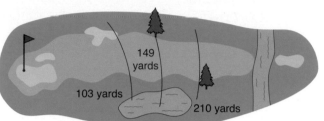

Figure 10.15b   Hole 2, 410 yards (374 meters), par 5.

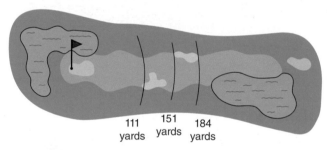

Figure 10.15c   Hole 3, 340 yards (310 meters), par 4.

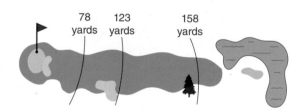

Figure 10.15d   Hole 4, 243 yards (222 meters), par 4.

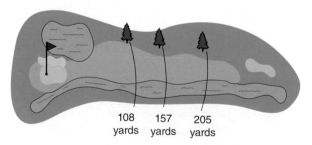

Figure 10.15e   Hole 5, 300 yards (274 meters), par 4.

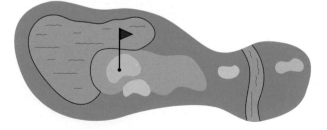

Figure 10.15f   Hole 6, 135 yards (123 meters), par 3.

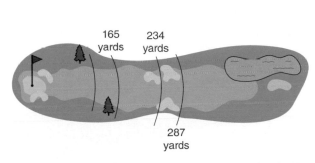

Figure 10.15g Hole 7, 490 yards (448 meters), par 5.

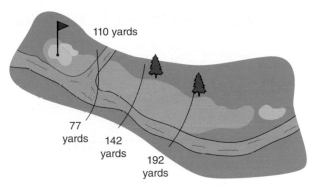

Figure 10.15h Hole 8, 366 yards (335 meters), par 4.

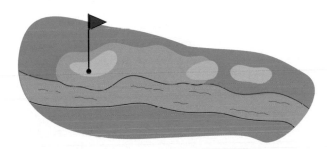

Figure 10.15i Hole 9, 123 yards (113 meters), par 3.

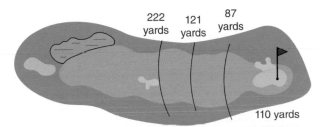

Figure 10.15j Hole 10, 475 yards (434 meters), par 5.

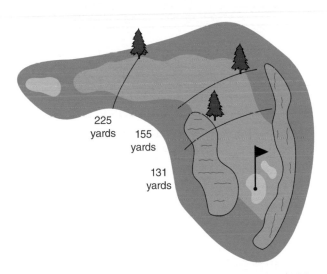

Figure 10.15k Hole 11, 400 yards (366 meters), par 4.

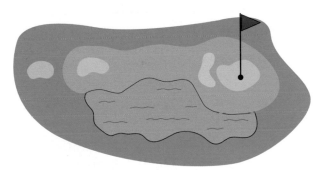

Figure 10.15l Hole 12, 120 yards (110 meters), par 3.

(continued)

Know the Course Drill 6 *(continued)*

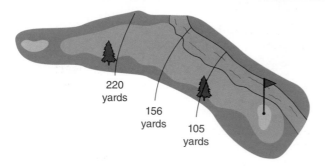

Figure 10.15m Hole 13, 410 yards (375 meters), par 4.

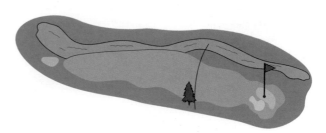

Figure 10.15n Hole 14, 310 yards (283 meters), par 4.

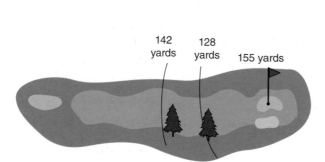

Figure 10.15o Hole 15, 235 yards (215 meters), par 4.

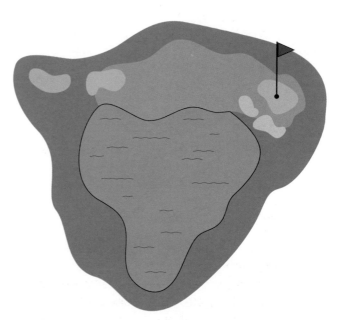

Figure 10.15p Hole 16, 122 yards (112 meters), par 3.

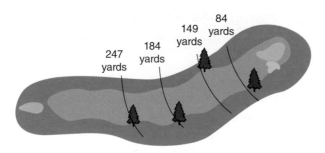

Figure 10.15q Hole 17, 491 yards (449 meters), par 5.

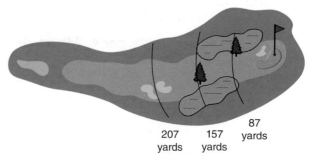

Figure 10.15r Hole 18, 317 yards (290 meters), par 4.

Score Your Success

Review your overall plan for all 18 holes, and score yourself based on the following criteria:

If you first determined from where on the fairway you wanted to hit your approach shot as you determined your tee shots = 2 points

If you attempted to play away from hazards = 3 points

If you played to the middle of the green on each approach shot = 2 points

If on par-4 and par-5 holes you used more clubs than just your driver from the tee box = 1 point

Your score _____ (of out a 59 possible points)

Answers for Know the Course Drill 4, Identify the Trouble

1. Out of bounds
2. Lost ball or unplayable lie
3. Water
4. Woods
5. Bunker

Answers for Know the Course Drill 5, Manage the Entire Hole

A well-designed golf hole provides you with many options. The clubs you select and types of shots you play will depend largely on your skill and ability to manage risks. Smart players accurately assess their skills and play each hole so as to minimize risks and eliminate the chance of running up large numbers on their scorecard. The answers that follow are only suggestions based on the authors' experiences with beginning and intermediate golfers. Compare your answers to ours and evaluate the way you considered each factor for the hole.

Hole 1 (figure 10.12), par 4, 341 yards (312 meters). Aim the tee shot to the middle of the fairway about 200 yards (182 meters), short of the sand on the right and trees on the left. This will leave you a 140- to 150-yard.

Hole 2 (figure 10.13), par 3, 168 yards (154 meters). With water before the green, large bunkers in front of the green, and the flag in the back part of the green, you need to select a club that will carry the ball at least 170 (155 meters) yards in the air to the middle of the green.

Hole 3 (figure 10.14), par 5, 502 yards (459 meters). This hole will require three shots to reach the green. It is better to play three low-risk shots. A 200-yard (182-meter) tee shot will get you over the lake and leave you short of the bunker, taking both hazards out of play. A second shot of 150 yards (137 meters) will get you to the middle of the fairway and leave you a third shot of 150 yards to the middle of the green.

Answers for Know the Course Drill 6, Managing Your Round

The better your strategy in a round of golf, the greater your chance of success. In figure 10.16, plot your strategy for each hole in a similar pattern to the manage the entire hole drill. Indicate the landing area for each shot and identify the club you would use for the shot.

Hole 1 (figure 10.15a), par 4, 254 yards (232 meters). A 170-yard (155-meter) tee shot aimed for the left center of the fairway will take the bunker on the right out of play and leave you with an approach shot of fewer than 90 yards (82 meters).

(continued)

Answers for Know the Course Drill 6 *(continued)*

Hole 2 (figure 10.15*b*), par 5, 410 yards (374 meters). Aim the tee shot for the right side of the fairway to avoid the water on the left. A 200-yard tee shot will leave 210 yards to the hole. Aim the second shot for the middle of the fairway for a distance of 140 yards (375 meters). This will take you past the bunker on the right and leave a pitch shot of 80 yards (73.15 meters) to the middle of the green.

Hole 3 (figure 10.15c), par 4, 340 yards (310 meters). Aim the tee shot just left of the bunker on the right side of the fairway. This will take the water on the left out of play. A tee shot of 200 yards (182 meters) will leave you with an approach shot of 140 yards (128 meters). With water on the right side of the green, aim your approach shot for the left or center of the green.

Hole 4, (figure 10.15*d*) par 4, 243 yards (222 meters). With a small green guarded in front by a large bunker, an accurate approach shot is needed. Therefore it will be necessary to get the ball closer to the green with the tee shot. The only hazard facing you off the tee is a fairway bunker on the left. Using your 150-yard (137-meter) club, aim the tee shot to the right side of the fairway. This will leave you with a 93-yard (85-meter) approach shot.

Hole 5 (figure 10.15e), par 4, 300 yards (274 meters). The fairway is widest approximately 200 yards (182 meters) from the tee box; this should be your landing area. Water runs the entire length of the left side of the fairway, so aim your tee shot to the right or center of the fairway. A good tee shot will leave you with a 100-yard (91-meter) approach shot. Bunkers and a water hazard line the right side of the green, and there is a water hazard to the left. Aim for the middle of the green.

Hole 6 (figure 10.15*f*), par 3, 135 yards (123 meters). The dangers on this hole come from the water that surrounds the right and back sides of the green and from the bunker on the front right. While an accurate shot to the middle of the green is optimal, the bailout area is short and slightly right. If your shot goes astray, a chip and pitch can save par. Select a club that will carry the ball no farther than 135 yards.

Hole 7 (figure 10.15*g*), par 5, 490 yards (448 meters). For a long hitter, this hole may be reachable in two shots. For the average player, it will take three shots to reach the green. The only serious trouble comes from the bunkers on the left and right sides of the fairway about 200 yards (182 meters) from the tee. A tee shot at 190 yards (174 meters) will take the bunkers out of play and leave you with 200 yards to the hole. A second shot of 125 yards (114 meters) would leave you with a full pitch shot of 75 yards (68 meters) to the middle of the green. A short three shot will help you avoid the bunkers guarding the green.

Hole 8 (figure 10.15*h*), par 4, 366 yards (335 meters). A tee shot of 200 yards (182 meters) aimed down the right or center will help you avoid the water on the left. Hit a 166-yard (151-meter) approach shot over water to the green guarded on the left by water. You will need to carry the ball at least 90 yards (82 meters) in the air to get over the water. There is a landing area over the water, so even if you are a bit short, you can still chip and putt for par. If you do not feel confident in getting the ball over the water, hit a 60-yard (55-meter) shot so that it stops well before the water, and make your third shot a 106-yard (97-meter) shot to the green. With the amount of water on this hole, it is better to reduce risk and play safely. Better a bogey than a high number.

Hole 9 (figure 10.15*i*), par 3, 123 yards (113 meters). With water on the left side of the green, aim to the right or center of the green with a club that will reach the hole.

Hole 10 (figure 10.15*j*), par 5, 475 yards (434 meters). A 200-yard (182-meter) drive will leave the average golfer short of the fairway bunker. A second shot of 150 to 175 yards (137 to 160 meters) to a wide fairway will leave a pitch or short iron approach to the green. A longer hitter could drive the ball down the left or center of the fairway to avoid the bunker, then use a fairway wood to get the second shot to the green.

Hole 11 (figure 10.15*k*), par 4, 400 yards (366 meters). This dogleg right hole is long and full of danger. Play safely to avoid errant shots or penalty strokes. A tee shot aimed toward the second pine tree on the left side of the fairway will leave you an open approach shot to the green. A drive of 200 yards (182 meters) still leaves 200 yards to the green. Consider laying up with a second shot of 125 yards (114 meters), leaving you a 75-yard (68-meter) pitch shot to the green. This should effectively take the fairway water hazards out of play and help you gain a short approach shot to a green surrounded by water hazards and a bunker.

Hole 12 (figure 10.15*l*), par 3, 120 yards (110 meters). The front bunker guarding the green means you will need plenty of club to reach the green. Choose a club that will carry the bunker and get the ball all the way to the hole; your 125-yard (114-meter) club would be a good choice. With water on the right, aim left of center on the green.

Hole 13 (figure 10.15*m*), par 4, 410 yards (375 meters). A 225-yard (205-meter) tee shot hit to the right center of the fairway will give you a chance to reach the green with a long iron or fairway wood and keep you away from the water on the left. If this long par 4 leaves you with more than 200 yards (182 meters) to the green after the tee shot, consider a second shot of 150 yards (137 meters), leaving you a pitch or short iron for an approach shot.

Hole 14 (figure 10.15*n*), par 4, 310 yards (283 meters). A 200-yard (182-meter) tee shot down the right side of the fairway will leave you with a middle or short iron approach. Be sure to take enough club to carry the bunker on your approach shot.

Hole 15 (figure 10.15*o*), par 4, 235 yards (215 meters). With a narrow fairway on this short hole, use a fairway metal (3-wood or 5-wood) off the tee for better accuracy. This will still leave you with a short iron to the hole.

Hole 16 (figure 10.15*p*), par 3, 122 yards (112 meters). Water and bunkers are on the right, so aim the tee shot left center of the green. Take enough club to get the ball to the hole.

Hole 17 (figure 10.15*q*), par 5, 491 yards (449 meters). A slight dogleg left means you can gain an advantage by aiming left or center with your tee shot. A 200-yard drive will leave you with a middle iron second shot (150 to 170 yards) and a middle or short iron approach shot (141 to 121 yards) to the middle of the green. Avoid the greenside bunker on the right by aiming slightly left of center.

Hole 18 (figure 10.15*r*), par 4, 317 yards (290 meters). This is a short hole but one wrought with danger. An accurate tee shot of 160 yards (146 meters) aimed just left of the fairway tree will get you past the fairway bunkers, keep you out of the water, and take the trees out of play. This will leave you with a 157-yard (143-meter) approach shot. Aim for the right side of the green to avoid the bunker guarding the left.

COURSE MANAGEMENT SUCCESS SUMMARY

Professional golfers spend several days playing practice rounds on the tournament course in preparation for the tournament. By playing these practice rounds, players become familiar with the length and features of each hole and develop strategies for managing the course. They determine which clubs they will hit and to what landing areas. They also consider options and how their strategy may change due to weather or their tournament standing. For example, a player may have an idea of alternative clubs to use in case the wind blows strongly on a hole with water hazards or if a downhill fairway begins to dry out from a hot sun. Course management is one area of golf that you can easily play like a pro because the skill is mental, not physical. Know your strengths, know the course, and plan an effective strategy, and you will find success on your scorecard.

Record your point totals from each of the drills in this step, and add them together. If you scored at least 180 out of 285 points, you're ready for the next step. If you scored 150 to 179 points, you're almost there; move on after reviewing the sections you think you can improve the most. If you scored fewer than 150 points, review the information and go through the drills again to raise your scores.

SCORING YOUR SUCCESS

Know Your Game Drills

1.	Yardage Guide	___ out of 26
2.	My Success Clubs	___ out of 8

Know the Course Drills

1.	Hole Strategy	___ out of 8
2.	Step Off	___ out of 38
3.	Phantom Threesome	___ out of 135
4.	Identify the Trouble	___ out of 5
5.	Manage the Entire Hole	___ out of 6
6.	Managing Your Round	___ out of 59
Total		___ **out of 285**

By completing this step, you have learned and practiced the essential skills of golf, from putting a ball into a hole to managing your game. You've come a long way and can now play golf competently. But like everyone who enjoys this wonderful game, you probably yearn to get even better. The next step will help you develop mental and emotional control on the course so that you can maintain your confidence throughout the round.

The Mental Game of Golf

As a game, golf can prove to be a stressful pursuit. The pressure to carry a shot over 100 yards (91 meters) of water, avoid the penalty of going out of bounds, or facing a lightning fast downhill putt can challenge the nerves of the calmest person. But to perform at your best in golf requires you be, if not relaxed, at least in control of your emotions.

Golf requires you to maintain mental and emotional control and stay in the psychological state in which you have the best possible chance to perform, from the first shot you hit to complete your round. Developing your shot-making skills is key to being a successful golfer, but those skills will not serve you well on the course if, when the pressure is on, you do not have the mental and emotional control necessary to execute shots when it matters most in the round. The best players in the world are great ball strikers and shot makers, but they are also great at performing those skills when it really matters. The world is full of golfers with great practice range swings and good practice or social round scores. But great golfers play well when the personal or competitive pressure is the strongest. Fortunately, like the physical skills in golf, the requisite mental and emotional skills can also be learned and mastered. This is the mental game of golf.

Feeling flow, or getting in the zone—that state where everything is effortless—is something we all do occasionally, usually without knowing how we actually got there. Finding the zone often requires learning about yourself, how you think, and what you see, hear, and feel when you play your best. It is also about learning how to practice this state of flow and the formula that gets you there. While it is not easy to learn to create the feeling of flow, like most skills it comes with understanding how it is achieved and then putting into practice what you learn.

LEARN FROM THE PROS

It is perhaps stating the obvious to say that the top players in the world are good at managing their game and emotions. Many golfers would agree that this is one of the key characteristics that distinguishes a world-class performer from an average tour player. Every player on the PGA and LPGA Tour has outstanding shot-making skills, but only those who can access their full potential when the competitive heat is on prevail. That is when players like Annika Sörenstam, Tiger Woods, Stacy Lewis, Luke Donald, and a few others stand out from the rest. To describe what these players do psychologically to perform so well is not easy. Individual differences are a factor; solutions that work for one golfer may not work for another. An American researcher, Deborah Graham, spent her doctoral thesis trying to discover the psychological difference between the players who win on professional golf tours and the players who do not. She concentrated on LPGA tour players, but she also included a few players from the PGA tour. Graham found that champions commonly possess the following qualities (*The 8 Traits of Champion Golfers: How to Develop the Mental Game of a Pro* 2000):

- A narrow focus, which helps them gather their attention for every shot. They can also relax and broaden their attention between shots.

- Abstract-thinking skills are average or above, allowing them to think strategically and creatively in picking the right club, strategy, and tactics.

- Emotional stability, which is that they show little or no reaction to good or bad shots.

- A higher level of dominance, making them more aggressive than the average player.

- They are tough and care less about others than the average person. They care about themselves and their game, and they are tough on themselves when needed.

- A high level of self-confidence, and do not stop believing in themselves when playing poorly.

- A high level of independence, which is an advantage when planning strategy and selecting a club. Off the course this is a good characteristic as well, because it helps them take responsibility for their lives and not let others bother them.

- Ability to modify arousal levels is somewhere between low and high. Parts of the game, such as putting, require low arousal while other parts require higher arousal. Generally speaking, too little arousal provides less energy while too much arousal lets feelings and reactions show, damaging focus and concentration.

The "click on, click off" is one method professionals will use to manage their games. A round of golf is long, often 5 hours for 18 holes. Staying focused for the entire time is challenging if not impossible. However, because it is crucial to find the optimal level of concentration for each shot, many professionals develop the ability to click on their concentration when they are about to hit the shot. Phrases such as *Step into the bubble* describe such preparation for a shot. Inside the bubble, good players will not let anything disturb them. After they play the shot, they step out of the bubble and might chat with the caddie or other players until it is time to step into the bubble for the next shot. The level of clicking on or off varies with the individual player. For example, Lee Trevino once said he could not play if he could not talk to the crowd or the other people around him. He had a very short period of clicking on. Other players, such as Nick Faldo, prefer not to talk during the round; it seems their period of clicking on runs from the first to the last shot of the round. Most likely, though, there is a difference in the level of concentration when playing a shot and when walking to the ball after a shot. Good players have the ability to stay inside the bubble when playing a shot and do not let internal or external distractions disturb them.

Preshot Routine

The importance of using a specific preshot routine is under debate. Research has not been able to show that improving the preshot routine improves performance. However, many players and coaches use a consistent preshot routine to help prepare for the shot and shut out internal and external distractions. The preshot routine can be thought of in two ways:

1. The physical routine players undertake when preparing for a shot. This involves the number of practice swings, the way the players aim and set up for the shot, the time of the routine, and so on.

2. The mental state players assume in preparing to play a shot. To accomplish this state, players complete a repeatable series of physical actions. However, players who are aware of their mental state and listen to internal signals may not need a specific physical routine, or they may need different physical routines each time to achieve the same state.

Without doubt, the most important part of the preshot routine is the state you are able to put yourself in as you step up to hit the shot. Good players can put themselves in a state of trust, focus, and comfort most of the time during a round. And they can do this on a regular, intentional, and consistent basis.

Legendary player, Arnold Palmer, once faced a 15-foot (4.5-meter) putt to win a major championship. When it was his turn, he simply stepped up to the ball and without hesitation stroked the ball into the hole. Afterward he was asked about what happened to his preshot routine and why he did not read the putt. He replied, "I already knew how to play the shot and did not want to disturb that by having second thoughts."

Finding Your Zone

Athletes in all sports try to find the zone. Being *in the zone* means achieving a mental state in which you are fully immersed in what you are doing and experience a feeling of energized focus, full involvement, and success in the process of the activity. When in the zone everything seems easy; you are in an optimal state of performance. For many golfers, this may include picturing the hole as being much bigger than it actually is, seeing fairways as wider than they are, and visualizing a path for the ball to roll into the hole. Players who have experienced the zone also say that while in the zone they do not think about failure and they have a very clear view of what they need to do (for example, seeing the target and not the water hazard).

The zone is probably not a state that others can teach you to reach because of individual differences in people's mental states. However, you have most likely experienced a state like this before, either on or off the golf course. With a few cues, you can experience it again and note some of the characteristics that will help you find it again and again. The first mental focus drill, My Winning Formula, will help you identify times when you have experienced the zone. It will also help you identify what the experience was like in terms of what you saw, how you felt, and what you heard. Perhaps your posture and body language are important. For example, you probably won't go around feeling sorry for yourself if you have a smile on your face. Body language can affect the physics in the body. When you know what your zone is like, the cues that describe it, and the things you can do to get there, it will be much easier for you to find the zone by choice rather than chance. The second mental focus drill, Repeating Your Winning Formula, will help you practice your cues and identify your progress in finding them on the golf course.

Some strategies that players have used to induce flow (get in the zone) may prove useful to help you manage your golf game. Mental rehearsal is a technique that usually involves closing your eyes and seeing yourself perform the mechanics required to hit the shot. Jack Nicklaus was known to use this technique. He described it as watching a video of himself hitting the shot, then rewinding the video and then executing the shot. A closely related technique is imagery. In golf, it often translates into picturing or imagining the flight of the ball to the target or the rolling of a putt into the hole. Pre-round routines are a third technique golfers use to relax and focus themselves for a round of golf. These routines may include having certain warm-up exercises, eating and drinking certain foods, or doing other activities that help the golfer to feel fully prepared to play in top form. A common technique among professional golfers is to have a game plan for playing a particular course. Decisions regarding clubs to be used, landing areas for golf shots, and places to land on the green can all be part of a game plan that helps you feel comfortable and ready to play. The important point is for you to select the strategy or routine that will help you feel relaxed, confident, and able to focus when you most need to be ready to hit your shots. In doing so, you will find your zone.

MISSTEP

While playing a shot, you are worrying about a water hazard, out-of-bounds area, or bunker instead of concentrating on executing the shot.

CORRECTION

This problem is often the result of not having made a clear decision on what to do for the shot. A clear decision means seeing, hearing, and feeling the shot, which will help keep out distractions. Try the Masters drill, and imagine the pressure or nervousness that might distract you. The Think Box and Play Box drill also may help.

Think Box and Play Box

Playing your best on a golf course requires a great deal of analysis and decision making. Course strategy, planning each shot, club selection, and other factors must be considered for scoring low. At the same time, the golf swing is a complex motor task. Conflictive thinking such as doubts about decisions you've made, thinking about swing mechanics, or worries about the outcome of the shot increase the chance of bad shots.

One method for dealing with this conflict is to separate thinking from playing with a decision line. This strategy has been described by Pia Nilsson and Lynn Marriott (*Every Shot Must Have a Purpose* 2005) as Think Box/Play Box. That is, do all your thinking behind the ball in the Think Box, then move into the Play Box, ready to play with no additional thinking required. The thinking involves deciding what type of shot and trajectory to hit, what club to use, and how to swing in order to produce the desired shot. When you have made your decision, cross the Decision Line, step up to the ball, and play the shot in the Play Box. Playing the shot is simply executing it. If you sense conflicting thoughts or worries, step back behind the Decision Line, and reconsider your decision.

Before hitting the shot, imagine it with as many senses as you can. Visualize the shot as it flies toward the hole, hear the sound of the club contacting the ball, and feel the swing. Not every golfer is able to visualize; for some people, other senses are stronger. You may find it easier to hear the shot or recall how it feels to execute it. On the putting green, Phil Mickelson will take three practice putting strokes before stroking the ball. The first practice stroke he intentional takes too strong, the second too weak, the third just right, and then he feels ready to make his putt. Brad Faxon, had a different approach to putting. He would stand behind the ball looking toward the hole. He would visualize the precise line his putt would travel and the speed it would travel. Then he would step up to his ball and make the ball do just what he visualized. What applies to putting works for all golf shots, including a full swing. If either Mickelson's or Faxon's techniques work for you, great; if not, find another way to mentally rehearse your shots.

Make it a habit to develop a basic game plan for every round you play, and make these decisions in your Think Box. Decisions should include the following:

1. For the shot at hand, decide what you want to do—what type of shot to hit (ball flight and trajectory), what club to hit, and how to execute the shot (setup and swing).
2. Make sure you have a clear idea of where the ball should land (target).
3. With as many senses as you can, imagine what the shot will be like (visualize the shot, hear the sound, and feel the swing).
4. Step up to the ball and into the Play Box. Without further thought, execute the shot.
5. If anything distracts you—noise, movement, or negative thoughts—step back, clear your thoughts, and go again.

MISSTEP

You are unable to reach the level of concentration you need for a shot.

CORRECTION

Overthinking, conflicting thoughts, and indecision are problems for any player. Any distracting thought, game-related or not, will take attention away from the shot. Perform the Rehearsal drill to increase your awareness of the task. Compare your execution with your rehearsal, and make adjustments to get better alignment between rehearsal and execution.

PLAN OF ACTION

Most good players have a plan of action for playing the course before they step to the first tee box. Such a plan will allow you to make many important decisions before you actually have to hit a shot. A plan of action will reduce the amount of thinking and decisions to be made on the course, and you will make many of the decisions when you are calmer and more objective than you will be once you begin playing your round.

MISSTEP

You find yourself thinking ahead to a possible score when you are playing well, or you dwell over a shot you missed earlier.

CORRECTION

Not staying in the present is a problem for many players. What you need to do right now should have your utmost attention. Try the Think Box and Play Box drill. Whenever your thoughts turn to things that will not help you, raise a "stop" sign and return to where you want to be.

Mental Focus Drill 1   My Winning Formula

The purpose of this drill is to train your mind to block out distractions and focus on your golf game in ways that will increase your performance. Sit or lie down in a quiet, comfortable place where you won't be disturbed. Relax and think back to a time when you experienced the zone—a round on the golf course, a game in another sport, or some other occasion when things went your way. Remember this event as vividly as you can. Try to experience in your mind everything that happened. Ask yourself, "What did I look like? What was my body language like? How did I walk? Was I slow or quick? What did I see? What did I hear? How did I talk to myself? What was my voice like? What did I feel? What did I think?"

While focusing on this event, or right afterward, make a list of things that you thought or felt during that zone experience. These factors are probably what helped you reach the zone. Common factors for golfers include the following:

- I am focused on the shot at hand.
- I walk with my head held high.
- All I see is where the ball should land.
- I trust my swing and my instincts.
- I follow my routine and I am relaxed.

Do this exercise 10 times over the next week or two, and rate your success as follows:

- Cannot see, hear, or feel anything; previous experiences are gone = 0 points
- Can visualize an experience close to the zone, but it is not golf-related = 1 point
- Can see or hear previous good performances on the golf course = 2 points

- Find something to add to your winning formula = 3 points
- Gain the confidence that you can experience this formula again during play = 4 points

TO DECREASE DIFFICULTY

- Have somebody videotape you when you are playing. Watch the tape, and try to experience the same thoughts and feelings you had during play.
- Make notes during a round while you are experiencing the zone and hitting good shots.

TO INCREASE DIFFICULTY

- Think about the zone while practicing, and try to incorporate it into your shots.
- Discuss your zone experience with a friend and compare notes.

Success Check

- Relax, think back, and let whatever comes up come up.
- Make notes after you finish reliving the experience.

Score Your Success

Your score _____ (out of 40 possible points)

Mental Focus Drill 2   Repeating Your Winning Formula

When you have identified a number of factors in your winning formula, practice getting to the level you need to reach for each factor that will allow you to play your best. For instance, what does *focused on the shot at hand* mean to you? Can you be more or less focused, and what will that level do to your performance?

When playing a round, give yourself a grade from 1 to 5 on each factor after you complete each hole. Note your score on each factor. After three holes, see what grade has come up most frequently; that is your score for those three holes. Every three holes, determine your most common score. After 18 holes, calculate your total score by adding the numbers of the 6 different 3-hole scores.

TO DECREASE DIFFICULTY

- Start on the putting green and set up 18 holes of putting. Score both the number of shots you take and how well you achieve your winning formula.
- Try your winning formula on the range without the distractions of playing the course.

TO INCREASE DIFFICULTY

- Divide the round into three-hole matches with yourself, and score yourself after completing three holes. Try to improve for each three-hole match.
- Ask a partner to distract you when playing shots. (See the Bubble drill.)

(continued)

Mental Focus Drill 2 *(continued)*

Success Check

- Pay attention to your keys to success.
- Work with your mindset and body language to come as close as possible to what is best for you.

Score Your Success

Your score _____ (out of 90 possible points)

Mental Focus Drill 3   **Think Box and Play Box**

This drill will help you to separate the decision-making portion of a golf shot from the execution of the golf shot. On the practice tee, place a ball on the ground, and pick a target for a shot. Place a club as a decision line 4 or 5 feet (about 1.5 meters) behind the ball (figure 11.1). The area next to the ball is the Play Box, and on the other side of the Decision Line is the Think Box. Stand in the Think Box, and decide what shot to hit. Pick a club, and feel or picture your swing and the ensuing golf shot. Cross the Decision Line, and step into the Play Box. Execute the shot with no further decisions or thoughts, trusting in your decisions. If you are disturbed by anything, step back into the Think Box and start over. Play 10 balls, scoring yourself based on the following criteria:

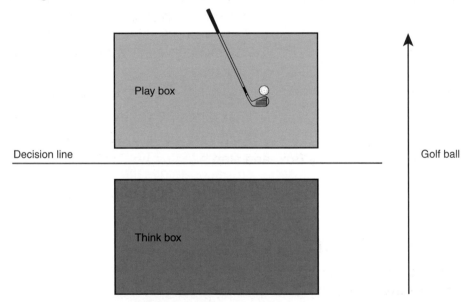

Figure 11.1   Set a club behind the ball as a visual decision line.

- Experience a lot of distracting thoughts while trying to hit the shot = 0 points
- Make a decision in the Think Box but lose it when in the Play Box = 1 point
- Make a decision, try to execute it, but get distracted = 2 points
- Get distracted in the Play Box, and step back to the Think Box to start over = 3 points
- Make a clear decision, and execute it with confidence in the Play Box = 4 points

TO DECREASE DIFFICULTY

- Hit with your favorite club until you feel comfortable.
- Try the exercise while putting on the practice green.

TO INCREASE DIFFICULTY

- Hit different types of shots (draw, fade, high, low), and vary your targets.
- Take the exercise to the course, and see if you can do it there.

Success Check

- Make sure the Decision Line is visual so that you can see the Think Box and Play Box.
- Any time you can't keep thoughts away in the Play Box, step back to the Think Box and start over.

Score Your Success

Your score _____ (out of 40 possible points)

Mental Focus Drill 4   Think Box and Play Box With Partner

For this drill, repeat the previous Think Box and Play Box drill, but this time take turns picking a target with a partner. When your partner plays, try to gently disturb him or her by making noise or moving. If you are distracted by your partner, step back and start over. Play at least five balls each, scoring yourself based on the following criteria:

- Experience a lot of distracting thoughts while trying to hit a shot = 0 points
- Make a decision in the Think Box, but lose it when in the Play Box = 1 point
- Make a decision, try to execute it, but get distracted = 2 points
- Get distracted in the Play Box, and step back to the Think Box to start over = 3 points
- Make a clear decision, and execute it with confidence in the Play Box = 4 points

TO DECREASE DIFFICULTY

- Hit with your favorite club until you feel comfortable.
- Try the exercise while putting on the practice green.

TO INCREASE DIFFICULTY

- Hit different types of shots (draw, fade, high, low), and vary your targets.
- Take the exercise to the course, and see if you can do it there as well.

(continued)

Mental Focus Drill 4 *(continued)*

Success Check

- Make sure you are clear about your Decision Line so that you can see the Think Box and Play Box.
- Any time you can't keep thoughts away in the Play Box, step back to the Think Box, and start over.

Score Your Success

Your score ____ (out of 20 possible points)

Mental Focus Drill 5   The Masters

While at the driving range, picture a golf course you know well, either from television such as Augusta National, site of the U.S. Masters, or an actual course you have played. Visualize yourself on tee box 1, and picture the first hole in front of you. Identify the left and right edge of the fairway, hazards, bunkers, and so on, making the visualization as real as you possibly can. If you have tournament experience or can guess what that might be like, try to imagine the nervousness or pressure you think you would have to deal with. Hit your first shot, and determine where the ball would end on your imaginary course. Play your next shot from that position with the appropriate club, and continue play until you reach the green or short-game area. Play at least nine holes. Give yourself 1 point for every fairway you hit off the tee and 2 points for every green you hit in regulation.

TO DECREASE DIFFICULTY

- Play an easier course with wider fairways and larger green areas.
- Imagine the pins in the middle of the greens.

TO INCREASE DIFFICULTY

- Play a more difficult course with narrower fairways and smaller greens.
- Imagine the pin placements in difficult spots such as behind bunkers or toward the edges.

Success Check

- Go through your normal routine when preparing for each shot.
- Use the decision line, think box, and play box.

Score Your Success

Your score ____ (out of 27 possible points for nine holes)

Mental Focus Drill 6   Rehearsal

On the driving range, in the short-game area, or on the course when faced with a particular shot, deliberately go through the preparation for the shot. After deciding which shot to take and how to execute it, rehearse the shot next to the ball, exactly the way you want to play it.

Try to store the feeling of the rehearsal shot in your memory, then execute the real shot and compare it to the rehearsal shot. When the rehearsal shot and the real shot match and the shot is good, you are done. If the real shot is not good, think about the differences between the rehearsal shot and the real shot. If there weren't any differences, practice and develop your shot-making skills to make you actual shots more like your rehearsed shots in terms of mechanics and tempo. If there were some differences, you need practice to be able to perform what you already know so you can play the shot you planned to play. Play 10 balls, and score yourself based on the following criteria:

- Played the shot but have no clue if it matched the rehearsal swing = 0 points
- Played the shot, but it was nothing like the rehearsal swing = 1 point
- Played the shot like the rehearsal swing, but it was not a good shot = 2 points
- Played the shot unlike the rehearsal swing, but it was a good shot = 3 points
- Played the shot like the rehearsal swing, and the shot was super = 4 points

TO DECREASE DIFFICULTY

- Play five shots with the same club, then another five with a different club.
- Start with short putts, and work your way out as you get the hang of matching rehearsed strokes to actual strokes.

TO INCREASE DIFFICULTY

- Make as big a difference between shots as possible. For example, hit a driver followed by a wedge.
- Perform the drill while playing on the course.

Success Check

- Make a clear decision on how you want to execute the shot.
- As vividly as possible, using all your senses, rehearse the shot.
- Play the shot, and compare it to your blueprint.

Score Your Success

Your score _____ (out of 40 possible points)

Mental Focus Drill 7 **The Bubble**

Playing successful golf is often about blocking out distractions. Distractions can come from inside, such as thoughts or feelings that get in the way of playing the shot as well as you can. Distractions can also come from outside, such as noise, movement, or other things that attract your attention. Fortunately, you can prepare to deal with distractions and practice staying in your bubble of concentration.

Team up with a friend, and take 10 balls each. For every ball, pick a different target, club, and shot to hit. When you get ready to play your shot, your partner should try to distract you in different ways, such as by making a sound, moving, saying something, or simply doing nothing (since you will be expecting something, doing nothing is a distraction). Score yourself based on the following criteria:

- Missed the shot completely = 0 points
- Played the shot, but was distracted and did not hit the target = 1 point
- Played the shot, was not distracted, but missed the target = 2 points
- Played the shot, was distracted, but hit the target anyway = 3 points
- Played the shot, was not distracted, and hit the target = 4 points

TO DECREASE DIFFICULTY

- Play five shots with the same club and then another five with a different club.
- Limit the distractions to a couple of predetermined options.

TO INCREASE DIFFICULTY

- Make as big a difference between shots as possible. For example, hit a driver followed by a wedge.
- Perform the drill while playing on the course.

Success Check

- Make a clear decision on how you want to execute the shot.
- Use the Think Box and Play Box.
- If you get distracted, step away and start over.

Score Your Success

Your score _____ (out of 40 possible points)

MENTAL AND EMOTIONAL CONTROL SUCCESS SUMMARY

No matter how good a golfer you are, you are not going to hit perfect shots every time. To become a great player, you will need to manage the mental aspects of the game both when playing well and when the game is not so good. Your play will be significantly enhanced if you can discover ways to get into the zone as you play. Finding your way there and staying there is the key to playing to your full potential. A number of drills can help you become better at executing shots you actually know how to hit. All of them focus on getting out of your own way; too much thinking usually messes things up.

Record your point totals from each of the drills in this step, and add them together. A score of 200 points or more indicates you are on your way to mastering the mental aspects of the game and you're ready for the next step. If you scored 150 to 190 points, you should be able to move on after reviewing and practicing the two drills you find the most difficult. If you scored fewer than 150 points, you have not sufficiently mastered the skills. Practice some more before moving on to the next step.

SCORING YOUR SUCCESS

Mental Focus Drills

1.	My Winning Formula	___ out of 40
2.	Repeating Your Winning Formula	___ out of 90
3.	Think Box and Play Box	___ out of 40
4.	Think Box and Play Box With Partner	___ out of 20
5.	The Masters	___ out of 27
6.	Rehearsal	___ out of 40
7.	The Bubble	___ out of 40
Total		___ **out of 297**

You are nearing the end of your journey to golf success. The final step is to develop ways to close in on making par. In the final step, you explore setting goals, practicing with purpose, and moving toward improving on the course.

12

Continuing to Improve

With knowledge of the rules, skills, and effective practice principles and an understanding of how to manage your golf game as well as the course, you are ready to accelerate your journey to become a successful golfer. How good you become will largely depend on a combination of motivation, practice, playing experience, and increased knowledge. As a game for a lifetime, golf will provide a constant challenge, and getting better will never grow old. It is a game you can play as little or as much as you like, with whomever you like, for as long as you like.

The first step to improving your game is understanding your bottom line in playing golf. In other words, at the end of a round, what is it that puts a smile on your face and gives you a deep sense of satisfaction? This final step discusses important topics that will help you continue to find success and enjoyment in the game of golf. Specifically, this step will help you enjoy your first (or next) round of golf, find a home course and a good instructor, obtain a handicap, learn how to play in tournaments, and include golf as part of your vacation and free-time plans.

PLAYING YOUR FIRST (OR NEXT) ROUND OF GOLF

For your enjoyment and the enjoyment of other golfers, you should develop sufficient skill and knowledge to successfully play your way around the course without taking too much time or losing too many golf balls. An average 18-hole round normally takes about 4 to 5 hours to complete. The first time you play, it's a good idea to ask an experienced golfer to play with you in order to show you the intricacies and etiquette of playing a round of golf. It will flatten your learning curve dramatically and increase your level of enjoyment greatly. If no one is available to take you out your first time, speak to the local golf pro and ask for advice. Golf pros are trained professionals who are knowledgeable in all aspects of the game, including how to successfully play—and enjoy—your first round of golf.

Finding a Golf Home

Most golfers who play on a regular basis have a place they consider to be their primary place to play and practice, their "golf home." A typical golf home will include a 9- or 18-hole course, sometimes multiple courses, and a driving range and putting green for practice. These are the basics, but as you will discover in this section, there can a great many more amenities in your golf home. Where you choose to call your home for golf largely depends on what facilities are conveniently located near you, what amenities and facilities are important to you, and how much you are willing to invest in your golfing experience. Some people choose a golf home based on where friends or family play. However, most people who play golf are friendly and love the game to such a degree that they will welcome anyone to join them in a round of golf.

Your golf home will be either a public or a member-only facility. As the names imply, public facilities are open to the public, and member-only facilities are open to club members and their guests. These facilities are described next.

PUBLIC FACILITIES

As the name suggests, public facilities are open to all members of the public regardless of age, gender, or playing ability. There are two types of public golf facilities: municipal or state-owned golf courses and privately-owned golf facilities. A municipal golf facility is owned and operated by the local or state government. As such, it is usually among the more reasonably priced facilities with a discount to residents. A municipal golf course usually includes a clubhouse with a pro shop for purchasing golf merchandise, changing facilities, a snack bar or restaurant, and restrooms. Most have practice facilities that include a driving range, short game practice area, and a practice putting green. The golf course can range from a minimum of a par-3 9-hole course (where all 9 holes are par-3 holes) to having several 18-hole golf courses.

For example, with 19 golf courses at 17 different facilities, the Los Angeles County Department of Parks and Recreation runs the largest municipally owned golf course system in the United States. The system offers affordable green fees, discount programs for senior citizens and students, and an extensive junior golf program. Thirteen of the courses are 18-hole regulation length, three are convenient nine-hole regulation length, one is a challenging 18-hole executive length (i.e., no Par 5 holes, with most of the Par 4 and Par 3 holes of shorter length than normal), one is 18-hole par-three, and one is nine-hole par-three.

Some of the greatest golf facilities in the world are privately owned and publicly available golf courses. While tee times may be difficult to get due to popularity, anyone can play the Old Course at St. Andrews (Scotland), Pebble Beach Golf Links, or the Ocean Course at Kiawah Island. Like municipal golf facilities, privately owned public golf courses will normally include a clubhouse with a pro shop for purchasing golf merchandise, locker rooms, and food service. Almost all will have a driving range, short game practice area, and a practice putting green. Again, the golf course can range from a minimum of a par-3 9-hole course to several 18-hole golf courses. Depending on location and amenities, a privately owned public course will usually cost a bit more than a publicly owned golf course but still less than a private course.

MEMBER-ONLY FACILITIES

A member-only golf facility (club) is owned and operated either by the club members or a private individual or group. Because of the exclusivity of these facilities, they are usually more expensive to play than public courses. Many member-only clubs require an initiation fee to join and then monthly dues regardless of how often you play. Member-only clubs vary widely in the amenities offered. Pine Valley, ranked the number one golf course in the United States by several publications, is a golf-only facility. In general, however, most member-only clubs include additional amenities, such as swimming pools, fitness rooms, tennis facilities, restaurants, card rooms, lounge areas, and locker rooms, and some even have overnight accommodations for members and guests coming from out of town. These are in addition to the traditional golf facility amenities such as a clubhouse, practice facilities, and at least one 18-hole golf course.

Back in the early part of 20th century in the United States, many people sought to escape the confines of city life, particularly on the weekends. Thus was born the idea of a country club. Country clubs are located outside city limits. They were designed as an easily accessible place for members and their families to come to enjoy a variety of outdoor activities such as golf, tennis, and swimming. Country clubs are still very popular in the United States.

Real estate developers in the 1950s and 1960s extended this idea by locating residential homes around golf courses and clubs. This led to the birth of what are now known as golf communities. While many of these community courses are member-only facilities, it is increasingly common to allow the public to play the course as well. The hybrid nature of these golf courses has led to the concept of a semi-private golf facility; that is, the facility has private members but also allows public access.

GOLF ADVENTURES AND TRAVEL

Having a home course insures you have a familiar place to play and practice. But it does not mean that you are restricted to a single course for your golfing days. Because golf is so popular worldwide, you can find a course almost anywhere. Discovering a new golf course increases your knowledge, experience, and enjoyment of the game. A golf adventure can range from playing a new course in your area with some friends, to traveling around the world to exotic locations with family or friends.

In the United States, many destinations offer all sorts of golfing experiences. If you care to steep yourself in the history and traditions of golf, perhaps a trip to Pinehurst, North Carolina to play famed Number 2 appeals to you. If you want to combine golf with other activities such as the beach, then perhaps a vacation to Sea Pines on Hilton Head Island or Torrey Pines in San Diego would be on order. If amusement parks are your thing, the golf courses in Disney World are world famous, and in the surrounding areas of Orlando you will have no difficulty finding golf courses to suit your taste and budget.

If international travel represents the sort of adventure you seek, then St. Andrews in Scotland, (also known as The Home of Golf) may offer an experience of a lifetime. Famous golf resorts can also be found in Asia, Europe, Central or South America and Africa. Book a tee time at Tromso (Norway) Golf Course, and not only will you be playing the world's most northern golf course, but in June or July you can play 24 hours a day in the sunshine. If a warmer climate has appeal, for $200 you can join the Equator Golf Club in Uganda, Africa. Play a round of golf there, and you can be among one of the few people in the world who can lay claim to having hit a golf ball from one hemisphere into another. The point is, there are few sports you can play that have the transportability of golf; you can play virtually anywhere at any time. Happy adventures!

FINDING A GOOD INSTRUCTOR

As your experiences and satisfaction in golf grow, you will want to continue to improve your game. Finding a good instructor will speed your progress in mastering and enjoying the game. In Harvey Penick's *Little Red Book* (1992), Penick writes, "Lessons are not to take the place of practice but to make practice worthwhile" (12). Connecting with a good instructor can help make practice more worthwhile.

A good teacher will help you set goals and will suggest practice activities to help you close in on par. Golf instructors are skilled at pinpointing exactly what will make the biggest difference on the course.

When looking for a teacher to help you improve, be sure to consider experience. Full-time instructors who have been on the lesson tee for at least 3 years are best. If they have been at it for more than 10 years, you know they are good enough to make a living at it. For playing experience, look for someone who was or still is a competitive golfer.

Credentials are the second key factor. Go with a pro. Your time, money, and game are too precious to place in the hands of an amateur. Look for a teacher who is PGA- or LPGA-certified. These individuals have successfully completed a rigorous educational program. To find a teaching professional in your area, try the websites for the PGA (www.pga.com) or LPGA (www.lpga.com).

Find a teacher who fits the way you learn. If you like technical, detailed information regarding your swing, look for a teacher who uses video equipment and stresses body position, angles, and swing speed. If establishing a relationship with the teacher is important to your learning, look for someone who focuses on your personal goals, emphasizes motivation and commitment, and asks lots of questions in an attempt to understand you and your game. If you seek a broader approach to learning that encompasses the rich traditions of the game, rules, etiquette, and established techniques in performance, look for the ambassadors of golf who believe golf is more than just chasing a ball for 18 holes. No single teaching philosophy is right for everyone, so decide what best fits your personality. Ask potential instructors to explain their teaching philosophy. The answers should guide your decision.

Simplicity is an art form. The human brain can process only so much information. A great teacher knows the most important piece of information that will make the biggest difference in performance. Lesser teachers will overwhelm you with information in an attempt to cure every symptom they see, because they haven't a clue as to what the disease is. When talking with a potential teacher, look for someone who will listen, set one or two goals at a time, and work progressively toward making you a better golfer.

The final key is you. If you are looking for a good teacher, you must be committed to becoming a good student. Practice what your coach tells you to in the way your coach tells you to. No one has ever improved in any sport simply by listening or reading. You've got to do it and do it properly again and again and again. This is why Henrik Stenson is one of the best golfers in the world—he practices regularly and often. When you find a good teacher, capitalize on your teacher's advice by applying it.

OBTAINING A HANDICAP

The USGA (United States Golf Association), the governing body of golf in North America, encourages golfers to post all of their golf scores online for purposes of establishing and maintaining a handicap. Formally known as a *handicap index,* a handicap allows you to compete against other golfers of different ability levels on an equitable basis, increasing the enjoyment of the game for you and your playing partners. The handicap index takes into account the average of your best scores as well as the difficulty of the course or courses you play. Simply put, your handicap is the average good score you would shoot on your home course or similar golf course.

In a tournament, your handicap levels the playing field when you to play against other players of differing abilities. For example, if your handicap index was 20 and in a tournament you shot 100, you adjusted or net score would be 80. If you were playing against a player with a handicap of 5 and he or she shot 85 for the round, their net score would be 80 and you would tie. The handicap permits players to compete on the basis of what they should score given their skills rather than their actual scores (also known as the gross score).

The USGA's system for recording the handicap scores is the Golf Handicap and Information Network, also known as GHIN. More than 12,000 golf clubs in the United States are associated with GHIN. To obtain a handicap index, you must first join a recognized golf club. Under USGA regulations, a golf club is an organization of at least 10 golfers that is licensed by the USGA Handicapping System, or a local, state or regional group licensed by the USGA through its GHIN reporting service. If you live in the United States then most, if not all, golf courses in your area will be official USGA golf clubs and support the handicap system. Once you determine which facility you would like to claim as your home course, you can inquire about obtaining a handicap at that club. You can then become a member by signing up and paying a nominal fee for the service. When you join a participating club, you will be given an ID and password to use to post your scores online. Most golf courses have an onsite computer dedicated exclusively to posting scores, so it is very convenient.

Once you post at least 20 scores, your handicap will be determined using your 10 best scores and calculated automatically by the USGA, taking into account the course rating and slope rating (course difficulty) of any course you play. Course raters are trained by the USGA and sent to new courses to rate each course. The raters consider factors such as hole lengths, green sizes, hazards, and fairway widths. After a thorough analysis, the raters give the course two scores: rating and slope. The higher the numbers are, the more difficult the course. This information is found on the scorecard for the course.

It is important you post all your scores, even scores when not played at your home course. The golf pro at your facility can answer any questions you may have about posting scores or questions about the system itself. It is easier than it looks, so don't be intimidated. And if you decide to play outside the United States, many courses require you to have a handicap card to prove that you have sufficient skill and knowledge to play a round of golf. For more information on obtaining a handicap, visit the USGA website at www.usga.org.

PLAYING TOURNAMENT GOLF

Most people who play golf do so for the sheer joy of playing. Golf offers a wonderful opportunity to apply your skills in a beautiful outdoor environment. Today's golf courses often resemble well-manicured parks and botanical gardens. You can also often find myriad social activities surrounding a golf course or club.

Golf is also a competitive game, and many players wish to take their game beyond the recreational level by testing their skills against other players in a tournament. The pressure found in a tournament tests your skill, knowledge, and fortitude. A tournament is a challenge that many players relish, though tournaments are not for everyone. You can gain a lifetime of enjoyment from golf without ever playing a competitive round.

However, if you believe competitive golf is a benchmark of your success as a golfer, you should try a tournament. For amateurs, the most competitive tournaments are hosted by the USGA, although state golf associations also host highly competitive tournaments. Private organizations and charities host tournaments for players who want a challenge but have limited time to commit to serious practice or extensive travel. Information on local tournaments is generally available at your local golf courses.

The two most common competitive formats are stroke play and match play. In stroke play, the player with the lowest number of strokes in a round is declared the winner. Stroke play is the format most often used on professional and collegiate tours. In match play, players compete to win the hole. The player with the lowest score on a particular hole wins the hole. The player to win the most holes is declared the winner. This format is most commonly seen in the Ryder Cup, Walker Cup, Solheim Cup, and similar team events but can also be used in individual competitions such as the World Match Play Championship.

Two other common formats are four-ball best ball and alternate shot. Four-ball best ball is played in pairs. Each golfer in a foursome plays her own ball. The lowest score recorded by a pair on each hole is the one that is recorded. Alternate shot is also played in pairs, and as the name suggests, one ball is played by the pair, with each member of the pair alternating turns. Player 1 tees off, player 2 plays the second shot, player 1 plays the third shot, and so on. Shots are alternated so the same player does not always tee off. These two formats are also popular in team competitions.

A format often used in amateur events is the scramble. The scramble is normally played in pairs but can also be played in threesomes or foursomes. Each player tees off on every hole. The team decides which drive is best and then each player on the team plays his second shot from that spot (one club-length drop). The team decides which second shot is best and they play from there, continuing until they hole the ball. Scores are recorded as stroke play, so only the shots that were actually used to put the ball into the hole are counted, regardless of which partner hit the shot that was used. This format is popular, because it gives the average golfer the chance to record scores like they see the pros shoot.

MEETING BENCHMARKS OF SUCCESS

Depending on your reasons for playing golf and your personal definition of success in the sport, you can use multiple benchmarks to gauge your success in golf. Discovering the friendly confines of a home course, expanding your knowledge and experience with a memorable golfing adventure, feeling the thrill of healthy competition in a charity tournament, and seeing consistent improvement in your skills all represent benchmarks for success in golf. Which benchmarks you chose to measure your success is entirely up to you. This section discusses benchmarks for success in terms of practice and play.

Practice

By now, you know there is no better way to find success in golf than by practicing the skills that will make you successful. In Freeman's *The Golfer's Book of Wisdom*, Gary Player notes, "The harder you work, the luckier you get" (46). To become successful at golf, you must become successful at practice. For many reasons, golfers sometimes find it difficult to regularly get on a golf course. Time, money, access, and physical limitations are just a few of the reasons. Some players find it easier to get to a practice ground than a golf course. Fortunately for these golfers—and all golfers for that matter—practice can be fun and rewarding and offer a benchmark of your success in golf.

You can use practice as a benchmark in two ways. First, at a practice ground you can find success measured in skill mastery. When practicing your putting, keep in mind a few games or challenges (see step 1 for suggestions) and see if you can improve your score over the last practice. The more skills you can improve and the more you improve in each skill, the more you will improve your overall skill as a golfer.

Second, for the recreational or amateur player, golf must be fun. If it isn't fun, why do it? On the practice ground, you can find pleasure in hitting a well-struck iron shot, splashing a ball out of a bunker, or sinking a dozen putts from a given distance. At our professional training camps, we spend considerable time discussing practice goals, effective drills, and technical information. Late one afternoon at one of these camps, Niclas Fasth, a Ryder Cup player, walked over to one end of the practice tee and started pitching balls to a green about 30 yards away. This wasn't in the practice plan, but as I watched him stroke shots in high, graceful arcs close to the pin, he turned and asked, "Is it OK to just hit shots because it's fun?" Niclas was concerned that inappropriate practice would detract from the high standard he demands from his golf skills. But what he had really done was remind us that golf should be fun. I told him, "Nothing wrong with it at all, Niclas." Enjoying practice is enjoying golf. If you enjoy practice, that is a benchmark of success.

Play

While practicing, learning, and improving should be enjoyable, most golfers measure their success on the golf course. For some golfers, that simply means getting onto a course for a round. Many who have a passion for the game find they don't have the time, money, support, knowledge, or courage to find their way to a golf course. The goal of almost every amateur golfer we know is to play more. This is not only a legitimate goal, it is an important goal. No matter what your reasons for playing this marvelous game, your goals will most often be fully realized on a golf course.

To this end, the number of rounds you play, whether they be 9- or 18-hole rounds, should be an important benchmark for your success. Identify the obstacles that prevent you from playing and work toward overcoming those obstacles. For example, find a course near your home that you can get to quickly. This will save you time. Perhaps you can find a municipal or public course that has low green fees or special rates on certain days. This will save you money. Perhaps when talking with friends or your golf instructor you could mention that you would like to find others of your ability and aspirations to play with. This will help you establish the support group with which to play. However you do it, find a way to get to the course. Playing the game is the best way to enjoy the game.

Success Summary

While this summary brings you to the end of the book, it hardly ends of your quest to become a successful golfer. You are encouraged to regularly revisit the steps to success and remind yourself of the key points that will make you successful. Practicing the drills in each step and recording points earned will allow you to measure your progress as a skillful and knowledgeable player. The techniques for putting, strategies for planning a practice round, and drills for pitching your ball close to the hole are all here. Only with knowledge and practice will you continue the step up your success in golf.

There are many ways to measure success and chart progress in golf. To find the measures that are most meaningful and give you greatest satisfaction begin by understanding what you like about playing this wonderful game. If your motivation is social or recreational, simply enjoy the camaraderie of your companions and the beauty of the golf course. If you are more competitive, develop a goal-based practice schedule and systematically chart your progress as you improve.

Golf has played a major part in our lives, both as players and coaches. We have enjoyed many beautiful places, met some wonderful people, suffered more than a few disappointments, and celebrated some unforgettable successes. No one has yet perfected this game, although players such as Jack Nicklaus, Annika Sörenstam, and Tiger Woods seem to come remarkably close. Like life itself, golf remains a challenge for us all. We can always get better, but we need to remember to rejoice in the rewards that playing golf brings. Golf is a game that you can enjoy for a lifetime. This book can help you on your way to becoming a successful golfer. Now it is time to put this book down. Go play. Enjoy the game of golf.

About the Authors

Paul G. Schempp is the director of the Sport Instruction Research Laboratory at the University of Georgia, where he also serves as a professor. He has spent the last quarter century studying the development of expertise in sport and coaching. Schempp has designed performance programs for the Swedish Golf Federation and Mexican national golf teams. He has coached several champions on the PGA and European PGA professional golf tours, including Jesper Parnevik, Richard S. Johnson, Niclas Fasth, and Fredrik Jacobson. As a scientific consultant to *Golf Digest*, he was instrumental in selecting America's 50 Greatest Teachers. A longtime consultant for the PGA of America, Schempp helped redesign the PGA's professional certification programs for golf instructors. He has also served on the National Education Advisory Board for the Ladies' Professional Golf Association (LPGA).

Schempp's groundbreaking research has made him a sought-after keynote speaker for professional associations and corporate conferences committed to improving performance. Clients include the American Society for Training and Development, BASF Corporation, Buckhead Business Association, Club Corporation of America, Condé Nast Publications, General Electric, National Institute of Education (Singapore), Professional Golf Association of America, Society for Human Resource Management, the Swiss Soccer Federation, Vistage, and USA Track and Field.

Schempp holds an EdD in human movement studies from Boston University and lives in Athens, Georgia.

Peter Mattsson serves as the director of elite performance at the Swedish Sports Confederation. He served six years as the director of coaching for the English Golf Union, where he was instrumental in the development of the current National Coaching Programme structure. Before coming to England, Mattsson was the head coach for the Swedish national teams, a role he held from 1998 to 2005. He has coached Swedish teams and individual players at numerous European and World Amateur Championships at the World Cup and at professional events on the men's and women's tours. Mattsson holds a BEd in physical education and is currently studying sport science with a focus on golf. He resides in Stockholm, Sweden.